Praise for *The*

D00362269

"*The I-Factor* clearly articulates that the ⌐ stem from how we engage ourselves."

—T. D. Jakes Sr., senior pastor, the Potter's House of Dallas; TDJ Enterprises; *New York Times* bestselling author

"Van Moody takes you on a biblically balanced, often painfully penetrating look—not just a look at the you in you, but a look at the God in you who defines and declares your destiny and worth."

—Kenneth C. Ulmer, D.Min, PhD; Faithful Central Bible Church; founder-CEO, the Ulmer Institute, Los Angeles, CA

"Small group leaders will love the summary at the end of each chapter. I loved it. I grew. You will too."

—Dr. Sam Chand, leadership consultant and author of *Leadership Pain*

"How refreshing to find a book that focuses on having a godly, healthy sense of self-worth!"

—Chris Hodges, founding and senior pastor, Church of the Highlands; author of *Fresh Air* and *Four Cups*

"A must-read for all those who aspire to leave an indelible mark and foot print on the earth."

—Dr. Leslie D. Ramiah, founder and senior pastor, New Creation Bible Church, Durban, South Africa

"*The I-Factor* is an essential key to reaching your next level in your understanding of yourself and then achieving the success of your dreams."

—Dr. Chris Hill, author, evangelist, senior pastor, the Potter's House of Denver

"Without reservation, I recommend *The I-Factor*."

—Jonathan Varner, director, Varner Family Ministries

"A true game changer! Rarely do I come across a book that convicts, challenges, and equips at the same time."

—DR. MATTHEW HESTER, AUTHOR; PASTOR,
DOMINION CHURCH INTERNATIONAL

"Of the dozens of books I've read in recent years, this is one of the best. It is an easy read, but its profound message can be life changing for anyone seeking inner peace and a life of significance and fulfillment."

—DOUG CARTER, SENIOR VICE PRESIDENT, EQUIP LEADERSHIP

"*The I-Factor* strengthened my personal relationship with myself, my wife, my family, and most notably a deepening of my ultimate relationship with God."

—ART FRANKLIN, EMMY AWARD–WINNING NEWS ANCHOR;
HOST OF CBS 42 MORNING SHOW WITH ART FRANKLIN

"If you want the keys to unlock a happier more fulfilling life, *The I-Factor* is the book for you."

—RUBEN C. STUDDARD, AMERICAN IDOL WINNER, THE BIGGEST
LOSER CONTESTANT, AND AWARD-WINNING ARTIST

"The revelatory insight that Van Moody shares in this book is more than life changing, it's world shaping."

—WARRYN AND ERICA CAMPBELL, TV PERSONALITIES;
GRAMMY AWARD–WINNING PRODUCER AND ARTIST; PASTORS,
CALIFORNIA WORSHIP CENTER, NORTH HOLLYWOOD, CA

"A thought provoking, challenging, and enlightening work that is a MUST-read for all people who strive to keep their hopes, dreams, and aspirations in check and on course."

—DR. C. E. GLOVER, SENIOR PASTOR, MOUNT BETHEL MINISTRIES

"If ever there was a time to understand yourself and the people you include into your world, it is now."

—MICHAEL PITTS, FOUNDING PASTOR,
CORNERSTONE CHURCH, MAUMEE, OHIO

"This book will definitely lead to transparency within yourself."
—HEZEKIAH WALKER, MULTI-GRAMMY AWARD-
WINNING ARTIST, PASTOR, AND RADIO PERSONALITY

"*The I-Factor* will become an essential read and a necessary reference for all those who are serious about fulfilling their dreams."
—DAVID G. EVANS, SENIOR PASTOR-TEACHER, BETHANY BAPTIST
CHURCH; BESTSELLING AUTHOR; CEO, DAVID G. EVANS MINISTRIES

"A great guide for mapping out a strategy to build a better future!"
—DALE C. BRONNER, D.MIN; BRONNER BROTHERS
MANUFACTURING; AUTHOR; FOUNDER AND SENIOR PASTOR,
WORD OF FAITH FAMILY WORSHIP CATHEDRAL

"I highly recommend this book to help anyone live out God's plan and purpose for their life!"
—MATT FRY, LEAD PASTOR, C3 CHURCH,
CLAYTON, NC; ARC BOARD MEMBER

"*The I-Factor* provides a mindmap for mental and spiritual health; it is the ticket to inner peace."
—DE'ANDRE SALTER, LEAD PASTOR, IMPACT CHURCH,
SOUTH PLAINFIELD, NJ; ENTREPRENEUR AND AUTHOR

"Get ready to be challenged to live a life you were meant to live and discover the keys of how to do it."
—BENNY PEREZ, AUTHOR; COFOUNDER AND
LEAD PASTOR, THE CHURCH LV

"Van Moody opens a vault of godly wisdom for us all. This is a must-read."
—DINO RIZZO, EXECUTIVE DIRECTOR, ARC; ASSOCIATE
PASTOR, CHURCH OF THE HIGHLANDS

"*The I-Factor* will help you master your relationship with yourself, enabling you to live your best possible life."
—RUSSELL AND SAM EVANS, LEAD PASTORS, PLANETSHAKERS
CHURCH AND MUSIC, MELBOURNE, AUSTRALIA

"A unique, greatly helpful, and inspiring book."

—TIM HALL, AUSTRALIAN EVANGELIST, PLANETSHAKERS
GLOBAL EVANGELISM, AUTHOR OF *GIANT KILLERS*

"*The I-Factor*'s most impressive quality is that it provides the necessary building blocks of recovery for all who truly desire personal transformation."

—WAYNE AND MYESHA CHANEY, TV PERSONALITIES; LEAD
PASTORS, ANTIOCH CHURCH OF LONG BEACH, CA

"Dr. Moody offers insightful and practical advice on how to 'get right with yourself,' so that your other relationships and endeavors may flourish."

—STEPHEN CHAPIN GARNER, SENIOR MINISTER, THE
CONGREGATIONAL CHURCH OF NEW CANAAN, NEW CANAAN, CT

"Enlightening, practical, and essential to all who seek to maximize the divine deposits God has made in them."

—JOSEPH WARREN WALKER, III, D.MIN.; SENIOR PASTOR,
MT. ZION CHURCH, NASHVILLE, TN; PRESIDING BISHOP, FULL
GOSPEL BAPTIST CHURCH FELLOWSHIP INTERNATIONAL

"I would recommend *The I-Factor* to anyone who desires to live their 'best' life."

—PAUL S. MORTON, SR.; FOUNDER, FULL GOSPEL BAPTIST CHURCH
FELLOWSHIP INTERNATIONAL; SENIOR PASTOR, CHANGING A
GENERATION MINISTRIES, ATLANTA, GA; OVERSEER AND CO-
PASTOR, GREATER ST. STEPHEN MINISTRIES, NEW ORLEANS, LA

"Definitely a 'how-to' book that not only makes for good reading, but also calls you into action."

—NEIL C. ELLIS, PRESIDING PRELATE, GLOBAL UNITED FELLOWSHIP;
SENIOR PASTOR–TEACHER, MOUNT TABOR CHURCH

"Provides not just an insightful, relevant, and practical tool for life change but a built-in personal coach that will help you turn your dreams into a reality."

—BRETT EASTMAN, PRESIDENT, LIFETOGETHER

"A magnificent book! Apply its timely principles for personal and spiritual success. Your life will change."

—DR. LEVY H. KNOX, FOUNDING BISHOP, LIVING WORD
CHRISTIAN CENTER, INTL. MINISTRIES AND KINGDOM
NETWORK OF CHURCHES INTL., MOBILE, AL

"A gift that needs no ribbon, just a reader who's ready to make the shift of a lifetime!"

—DR. NICOLE LABEACH, CEO, VOLITION ENTERPRISES, INC.;
EXECUTIVE AND LIFE COACH; AUTHOR, *A WOMAN'S TRUE PURPOSE*

"For anyone who wants to live fuller, greater, and with more impact."

—ROB KETTERLING, FOUNDER AND LEAD PASTOR, RIVER
VALLEY CHURCH, APPLE VALLEY, MN; AUTHOR; SPEAKER

"A guide for understanding yourself and leading yourself with excellence . . . so you can help others like never before."

—RYAN FRANK, PASTOR, PUBLISHER,
ENTREPRENEUR, LEADERSHIP COACH

"Get ready to be challenged, inspired, and maybe even offended at times as you flip through the pages of this book."

—MARTIJN VAN TILBURGH, CEO, FOUR RIVERS MEDIA;
COFOUNDER, THE LEVERAGE GROUP AND KUDU PUBLISHING

"By helping us to find ourselves, Pastor Van Moody leads us to stop making excuses and blaming others, and take personal responsibility for who we become and who we are called to be."

—DR. KIM BROWN, SENIOR PASTOR, MOUNT LEBANON CHURCH,
VA AND NC; CHURCH PLANTER; AUTHOR, *MARRIAGE TALK*

"Van Moody has a keen understanding of human problems and the solutions we need to advance."

—DR. WALTER S. THOMAS, SENIOR PASTOR, NEW
PSALMIST BAPTIST CHURCH, BALTIMORE, MD; EXECUTIVE
AND PERSONAL COACH; AUTHOR AND EDITOR

"Getting ahead, achieving greatness, and fulfilling God's purpose for our lives begin with knowing who we are and why we're here. Van Moody helps us to discover those things in *The I-Factor*. I highly recommend reading this book!"

—HENRY FERNANDEZ, SENIOR PASTOR, THE FAITH
CENTER, SUNRISE, FL; SPEAKER; BESTSELLING AUTHOR,
FAITH, FAMILY, AND FINANCES; ENTREPRENEUR

"*This is a must-read* . . . I believe that the world is going through an identity crisis and this book is the answer."

—DR. GEORGE SEARIGHT, FOUNDER AND SENIOR PASTOR, ABUNDANT
LIFE FAMILY WORSHIP CHURCH, NEW BRUNSWICK, NJ

"As you read these pages, be prepared to be transformed from the inside out!"

—DR. FREDERICK DOUGLASS HAYNES, III; SENIOR PASTOR,
FRIENDSHIP-WEST BAPTIST CHURCH, DALLAS, TX; ACTIVIST

"A practical, readable, compelling guide to self-actualization and greatness."

—DR. JOE SAMUEL RATLIFF, PASTOR, BRENTWOOD
BAPTIST CHURCH, HOUSTON, TX

"This book, if applied to daily life and relationships, will be life changing!"

—LAYNE SCHRANZ, EXECUTIVE PASTOR, GROW LEADERSHIP NETWORK
DIRECTOR, CHURCH OF THE HIGHLANDS, BIRMINGHAM, AL

"The ultimate guide for tapping into your core strength in order to walk into your destiny."

—ODELL DICKERSON, JR., M.B.A.; CEO, NEW
PSALMIST BAPTIST CHURCH, BALTIMORE, MD

"Van Moody will guide you to a better you—a you that obtains and maintains healthy relationships that last. This is the book you need to read now."

—PHIL MUNSEY, CHAIRMAN, CHAMPION NETWORK OF
PASTORS WITH JOEL OSTEEN/LAKEWOOD CHURCH

"Each chapter is scripturally grounded as well as personally focused and culturally relevant."

—DR. CRAIG L. OLIVER, SR.; SENIOR PASTOR,
ELIZABETH BAPTIST CHURCH, ATLANTA, GA

"I found this book refreshing, enlightening, and inspiring."

—RUCKINS MCKINLEY D.D., AUTHOR AND SPEAKER

"Thank you, Pastor Moody, for this valiant and forthright road map into becoming who I was intended to be, the real me!"

—DR. B. COURTNEY MCBATH, SENIOR PASTOR,
CALVARY REVIVAL CHURCH, NORFOLK, VA

"Establishing the order from the inside out will definitely help bring the healing we need as individuals, as the kingdom, as the church, and as a country! Thank you, Van Moody, for this amazing body of work!"

—TYE TRIBBETT, GRAMMY AWARD–WINNING SINGER
AND SONGWRITER; TV HOST, BET's JOYFUL NOISE

"Pastor Van keeps it real and practical for all who are serious about succeeding on this journey of life."

—DR. JERRY L. CANNON, PASTOR, CN JENKINS MEMORIAL
PRESBYTERIAN CHURCH, CHARLOTTE, NC; EVANGELISM COACH; FORMER
PRESIDENT, THE NATIONAL BLACK PRESBYTERIAN CAUCUS (PCUSA)

THE I-FACTOR

HOW BUILDING A GREAT RELATIONSHIP
WITH YOURSELF IS THE KEY TO A
HAPPY, SUCCESSFUL LIFE

VAN MOODY

NELSON
BOOKS

An Imprint of Thomas Nelson

© 2016 Vanable H. Moody, II

All rights reserved. No portion of this book may be reproduced, stored in a retrieval system, or transmitted in any form or by any means—electronic, mechanical, photocopy, recording, scanning, or other—except for brief quotations in critical reviews or articles, without the prior written permission of the publisher.

Published in Nashville, Tennessee, by Nelson Books, an imprint of Thomas Nelson. Nelson Books and Thomas Nelson are registered trademarks of HarperCollins Christian Publishing, Inc.

Thomas Nelson titles may be purchased in bulk for educational, business, fund-raising, or sales promotional use. For information, please e-mail SpecialMarkets@ThomasNelson.com.

Unless otherwise noted, Scripture quotations are taken from the Holy Bible, New International Version°, NIV°. Copyright © 1973, 1978, 1984, 2011 by Biblica, Inc.° Used by permission of Zondervan. All rights reserved worldwide. www.zondervan.com. The "NIV" and "New International Version" are trademarks registered in the United States Patent and Trademark Office by Biblica, Inc.°

Scripture quotations marked AMP are from the Amplified° Bible. Copyright © 1954, 1958, 1962, 1964, 1965, 1987 by The Lockman Foundation. Used by permission. (www.Lockman.org)

Scripture quotations marked KJV are from the King James Version. Public domain.

Scripture quotations marked THE MESSAGE are from *The Message*. Copyright © by Eugene H. Peterson 1993, 1994, 1995, 1996, 2000, 2001, 2002. Used by permission of Tyndale House Publishers, Inc.

Scripture quotations marked NKJV are from the New King James Version°. © 1982 by Thomas Nelson. Used by permission. All rights reserved.

Scripture quotations marked NLT are from the *Holy Bible*, New Living Translation. © 1996, 2004, 2007, 2013 by Tyndale House Foundation. Used by permission of Tyndale House Publishers, Inc., Carol Stream, Illinois 60188. All rights reserved.

Scripture quotations marked HCSB are taken from the Holman Christian Standard Bible°. Copyright © 1999, 2000, 2002, 2003, 2009 by Holman Bible Publishers. Used by permission. HCSB° is a federally registered trademark of Holman Bible Publishers.

Any Internet addresses, phone numbers, or company or product information printed in this book are offered as a resource and are not intended in any way to be or to imply an endorsement by Thomas Nelson, nor does Thomas Nelson vouch for the existence, content, or services of these sites, phone numbers, companies, or products beyond the life of this book.

ISBN 978-0-7180-7758-7 (eBook)

Library of Congress Cataloging-in-Publication Data

Names: Moody, Van, 1975- author.
Title: The I factor : how building a great relationship with yourself is the key to a happy, successful life / Van Moody.
Description: Nashville : Thomas Nelson, 2016. | Includes bibliographical references.
Identifiers: LCCN 2016008305 | ISBN 9780718077563
Subjects: LCSH: Self--Religious aspects--Christianity.
Classification: LCC BT713 .M66 2016 | DDC 248.4--dc23
LC record available at https://lccn.loc.gov/2016008305

Printed in the United States of America

16 17 18 19 20   RRD   10 9 8 7 6 5 4 3 2 1

The Lord does not look at the things people look at. People look at the outward appearance, but the Lord looks at the heart.

—1 Samuel 16:7

To my amazing wife and beautiful daughter and son

*To the Worship Center Christian Church: the
wonderful people I get to do life with*

To everyone who desires successful living from the inside out

Contents

Introduction

ON JUNE 25, 2009, THE DEATH OF MICHAEL JACKSON shocked the world. Without warning, one of the world's most popular recording artists was gone, his unmistakable voice silenced at the age of fifty. His passing sent a surge of disbelief and sadness across the country and around the world. People simply could not believe he was gone and immediately began asking, "What happened?"

I would venture to say Michael Jackson was universally acknowledged as a brilliant entertainer, but he was also regarded as eccentric and seemed content to live with an air of mystery. Questions and controversy sometimes surrounded him, but his talent was tremendous and his unforgettable songs were phenomenal successes. Within certain age groups, you could go almost anywhere in the world and find someone to quote lyrics from "Billie Jean" or "Man in the Mirror."

Before the world fully absorbed the shock of Jackson's passing, another piece of news emerged, one that was even harder to believe: His death was not the result of a random accident or some undisclosed illness. It was the result of an overdose of medication prescribed to help him sleep. People immediately began asking why. If they thought about it very long, they might have realized that not being able to sleep is often rooted in some type of internal torment. At a basic physiological level, it's the inability to find peace and rest. Michael Jackson, a musical icon about to embark on a world tour, seemed to have it all in many ways. Why couldn't he sleep at night?

While I cannot comment on the specifics of Jackson's situation, I don't think any external circumstances led to his demise; I think what caused him to take a lethal dose of sleeping medication was a problem in an often-overlooked dynamic I call the I-factor. Let me explain.

When I refer to Jackson's I-factor, I am talking about his relationship with himself—apart from all the applause and accolades he received from the public and apart from the affection he experienced in private relationships with friends and family. Jackson's enormous audience knew him as a great entertainer and, from all appearances, as a sensitive and generous human being. They knew his public persona, but they also had glimpses of a troubled life beneath his designer clothes, hats, and sunglasses. He had earned great fame and prestigious awards. But underneath those trappings, he was miserable—so miserable that he reached a point where he could not even sleep. And so his I-factor issues robbed his family of a son and a brother, his children of a father, and the world of one of the greatest entertainers of my lifetime.

Jackson's struggles were not unique, not by a long shot. Throughout history, people with remarkable talent or impressive positions have come to surprising and terrible ends—people like the singer Amy Winehouse, actor Heath Ledger, writer Ernest Hemingway, painter Vincent van Gogh, and the ancient Egyptian queen, Cleopatra. Clearly, an inability to manage success is a problem with a long history and a challenge that still threatens people today.

The common denominator between Jackson and these others is that all of them had achieved great success—or were solidly on the path to great success—but for some reason crashed and burned. I believe the problem lies in the I-factor.

The connection in the stories of these individuals is that some personal weakness took them from the pinnacle of success to total disgrace. While their scandals were public, what led to each scandal was deeply private. None of these individuals can blame their downfalls on anyone else; each was solely responsible. The specific contributing element to the downfall was different in each situation, but it was always something unrelated to his or her intelligence, personality, abilities, or fame and fortune. The reason was something deeply personal and private: something was faulty in their relationships with themselves.

Maybe you cannot relate to people with such fame, fortune, and perceived success, but you know exactly what I mean when I talk about people who have a longing to succeed but keep tripping themselves up. Maybe that's exactly what's happening to you. You have desires, goals, abilities, initiative, motivation, energy, and solid plans. You have all the right credentials, and to any casual observer you are positioned to succeed. From the outside looking in, there's no reason you shouldn't be able to live your dreams. Yet you make a certain amount of progress down the path of your potential, and then something happens. You get derailed. It's happened enough times to become a pattern, and your greatest source of frustration is that you simply cannot put your finger on the problem. Maybe the problem seems different every time it happens, and that only adds to your confusion. I have great news for you: this book will help you identify the problem, understand it, and solve it, removing the obstacles that have hindered the success you long for and the greatness that awaits you.

So what exactly is the I-factor? I will explain it in greater detail as this book unfolds, but in a nutshell, it's how people think about themselves, feel about themselves, and relate to themselves. It's a combination of dynamics that converge to form the totality of a person's relationship with him- or herself. It's more than self-worth or self-respect. It goes beyond matters of character and motives. It reaches past a sense of significance or a perception of purpose. It does include relational skills with other people, but it has *everything* to do with one's relationship with oneself. It's about managing yourself—and your whole life—well.

Of course, I-factor problems are not limited to the world's rich and famous. Ordinary people face the same struggles every day. The problem with the I-factor is that it's so internal. It's often a massive personal struggle, well camouflaged by talents and abilities, personality and charisma, or accomplishments. We shouldn't be deceived by the cover-up; almost everyone struggles with the I-factor in silence, with as much anonymity as possible. No one seems to want anyone else to know how difficult and brutal the fight can be, which is a shame because so many people are in it.

In my book *The People Factor,* I wrote: "Every relationship you have influences your life. *There are no neutral relationships.* Each one lifts you up or weighs you down. It moves you forward or holds you back. It helps you or it hurts you."[1] All these statements are true, and I believe them as strongly today as ever. I also understand a parallel truth about relationships: it's your relationship with yourself that trumps every other association in your life. Everything I believe about the power of relationships with others, I believe even more about your relationship with yourself. It can be the most dangerous relationship you ever have, or the most awesome one. It is the difference-maker between success and failure. No one can derail your destiny as quickly or effectively as you can. However, no one can position you for success and for the fulfillment of your dreams as well as you can.

The three ingredients for your best possible life are a great relationship with God, a great relationship with yourself, and great relationships with others. I've written at length about your external relationships in *The People Factor.* In *The I-Factor,* I'm writing about your internal relationship. If your relationships with God and others are healthy and you also have a strong, positive relationship with yourself, you will be unstoppable. There will be no limits to what you can achieve and who you can become.

Over the past few years, I have been astounded by stories of people who could not manage some aspect of their lives and ended up dying young or in public disgrace. My goal in *The I-Factor* is to put a stop to the sad stories of defeat and help people become the main characters in their own success stories. In this book, I hope to rip away the veil of secrecy covering people's deepest and most intimate struggles in such a way that those struggles ultimately give way to personal victories. I want to help people see beneath the surface of their lives so they can understand the source of their greatest struggles, deal with the ways those struggles impact their lives, avoid the personal disasters their struggles may lead to, and ultimately live their dreams. I believe many people ask themselves more often than they admit, "How do I deal with myself?" and I've written this book to help answer that question. I'm convinced that winning the battle with the I-factor may be the most important step in bringing about personal wholeness, security, and success.

Winning the battle with the I-factor takes a proper understanding of three dynamics: identity, significance, and perspective. You'll see these words mentioned, explained, and elaborated on throughout the book. They are all necessary to a healthy relationship with yourself and foundational to the development of a strong I-factor. When you understand your identity, you know who you are, and that's the foundation of everything. When you understand your significance, you get in touch with the purpose and the greatness for which you were created. When you understand perspective, you can view the problems you face as stepping-stones to greatness instead of stumbling blocks. The right perspective will enable you to walk across difficulties to your destiny instead of allowing them to stop you in your tracks.

Are you tired of working toward personal or professional success and falling short? Are you frustrated over the little things that seem to trip you up on the path to your fullest potential? Are you wondering, deep down inside, if some of these things may have more to do with your relationship with yourself than with circumstances or people around you? Do you ever find yourself asking, "What am I doing wrong? Why can't I ever seem to make it?" Or, do you simply want to learn how to live your best life by removing all the potential obstacles that may arise so you can pursue your destiny with wisdom?

If you can answer yes to any of these questions, chances are there's more going on inside of you than your appearance or persona would indicate, and as you continue reading this book, you'll find yourself on an amazing journey of hope. I have written it with the profound conviction that you are destined for greatness and that the practical principles and biblical truths in this book will help you get there. This book can change your life for the better, and that's exactly what I am believing for you.

More Than Meets the Eye

*If you want to be truly successful, invest in
yourself to get the knowledge you need to find
your unique factor. When you find it and focus
on it and persevere your success will blossom.*
—SYDNEY MADWED

"IT'S BEEN EIGHTY-FOUR YEARS," RESCUED PASSENGER Rose DeWitt Bukater reminisced in the movie *Titanic*, "and I can still smell the fresh paint. The china had never been used. The sheets had never been slept in. *Titanic* was called the 'Ship of Dreams.' And it was. It really was."[1]

I'm sure you have heard about the majestic passenger ship, *Titanic*. It was the finest vessel of its day—larger, faster, and better equipped than any other. It boasted all the engineering and shipbuilding expertise of the times and every luxury its wealthy travelers were accustomed to. The ship had been called unsinkable, and no doubt those aboard felt safe, pampered, and privileged.

If ever a ship seemed destined for success, it was the *Titanic*. No one could have possibly imagined that *this* ship would go down. It would go down in history, for sure, they must have thought, because it was such an excellent vessel, but they were also convinced it could withstand any challenge it met at sea. An employee of the *Titanic*'s

1

parent company, the White Star Line, said, "Not even God himself could sink this ship."[2]

But at 11:40 p.m. on Sunday, April 14, 1912, only five days into its voyage from Southampton, England, to New York City, the *Titanic*'s lookout sent an urgent message to the bridge: "Iceberg, right ahead." Less than forty seconds later, the ship hit the iceberg. Within three hours, the celebrated vessel rested at the bottom of the frigid Atlantic Ocean, and more than fifteen hundred lives were lost.[3]

The lookouts in the crow's nest did not have binoculars. Had a simple pair of binoculars been available, someone could have seen the iceberg ahead, and one of the greatest tragedies in maritime history might have been avoided. As it happened that day, the time elapsed between the first sighting of the iceberg and the ship's impact was a little more than thirty seconds.[4] Here's my point: the *Titanic* sank not because the iceberg was in the ocean, but *because no one saw it in time to steer clear of it.*

As I researched the iceberg the *Titanic* hit, I saw varying statistics about its size. One source said the iceberg was estimated to have been about six hundred feet long, with five hundred feet of it below the ocean's surface and one hundred feet visible above the water. I also learned that typically, seven-eighths of an iceberg is underwater, which means slightly more than 10 percent of an enormous mass of ice would be visible to a captain or a ship's crew.[5] Where icebergs are concerned, what's under the surface, invisible to the naked eye, does much more damage than the part of the iceberg people can easily see. This was certainly true for the *Titanic.*

Believe it or not, the story of the *Titanic* and the theme of this book, the I-factor, have a lot in common. Let me explain. Many people in the world have all the trappings of success. Like the *Titanic*, they are decked out with everything the world finds impressive. They not only have good looks, designer clothes, the best car, and the right address, they also have a sterling educational pedigree, a broad social and professional network, strong skills, and a bright mind. Everything about them seems destined to succeed—just like the *Titanic*. If there were ever any sure bets for success, they would be on these people.

But sometimes these people crash and burn—and no one understands why. The reason is that the world places such high value on who we are on the outside and pays little attention to who we are on the inside. To use the metaphor of an iceberg, it's what's under the surface that can sink a person's whole life, not what's visible to others. The totality of the difference between success and failure is not in any degree we obtain, position we hold, label we wear, car we drive, or amount of money we have. The difference is what's on the inside of a person, who he or she really is at the core, underneath all the trappings and accessories of success. It's those internal dynamics that will cause us to sail or to sink as we go through life. While relationships with other people are vitally important, your relationship with yourself, which is part of what the I-factor is all about, is even more important.

The *I* in *Lie*

How does the I-factor precipitate a person's downfall? One of the stories that best illustrates my point happened to a man you probably have heard of. In 2007, he was named one of *Time* magazine's most influential people in the world. He was the National Father of the Year in 1996. He's appeared on *Sesame Street, Saturday Night Live,* the Olympics, and *Late Night with Jimmy Fallon,* just to cite a fraction of his television experience. This man has won twelve Emmy awards, and as of December 2014, his salary was ten million dollars per year. His personal brand seemed untouchable and his celebrity credentials were strong. Just three months later, in February 2015,

3

he was suspended from his job without pay and had lost not only his influence, but his credibility too. I'm sure you know who I'm describing, former NBC news anchor Brian Williams.

Williams was part of a fairly exclusive lineage. At one time in the United States, before the days of cable news, the most powerful voices in media belonged to the men who occupied the anchor chairs at the big three networks: ABC, CBS, and NBC. With recognizable voices and just the right amount of gravitas, they were media kings. When they reported the news of the day, people believed them. People had no reason not to believe them. Viewed as trustworthy American icons, they held the public trust for decades.

When Brian Williams ascended to the helm of *NBC Nightly News* in December 2004, the evening news anchor job was still admirable and considered quite an accomplishment, even though by then a host of other news broadcasts had joined the big three. Williams quickly became one of America's favorite news anchors, a popular and reliable source for the important information and stories of each day, and he typically outscored his competitors in the rankings of evening news broadcasts. By all appearances, he had reached the pinnacle of success. Had he chosen to do so, he should have been able to cruise his way into retirement from his seat behind the evening news desk. The respect he had gained in about ten years was his to lose—and lose it he did. Big time.

> While relationships with other people are vitally important, your relationship with yourself, which is part of what the I-factor is all about, is even more important.

He did not lose it over a major scandal or some type of serious journalistic error. He lost it because somewhere in the midst of all his fame and fortune, he was not satisfied. He wanted more—more acclaim, more oohs and aahs, perhaps a chance to show a little more bravado on the television screen. In the quest for even more than he already had, he told a lie. Actually, he told several lies, but the one that really got him in trouble was that he had been in Iraq in 2003, riding in a helicopter that came under heavy enemy fire and was hit by a rocket-propelled grenade.

I assume the world would have believed him had crewmembers who *were* in the helicopter that was hit not called his bluff in *Stars and Stripes*. That was the beginning of the end for Williams at the anchor desk. After six months of suspension, NBC gave the anchor job to Lester Holt and relegated Williams to the position of breaking news anchor on MSNBC and breaking news anchor for NBC live special reports, a significant demotion to say the least.

Why?

Many people have questioned why Williams embellished his story. From the moment I first heard about it, I could make only one assumption: the reason had something to do with his I-factor. I did not know all the details or realize he would ultimately admit that the helicopter story, and others that were also embellished, were "clearly ego driven," and born of *"the desire to better my role in a story I was already in"* (emphasis added).[6]

A quote from the website Politico characterizes the situation accurately: "You'd think that Brian Williams, a mega-successful, handsome, funny, high-status millionaire journalist wouldn't need laurels beyond the ones he's already collected. You'd be wrong."[7] The Politico writer instinctively understood that what Williams did left much of America scratching our collective head, totally baffled.

I mention this story because of its shock value and its connection to the I-factor. People all over America and even around the world were stunned that a US media darling could fall so far, so fast. They were even more stunned that the wound to his career and his character was self-inflicted. I cannot count the number of times I read or heard someone say, "Why would he do this to himself?" The incredulity in our country was palpable for days after the story broke. As a culture, no matter how many times we witness it, we still marvel at the way people sabotage themselves.

When we orchestrate our own demise or our own delays on the road to success, we try to explain it away. Sometimes, though, those explanations are faulty because our insights into our own souls are not as sharp and clear as they should be; they are dulled and clouded by our desire to view ourselves in the most positive ways, instead of the most honest ways. These personal struggles, along with our continued bafflement over why other people do what they do, all happen for the same reason: we do not yet fully understand the I-factor.

What's the Problem?

How many times have you heard a shocking story similar to the one about Brian Williams—when someone in your community, your country, or the world seemed to have it all together and then, to the amazement of most people, suffered a tragic fall? These types of scenarios surprise and confuse us. Depending on the situation, one question floods our minds: How could this have happened? Then we go on to tell ourselves that the person who crashed and burned was so smart, so good looking, so funny, so talented, so strong, so prosperous, or so savvy—whatever adjective applies. This kind of thinking is so common in America that I'm not sure we realize how problematic it is.

We have a tendency to assess and esteem people based on their external qualities. We look at their tangible assets, such as educational credentials, physical attractiveness, financial strength (or apparent financial strength, which may be nothing more than debt), professional experience, social position, or worldly influence, and we assume these people are successful. We also look at their intangible qualities, such as personality or charisma and intelligence, believing these attributes make people successful.

We take the same approach toward ourselves. When we struggle to get the job we want; the relationship we want; the influence we want; or the house, car, or designer clothes we want, we immediately try to fix something external. We go back to school; we get another certification; we find a mentor; we lose weight and get in shape; we moonlight until we have enough extra money to buy the possessions we think will make us feel better about ourselves. Sooner or later, though, we realize that none of those things solved our real problem. They may have provided some temporary relief, but when we look in the mirror each day, we still see the same person wrestling with the same challenges.

While external factors do contribute to success in certain ways, none of them and no combination of them form the bedrock for a successful life. They can take people part of the way toward true success, but they can't keep them there. In order to attain and experience genuine success, the I-factor is another element that must be involved. It's often a silent partner in the formula for success; it's also the most important one. It may be something you have never considered and no one has ever told you about.

The I-factor is as intensely personal a matter as there can be. It affects your relationships with others, but it is the basis of everything about your relationship with yourself. It's completely unrelated to everything a person has working for him on the outside; it's all about what's happening on the inside—thoughts, emotions, motives, self-talk. It's the foundation of the way you relate to yourself. While self-esteem and self-respect are closely related to the I-factor, they don't encompass all of it. The I-factor also includes a person's innate integrity. It's the often unseen "why" behind what you think, say, and do. It's a combination of internal dynamics that forms your identity, shapes your character, and influences your life far more than you may realize.

Think again about Brian Williams. His lie about being in a helicopter under enemy fire was not the biggest problem. The biggest problem was whatever was happening inside of him that caused him to tell that lie and others. A person with a weak or negative I-factor would understandably lie in that way—because something on the inside felt deficient. In Williams's case, as he admitted, he wanted "to better [his]role in a story [he] was already in."[8] So that's part of the story behind the story, part of the psychological explanation for what he did. But the question that leads us to I-factor issues is this: *Why* did he want to better himself, as good as he already was? The answer is that deep inside he still felt lacking—not good enough—in some way. None of the acclaim or fame or fortune was enough to empower him to see himself as many others saw him. They saw him as nearly perfect; he saw himself as needing to beef up a story so he would seem better. That's an I-factor problem.

> While external factors do contribute to success in certain ways, none of them and no combination of them form the bedrock for a successful life. They can take people part of the way toward true success, but they can't keep them there.

Though we seem to be hearing about more and more such situations on the news websites these days, I-factor problems are not new. They stretch back for centuries, at least as far as the Old Testament, in the story of two young men I will share later in this chapter.

You Are the Key to Your Success

Often, when people fail to reach their goals, fall short of achieving their destinies, or tumble from a place of position or prominence, they quickly begin playing a blame game. Almost immediately, they find a reason that things did not work out as they had hoped. Usually, it's something like this:

- "Well, that opportunity didn't work out for me because that company never hires people from the school I went to."
- "I didn't get the job because of my gender."
- "I ended up with this addiction because I needed something to numb the pain of my past."
- "My marriage fell apart because my parents were divorced and they did not teach me the relational skills I needed."
- "I'm deep in debt because of all the designer clothes and the car I had to buy in order to make a good impression on my coworkers."
- "I never finished school because I couldn't get the grants I needed."
- "I'm overweight because I have to cook for my kids and they won't eat anything healthy."

I have heard people blame their problems and shortcomings on everything from their parents to their children to the government to race, age, or gender, or to the neighborhood where they grew up.

When disappointments or troubles happen to Christians, they often blame the enemy, making comments such as, "The devil is trying to steal my destiny!" or, "I'm under attack from the enemy! He's hindering my success!" While I am quick to affirm the reality of spiritual warfare, I also think spiritual warfare is cited as the reason for many things that have absolutely nothing to do with the spiritual realm.

The hard but absolutely transformative truth of the I-factor is that, more often than not, no person, no organization, and no situation is responsible for what happens in our lives. Almost always, something within us as individuals is what causes our greatest frustrations. Many times, we are our own worst enemies. The good news is that as we resolve our I-factor issues, we become our own best friends and biggest helpers.

Are You Your Own Worst Enemy or Your Own Best Friend?

The I-factor ultimately determines whether we will help ourselves or hinder ourselves as we go through life. People with weak, negative I-factors become their own worst enemies, while people with healthy, positive I-factors end up being their own best friends. The following table compares the mind-sets and behaviors of those who sabotage themselves and become their own worst enemies with those who position themselves for success:

PEOPLE WHO SABOTAGE THEMSELVES	PEOPLE WHO POSITION THEMSELVES FOR SUCCESS
Allow their egos to get in the way of everything else	Are secure in who they are, yet humble
Refuse to take advice or receive help	Seek and implement good advice from others
Criticize themselves	Accept themselves
Cannot manage their anger, greed, jealousy, lust, or other negative emotions	Know how to manage anger, greed, envy, sexual temptation, and other potentially negative emotions in healthy ways
Fear failure	Are not afraid of failure, but are eager to learn from it

Will not try again after they make mistakes	Always try again if they do not succeed at first
Lack self-confidence	Have healthy self-esteem and an appropriate measure of self-confidence
Won't pay the price necessary to achieve success	Work hard and pay the price for success
Are not content with what they have while they try to better themselves	Are satisfied with what they have and will work for something better
Will not take responsibility for their lives	Take responsibility for their thoughts, feelings, words, and behaviors
Are negative and fault-finding, frequently blaming others for their own shortcomings	Are optimistic and positive
Allow other people to use them	Are willing to help others, but will not allow themselves to be used
Are overly eager to please	Care more about preserving their integrity than pleasing people
Will not take risks	Are willing to take appropriate risks
Have unrealistic expectations	Set expectations that are reasonable and realistic
Are willing to compromise their integrity to get what they want	Will not compromise their character, even if it means not getting what they want
Have talents or abilities, but not character or discipline	Make sure their character and integrity co-exist with their gifts and abilities
Do not know how to deal with pain and disappointment in a healthy way	Deal with pain and disappointment in healthy ways

The Little Letter That Makes a Big Difference

My study of the I-factor started with the fascinating but sad story of two young men whose lives came to a tragic end. Their names were Hophni and Phinehas, and they were the sons of Eli, a priest in Israel. This means they, too, were priests, but as we will see, they only served the Lord externally; they held no honor for Him in their hearts.

The first insight Scripture gives us into these two men and the disconnect between what they did outwardly and who they were inwardly is in 1 Samuel 2:12 (HCSB): "Eli's sons were wicked men; they had no regard for the LORD." *The Complete Word Study Dictionary of the Old Testament: NIV* notes that the word *wicked* means "worthless" and "good for nothing."[9] In other words, no matter what they did or who they were with, they brought no value to the situation. To further understand this verse, we see that in the *NIV Study Bible*, the annotation to this verse explains that "had no regard for the Lord" literally means "did not know." It goes on to say: "In Old Testament usage, to 'know' the Lord is not just intellectual or theoretical recognition. To know the Lord is to enter into fellowship with him and acknowledge his claims on one's life. The term often has a covenantal connotation."[10] Based on this explanation, we can assume Hophni and Phinehas were estranged from God and uninterested in the things of God, even though they were priests. We also know that they were greedy, irreverent, and involved in sexual sin (1 Sam. 2:12–17, 22), serious I-factor issues.

Even their names point to the fact that they were not dedicated to the ways of the Lord. Hophni means "fist-fighter" and Phinehas means "mouth of a serpent."[11] Any time anyone called these men by their names, that person was reinforcing these negative descriptions of them. To the worshippers in the temple, Hophni and Phinehas may have appeared to be successful in their responsibilities of serving the Lord, but they clearly had many faults and weaknesses. Their private failures undermined their public success.

After the description of Hophni and Phinehas, we are told a prophet visited their father, Eli, with strong words spoken on God's behalf: "Why do you honor your sons more than me by fattening yourselves on the choice parts of every offering made by my people Israel?" (1 Sam. 2:29). The prophet concluded his message with these chilling words: "And what happens to your two sons, Hophni and Phinehas, will be a sign to you—*they will both die on the same day*" (v. 34, emphasis added).

Sure enough, on a tragic and dramatic day, both Hophni and Phinehas died in a battle that ensued when the Philistines slaughtered many Israelites and captured the ark of God (1 Sam. 4:10–11). At that time, Eli was ninety-eight years old and when a messenger told him all that had happened, he fell backward out of his chair, broke his neck, and died (vv. 17–18).

At the time this happened, Phinehas's wife was pregnant. When she heard that the ark had been captured and that Phinehas, Hophni, and Eli were all dead, she went into labor. According to Scripture, she "was overcome by her labor pains. As she was dying, the women attending her said, 'Don't despair; you have given birth to a son.' But she did not respond or pay any attention" (vv. 19–20). Before she died, however, Phinehas's wife "named the boy Ichabod, saying, 'The Glory has departed from Israel'—because of the capture of the ark of God and the deaths of her father-in-law and her husband. She said, 'The Glory has departed from Israel, for the ark of God has been captured'" (vv. 21–22).

To further understand the significance of Ichabod's name, it's important to also understand the meaning of the word *chabod*, without the *I*. In Hebrew, *chabod* is the opposite of *Ichabod*. *Chabod* refers to the full weight or splendor of God's glory.[12] The word *glory*, especially in its Old Testament sense, seems old-fashioned and outdated in our current day, but the modern definition of *glory* is this: "public praise, honor, and fame; something that brings praise or fame to someone or something; something that is a source of great pride."[13] Based on this definition, it's reasonable to say that whatever we view as "success" is our "glory." It's what earns us public praise, honor, and recognition; it's something in which we take pride. With that in mind, let's think again about Ichabod.

The difference between *Ichabod*, meaning "no glory" and *chabod*, meaning "the full measure of glory" is one tiny letter—the letter *I*. That's the letter that changes everything. In biblical times, it made the difference between glory and no glory. Today, it makes the difference between success and failure, not because of its connection to those words, but because of the person to whom it applies. Almost always, the difference between victory and defeat in life is "I." The ability to succeed or not resides within us. Yes, there are times when other people help us succeed or when circumstances seem to fall into place perfectly, setting us up for the breakthroughs we need. And yes, there are times God moves on our behalf in astonishing ways to help us get where we need to be. But generally speaking, success rises and falls on each individual who pursues it. One of the truths of life, although it can be painful, is this: we are often the greatest hindrances to our success and the greatest barriers to everything God wants to do in and through our lives. That's what the I-factor is all about.

The I-Factor: It Must Be Dealt With

One of the biggest problems in our society is that so few people recognize or acknowledge the I-factor. Everybody has one, but many people don't realize that. In some people, it's positive; in some it's negative. In some people, it's weak; in others it's strong. For most people, though, it's a struggle because it goes unnoticed and therefore unaddressed. It's like a stealth bomber that wreaks havoc in a person's life, while the person has no idea the bomber is even in flight.

As far back as Hophni and Phinehas's day, people have been clueless about the I-factor and about how much it has to do with what happens to them. In the case of the two brothers, Israel was at war with its enemy, the Philistines. At one point in the battle, the Israelites kept asking, "Why? Why are we being defeated?" They did not recognize their greatest weakness—that God was not with them. Even worse, they did not realize the reason He was not with them was because of the I-factor issues of the priests, Hophni and Phinehas. The Israelites thought simply regaining the ark of the covenant would be enough to guarantee their victory. It wasn't—because doing the right things externally is never sufficient. In fact, the Israelites were defeated long before the battle even started because their leaders never addressed their I-factor issues.

In many ways, life is a battle, just as real as any military conflict. People wrestle with financial issues, relational issues, bad habits and addictions, poor choices, trying to get ahead personally and professionally, and a host of other challenges that everyday life presents. Like it or not, in order to succeed we have to fight. We have to fight external enemies, but we also have to fight the internal forces that cause us to sabotage ourselves.

In order to win the battles necessary to succeed in life, we have to start with three things. First, we need to recognize the I-factor. We need to realize that not every hindrance, delay, or challenge we face is external. Some of them—some of the most potent—are internal. Second, we need to deal with the weaknesses and negative aspects of our own I-factors. This may not be a quick-and-easy process, but the rewards will be tremendous. Third, we need to replace the faulty elements of our I-factors with strong, healthy ingredients. As we do this, we turn the things that hinder us into things that will help us.

I believe you are destined for so much more than you are currently experiencing. I am convinced your life can be so much better than it is now, and so much better than you have ever imagined. I know you have many gifts, skills, talents, and dreams just waiting to take you to the next level of greatness. No doubt, you have many of your externals in order, but perhaps you know deep down that something—something you cannot perceive clearly and may not be able to articulate, but you know it's there—is holding you back from the life you long for. There's a good chance that "something" is related to the I-factor. This book will help you resolve your I-factor issues so you can experience all the greatness for which you were created.

Internal Building Blocks

- True success is not dependent on external resources or evident in the so-called external trappings of success. It comes from what's inside you.
- The most important relationship you will ever have in your life is the relationship you have with yourself.
- The way you manage yourself internally determines whether you become your own best friend or your own worst enemy, whether you help yourself or hinder yourself on the journey to success.
- Three secrets to success are to recognize your own I-factor and understand the importance of a healthy relationship with yourself, deal with your internal issues and struggles, and work to replace weak aspects of your I-factor with strong ones.

———————— Strengthening Your I-Factor ————————

1. Based on this chapter, what does the I-factor mean to you?
2. How would you describe your relationship with yourself?
3. Why is your I-factor your most important key to success?
4. What do you believe to be your most significant I-factor weakness and how can you strengthen and improve it? (Please see chart on pages 10–12.)
5. What do you believe to be your biggest I-factor strength and how can you use it to take yourself to a new level of success and greatness? (Please see chart on pages 10–12.)

It's Time to Peel the Onion

*Success in any endeavor depends on the degree
to which it is an expression of your true self.*
—RALPH MARSTON

THE ISSUE OF PERSONAL IDENTITY IS A HUGE COMPONENT of anyone's I-factor. Everything you think, everything you do, and the entire way you see and relate to yourself flows from your sense of identity—your personal assessment of who you are and why you are significant. Your identity is the compass that guides you through every aspect of your life and keeps you grounded and centered in the things that matter most to you.

When people are not secure in their identities, they waste much of their time in efforts to fulfill the unreasonable expectations that others have placed on them. Many individuals have crashed and burned not because of their own inabilities or weaknesses, but because they have tried to be something they were not in an effort to please people who never should have had so much influence in their lives.

Trying to please or impress other people, or to live up to their expectations, is exhausting and frustrating. People rarely succeed at it because when they do it, they suppress and deny their true selves as they pretend to be smarter, wealthier, more attractive, more charismatic, more gifted, or more connected than they really believe themselves to be. If they only knew how valuable they actually are, they could save so much energy, be so much more authentic, and enjoy life so much more.

The process of discovering your personal identity is one of the most rewarding journeys you will ever take. It's not easy, but when you begin to find out and tap into who you really are, apart from all the trappings of your life, I believe the results will invigorate you, empower you, and take your breath away. I liken this process of self-discovery to an activity we're all familiar with—the peeling of an onion.

When you peel an onion, you remove one layer at a time until you get to the core of the onion, which began as an onion seed. Just as the onion started with a seed, you also started as a seed, biologically speaking, the seed of life. That seed carried everything about you, and the unique DNA code of who you are—your identity—was in it. Over time, many layers have piled on top of that unique identity, layers of experience, layers of fear, layers of disappointment, and layers of so many other things. Getting back to the core of who you are, the seed, allows you to live from the healthy place of your true identity.

You figure out who you really are and why you are so valuable one discovery at a time. Often, before you get down to the core of who you really are, you first have to strip away who you are not. Just like peeling an onion can sting your eyes and stink up your kitchen, uncovering your true identity can be messy and painful. Just as there are times you have to step away from the onion because your eyes are watering so profusely, there will be times you have to back off on your journey of discovery because it's so intense. I don't pretend that the process is easy, but I promise that it's a supremely worthwhile endeavor. Failure to do it will forever bind you to the emptiness of trying to define yourself according to what you do in life instead of who you are, to what someone did to you or said about you, to circumstances beyond your control, or to what has happened in your past. But if you'll do the work of finding out who you really are, it will shape and shift your entire life in all the best ways.

Your Identity Is Not Based on What You Do

Bible teacher Joyce Meyer has a well-known quotation that summarizes identity in just a few words: "You must separate your *do* from your *who*."[1] In other words, who you are is totally separate from what you do. Your identity comes from God and is revealed in His Word. Yet many people are unaware of this truth, so they go through life defining themselves in terms of their accomplishments or activities instead of their internal realities. As an example, think about how many times you have overheard a conversation like this:

"Hi, I'm John."

"Hi, John. I'm Darrell. Nice to meet you."

"Nice to meet you, too, Darrell. Tell me about yourself."

"Well, I'm an accountant and a running enthusiast."

John might then respond with the fact that he is an engineer and a guitarist in his spare time.

At the end of a conversation like this, both men end up finding out what the other one *does*, but they know little about who the other one *is*. Unfortunately, much of our social system in the United States is built on knowing what people do, not on who they are. This happens not only in relationships with others, it also happens in our relationships with ourselves. Because we find it easier to focus on our actions than on our inner beings, we default to talking about who we are in terms of

> You figure out who you really are and why you are so valuable one discovery at a time. Often, before you get down to the core of who you really are, you first have to strip away who you are not.

what we do—when, in reality, they are two separate aspects of our lives.

In order to live successful lives, we cannot define ourselves by or try to find our value in what we do in life. What we do includes not only our chosen professions but also all our external qualities. We need to define ourselves and find our worth in who we are on the inside. Identity is not about what's readily visible to casual observers—good looks, stylish clothes, a house in the right neighborhood, professional or personal accomplishments, or even intellect or charisma. Identity is about what God has put deep inside of us, not only our uniqueness as individuals, but also the spiritual realities He has deposited in us as believers. When we perceive those gifts rightly, we draw strength and pursue our destinies based on all He has placed inside of us, not on anything we could gain through human effort.

Perhaps you saw the movie *Gladiator*, which is a phenomenal story of the power of identity. In the movie, Russell Crowe plays Maximus, an outstanding general in the army of the Roman emperor, Marcus Aurelius. Aurelius's son, Commodus, expects to succeed his father as emperor, but Aurelius knows Commodus is unfit to rule and chooses Maximus instead. Hearing this news, Commodus flies into a rage and kills his father. He arranges for Maximus to be arrested and killed, and he orders Maximus's farm burned and his family murdered. After this trauma, as Maximus wanders in the desert, a North African slave owner captures him and requires him to work as a gladiator.

Maximus quickly becomes a skilled gladiator, winning victory after victory and becoming popular with the local audience. The people, however, do not know who he is, because he fights in a mask. They only know him as "the Spaniard." Eventually he ends up back in Rome in the fighting ring with Commodus, who has no idea Maximus is still alive.

Commodus begs the Spaniard to identify himself, and when he finally does, Commodus is stunned and the audience in Rome is thrilled. Their hero has returned! Maximus's soldiers rally around him, and Commodus knows his days are numbered. In his jealousy and desperation to retain the throne, he challenges Maximus to a duel. Prior to the match, he stabs Maximus. Despite his wound, Maximus fights on, eventually killing his longtime rival. After Commodus's death, Maximus's stab wound becomes fatal, and he requests with his dying words that the important reforms needed in Rome finally become realities and that the gladiators with whom he was imprisoned be freed.

The reason Maximus was victorious in the end was that he never lost his sense of identity. He went from being a general in the Roman army to being a prisoner, but he did not let that change who he was. He never appropriated the mind-set or the bearing of a prisoner. His "do" changed radically, but his "who" never did.

Many people today believe their identities are in what they do. There are large numbers of people who, if they lost their jobs tomorrow, would suffer a great deal emotionally. They would question their self-worth and their value to the world around them, when in reality nothing about who they are or what they can contribute would change at all. Those things would stand firm; the professional expression of those things would simply be removed.

Perhaps you have heard, as I have, of men whose identities were so tightly tied to their ability to provide for their families that they killed themselves after losing their jobs and not being able to find what they considered appropriate employment. These situations are tragic in every way, and their bottom line is that those who committed suicide never understood how valuable they were, with or without a job. They never separated their *who* from their *do*, and their failure to do so was devastating.

When you know your *who* and are firmly established in your

identity, you can lose your do and bounce back to bigger and better "*do*"s. Failure does not keep you down when you know who you really are. Many people seem to believe their *do* makes their *who* possible, but the truth is the other way around: your *who* makes possible everything you do.

I want to encourage you to take a hard look at your life. Examine what you do and ask yourself how it makes you feel. Do you feel important because you are a CEO, a COO, a CFO, or some other executive—or do you feel important because you are you? Do you believe life is worth living as long as you are raising smart, well-mannered children or coaching a winning football team—or is life worth living because of the positive internal resources you can offer the people around you? Are you fulfilled because you've earned the respect of your community—or do you feel fulfilled because you have the qualities that earned the respect in the first place?

> When you know your *who* and are firmly established in your identity, you can lose your *do* and bounce back to bigger and better "*do*"s.

As you begin peeling the onion of who you are, these questions and others will probably come to mind and will take time and effort to answer. You may have to face some unpleasant realities about how much weight you have been attributing to your *do*, when it rightfully belongs to your *who*. The only way to move toward a better, happier, psychologically healthier life is to start investigating where you really find your identity and then make whatever changes are needed.

Your Identity Is Not Based on Circumstances

Everyone's life is affected at some point by situations outside of his or her control. When these things happen, many people allow them to define who they are—whether it's being born without the advantages other people enjoy, the breakup of a family during childhood, a serious accident or injury, the loss of a job and a paycheck, an illness, or a teenage child's bad decisions.

One of the best stories I know of a person who refused to allow circumstances beyond his control to contribute to his identity is about an amazing man whose inventions years ago probably still impact your life today. His story is so inspirational that he has become almost a living symbol of what it means to overcome seemingly insurmountable personal obstacles and achieve success. His name is George Washington Carver, and he is famous for his work as an inventor and for his creativity in finding more than three hundred beneficial uses for the peanut, including mayonnaise, shampoo, nitroglycerine, and axle grease.[2] At a time when the boll weevil threatened to destroy the economy of the South by wiping out the cotton crop, Carver's inventions inspired struggling farmers to plant and harvest peanuts instead of cotton, arguably saving this entire region of the United States from financial disaster.[3] His accomplishments are remarkable not only because of their creative and scientific value, but also because the man overcame his personal history. Against all odds, he persevered with the help of the family who raised him, even though he was not their biological child.

During the Civil War, one-week-old George was kidnapped from the home of his owner, Moses Carver. One of Mr. Carver's employees found the baby and returned him to the Carvers' home. Mr. Carver and his wife took the boy in, raised him, and were determined to provide him with an education.

In those days, schooling was not readily available to African American children, and none of the local schools would admit George as a student. So Mrs. Carver taught George to read and write. Even after the end of slavery, George continued to live with the Carver family and Mrs. Carver remained his teacher for several years.

Eventually, George was able to go to a school about ten miles from the Carvers' home. He was then accepted at a college in Kansas and planned to attend—until school officials changed their minds about him because of his race. Later, George became the first black student at Iowa State Agricultural College, where he excelled in his studies and received both a bachelor's and a master's degree.

George Washington Carver established himself as a brilliant botanist, teacher, inventor, and administrator. He ran the agriculture department at the esteemed Tuskegee Institute, and under his leadership, the department gained national respect and renown. He became one of America's foremost intellectuals in his day, serving as an advisor to President Theodore Roosevelt. On the international scene, he advised India's leader, Mahatma Gandhi, on issues of agriculture and nutrition.

At the beginning of George's life, nothing suggested he would ever be able to learn or go to school, much less enjoy worldwide esteem. But his curiosity, diligence, and perseverance paid off, and he went from being a slave child to being a globally respected scientist and leader. Of course, his brilliance took him to places he once only dreamed of going and gained him the trust of world leaders and the admiration of generations of Americans. But had the Carver family not cared for him and raised him as their own, his intellect would never have been given a chance to develop and his creativity might not have been channeled in the right direction. The education the family provided gave him the foundation he needed for a life of phenomenal success.

I can imagine that George Washington Carver never forgot he was born a slave. That could have resulted in all sorts of I-factor issues for him—feelings of inferiority to others, feeling he was a victim, anger over his lot in life, or fear of having big dreams. He could have squandered the opportunities the Carvers gave him, especially after he had endured race-based rejection from several schools. But he didn't. He chose to believe in himself and his abilities, and to take advantage of his opportunities. He did not let obstacles stand in his way, nor did he allow the opinions of others (especially those who denied him entrance to school) to change his estimation of himself. He did not allow the circumstances into which he was born to define his view of himself. In fact, that identity became the fuel of his accomplishments. His *who* was the internal engine that drove everything about his life. When your *who* defines and drives your life, opposition, obstacles, and even unfair treatment are not allowed to become determining factors about who you are.

When Carver died on January 5, 1943, President Franklin D. Roosevelt sent this message: "All mankind are the beneficiaries of his discoveries in the field of agricultural chemistry. The things which he achieved in the face of early handicaps will for all time afford an inspiring example to youth everywhere."[4] George Washington Carver had a strong I-factor that became the cornerstone of his success because he made the mental and emotional transition from a slave to a son.

Your Identity Is Not Based on What Happened to You

The Bible tells the poignant story about a person who had no idea who he was, no sense of identity, and who lived more like a slave than a son—Mephibosheth, a grandson of Israel's King Saul, a tragic historical figure. Mephibosheth is a powerful picture of someone who did not know who he was and who lived beneath his privilege as a result. We can learn some valuable lessons from his life.

King Saul was King David's predecessor on the throne of Israel. He started out well but ended up a tormented man jealous of the young David destined to rule after him. When David had the opportunity to kill King Saul, he restrained himself, twice (1 Sam. 24:1–7; 26:7–11). One reason for David's kindness toward Saul was his friendship with Saul's son Jonathan. Years after Saul and Jonathan had died, David remembered his friend and asked a question: "Is there anyone still left of the house of Saul to whom I can show kindness for Jonathan's sake?" (2 Sam. 9:1). He discovered that Jonathan had a son who lived in poverty in a place called Lo-Debar, so he sent for him. Their first conversation recorded in 2 Samuel 9:6–8 is remarkable:

> David said, "Mephibosheth!"
>
> "At your service," he replied.
>
> "Don't be afraid," David said to him, "for I will surely show you kindness for the sake of your father Jonathan. I will restore to you all the land that belonged to your grandfather Saul, and you will always eat at my table."
>
> Mephibosheth bowed down and said, "What is your servant, that you should notice a dead dog like me?"

Clearly, Mephibosheth had an I-factor problem. There he was, with King David offering to completely restore all his family had lost and to treat him as family by moving him into the palace and including him at the king's table for every meal. Mephibosheth thought so poorly of himself that he could not even acknowledge David's grace and favor. All he could focus on was what a wretch he was, in his opinion.

When we hear of a prince living in poverty, viewing himself as "a dead dog," and being rescued by his father's friend, we have to wonder how he ended up that way. It goes back many years, to a time when Mephibosheth was very young and Saul's family members were forced to flee their home (2 Sam. 4:4). A nurse gathered

Mephibosheth in her arms to carry him to safety, but in her haste, she tripped and dropped him, which is how he became crippled. The critical I-factor lessons in Mephibosheth's story are twofold: Anyone can lose his or her sense of identity, even the grandson of a king, but anyone can also recover and regain it. Second, one of the most important aspects of regaining a sense of identity is to deal with what has happened in the past. Bad things do happen to people. Sometimes those things are tragic and completely outside of the victim's control. In those circumstances, individuals can choose to live with the negative consequences of what others have done to them (or allowed to happen to them), or they can choose to overcome.

I am certain Mephibosheth's nurse did not mean to drop him. No doubt, it was an accident. She was trying to help him, but he ended up hurt—permanently—despite her good intentions. Many people, maybe even you, can relate to Mephibosheth's predicament. Perhaps something deeply wounding has happened to you, and it was not your fault. The person who caused the damage may not have intended to hurt you and may feel terrible about it now. But the facts and the consequences of the situation are what they are; you can't change them, but you can change the way you allow them to affect you. What happened to you is external; what you do with it is internal. You have a choice: you can focus on what happened or you can focus on who you are. Who you are has absolutely nothing to do with what has happened to you.

Had Mephibosheth chosen to focus on who he was, he could have experienced restoration much sooner than he did; he lived in poverty in Lo-Debar for way too long. David had a track record of kindness toward Saul's family, and had Mephibosheth simply made the effort to reach out to David, he would not have struggled in deprivation for so long. Had he viewed himself as the royalty that he was instead of as a dead dog, his entire life would have been different.

What happened to Mephibosheth was external, not internal. Although it affected him dramatically, it did not have to change who he was or how he viewed himself. If you have struggled with allowing your past to define you, one of the best things you can do is break free from it. So how do you move beyond the things that have hurt you, handicapped you, or hindered your pursuit of your destiny? Let me offer four observations many people have found helpful: Things happen. Freedom comes from forgiveness. Who you are is much more important than what happened to you. Changing what you can change is important.

Things Happen

Life is not always a bed of roses. Good things do happen to people, but bad things happen too. It's just part of living. Many times, when circumstances are extremely painful or have caused problems for us, we may be tempted to deny them. We may blame our troubles on other things because the real culprits are too painful to deal with. This is especially true for victims of sexual abuse or assault. It can also apply to people injured in car accidents when the other driver was intoxicated, for parents or siblings of people who bring shame or embarrassment to their families, or for hard-working individuals who may end up out of a job due to the sale of a company or other circumstances beyond their control. Many people have these situations and others like them in their pasts. In most cases, these people cannot help what has happened to them. They can only decide that they will not allow these things to define them.

If something in your past truly has put certain limitations on your present circumstances, one of the healthiest things you can do is to accept it as a part of your life's journey but refuse to see it as the defining moment of your life. You are not the product of the things that have happened to you. You're bigger and better than that.

Freedom Comes from Forgiveness

I know many people who have had negative experiences in their lives. Some of them view themselves as victims who will never heal, and some see themselves as overcomers. Often, what makes the difference between the two mind-sets is whether people choose to forgive those who hurt or offended them.

You will find more detail about forgiveness later in the book, but for now I simply want to encourage you to take the most important step in your healing journey—forgive. You may need to forgive the person or people involved in the circumstances that hurt you. In some cases, you may also need to forgive yourself for blaming others when you could have taken responsibility for yourself or for lingering in your pain when you had opportunities to be healed. As one version of an anonymous old saying goes, "Harboring unforgiveness is like taking a drink of poison and hoping it will kill somebody else." Not being willing to forgive will keep you in bondage to your past and to the people involved in your previous pain; it will form an invisible bond that connects you to that situation and all its negativity.

No matter who was involved in the tragic or unfortunate things that have happened in your past or what their specific roles were, the only way to set yourself free from them is to forgive them. You'll be amazed at the freedom, strength, and new perspectives on life that will come to you when you do.

Who You Are Is Much More Important than What Happened to You

I am convinced that Mephibosheth's biggest problem was obsessing about what happened to him instead of thinking about who he was and what he could become. He seems to have fixed his gaze on what he could not do instead of what he could do.

As you move forward in your life, let me encourage you to

stay focused on your identity, not on the incidents that have happened in the past. If you will put past events behind you and build up who you are on the inside, you'll soon find yourself with a whole new outlook on life. You will gain the ability to dream again and to develop the motivation to go after your destiny like never before.

When you wake up every morning and feel a familiar physical or emotional pain from some previous trauma, you have a decision to make. You can say something like, "Oh, there's that pain again. I feel it every single day. I remember when it happened . . . I'll never get over it." Or you can say, "There's that pain again. I feel it, but it doesn't define me. I'm not a victim of the circumstance that caused that wound. I forgive the people involved in it. I am determined to move beyond it. I am bigger than my past and stronger than anything that would try to hold me back."

Changing What You Can Change Is Important

Based on what we know about Mephibosheth's story, one of his failures is he never tried to better himself. He allowed himself to live in Lo-Debar to the point that the spirit of Lo-Debar seeped into his very being and became part of who he was. He saw himself as no better than a dead dog, when he was actually a prince! This is what happens to people who wallow in their pasts; they lose their desire and ultimately their ability to change. If you are in this situation, I pray you will take action and begin to look at what can be different. It may be something extremely small, but small beginnings are very important.

Think about an athlete who suffers an injury during a ball-game. Let's say that athlete once dreamed of playing professional sports because of his love for baseball, football, or basketball. If the injury is debilitating, he may not be able to play on the professional level, but he could pursue sports broadcasting, sports medicine, sports marketing, employment in the front office of a major league team, or he could strive to be a sports agent. If the injury is not permanent and he allows himself to laze around in bed instead of doing the work his recovery requires, he could end up permanently incapacitated. But if he chooses to work on getting better every day, he could regain his health and strength and find ways to participate in the sport he loves, even if he cannot actively participate on the field or on the court.

In many situations, people allow themselves to become stuck in their pain or in the disappointment that they can no longer do what they've always wanted to do. But that does not mean they cannot do anything at all. The key to moving forward in life is to do what we can do and to change our circumstances in every possible way instead of letting them overcome us and shut us down.

All Those Good Things Are for You!

As I mentioned earlier, Mephibosheth is a picture of so many people who are not established in their identities. One way to know when someone is struggling with this issue is when he or she looks at other people and thinks, *They will have the breakthroughs they need. Everything will turn out fine for their families. Something great is going to happen for them, but not for me.* This is the mentality of people who do not know their true worth, not the viewpoint of those who know who they really are. Perhaps you have even found yourself thinking this way.

Mephibosheth's story applies today to people whose negative I-factor issues have caused them to miss out on the very best life can offer them. If your past has caused you to believe certain things that simply are not true about your identity, you can have a fresh start and you can go on to have a great life full of good things. All you have to do is realize that your *who* is not your *do*. Whether your *do* is based on something you did to yourself (such as making an unwise decision) or something someone else did to you (such as hurting you, cheating you out of something you had earned, betraying you, or abandoning you) it's in the past. You don't have to take it into your future.

As you look ahead, I hope you will believe that greatness awaits you. Your past does not have to stand between you and your success. You don't have to carry your past with you or even look back and try to remember it. You can move forward without the baggage of the days behind you and enter into the amazing days ahead of you with the freedom and strength that come from knowing who you are and living from that core.

─────────── Internal Building Blocks ───────────

- The process of discovering your personal identity—your own assessment of who you are and why you are significant—is one of the most rewarding journeys you will ever take. It's like peeling an onion. You remove the layers of expectation, frustration, and disappointment from your life, and you discover who you really are.
- Trying to please or impress other people or to live up to their expectations instead of living out of your true identity is exhausting and frustrating. The only ticket to real success is to be who you really are.
- Your identity is based on who you are, not on what you do.
- Your past does not define you, nor does it have to determine your present or your future.
- There are at least four ways to break free from your past. First, realize that things happen, and they can and must be dealt with in healthy ways. Second, understand that forgiveness leads to freedom. Third, realize that who you are is much more important

than what happens to you. And fourth, in any situation, it's important to be proactive and change what you can change.

Strengthening Your I-Factor

1. What are some of the layers you need to peel back in order to reveal your true identity?
2. How would you define your true identity?
3. Have you ever worked hard to please someone or live up to his or her expectations? Did that situation allow you to express your true identity, and was it ultimately good for you?
4. What is the most valuable discovery you have ever made in finding out who you really are?
5. One of the ways to break free from your past is to realize that who you are is much more important than what has happened to you. In your life, what has happened that has become so big that it now overshadows who you are? How might you change the way you think about yourself and your true identity in order to put that situation in proper perspective?

The Best-Kept Secret of
Sustained Success

*The toughest thing about success is that
you've got to keep on being a success.*
—IRVING BERLIN

SOME PEOPLE SEEM TO KNOW EXACTLY WHAT TO DO TO reach the pinnacle of success, but they know little about how to stay at the top of their game once they get there. They may enjoy achievements and acclaim for a while, but then something happens and they lose their position. Almost always, they fall because of something internal, some kind of I-factor issue. I realize that in certain situations, such as a hostile takeover when the CEO of a company loses his or her job, other people may be responsible for someone's downfall. But most of the time, people who reach a level of success and cannot maintain it have only themselves to blame.

Some people fail to succeed; others succeed only to then become very successful at failure. In some ways, the internal dynamics needed to reach a point of success are different from those required to stay successful. Reaching a goal often takes one set of skills and personal resources, while living at that new level takes other skills. For example, for some people, ambition and determination are the top-priority attitudes while they are seeking success. Once they reach the success for which they've labored, ambition fades or gets redirected because it's no longer needed in the way it once was. Then responsibility takes over, and the pressures of responsibility are different from the pressures of ambition. That's why some people seem to attain success quickly and then lose it just as speedily.

> Reaching a goal often takes one set of skills and personal resources, while living at that new level takes other skills.

Whenever a person has a weak or faulty I-factor, long-term and sustained success will be difficult. But I truly believe anyone can achieve and sustain success if his or her I-factor is strong and healthy. No matter what an individual's personal definition of *success* is, he or she can get there and stay there, as long as the I-factor is right.

Success Isn't Necessarily Permanent

Xerxes I of Persia
Anna Nicole Smith
Lance Armstrong
Jimmy Swaggart
Leona Helmsley

These people are seemingly as different as they can be, but they all have one thing in common: they suffered in life because of a personal weakness that took them from the pinnacle of success to total disgrace. In each situation, the specific contributing element to the downfall differed, but it was something related to the I-factor.

The ancient King Xerxes I of Persia allowed his ego to cause him to underestimate a powerful Greek army that eventually defeated him. Anna Nicole Smith's hunger for attention, glamour, and wealth left her empty and miserable; ultimately she died of a drug overdose. Lance Armstrong's quest for dominance and fame caused him to cheat by using illegal substances. Jimmy Swaggart's inability to control his lust led to his being defrocked and losing what was once a popular ministry. Leona Helmsley's greed and arrogance ended with a seven-million-dollar fine and eighteen months in prison.

These individuals reached great heights of success and then fell, but the same dynamics that toppled them are the basic reasons why other, less well-known people have the potential to succeed, yet never do. These people never reach positions of visibility and influence, never see their stories in the news. They suffer in obscurity, well aware of their potential, but unable to reach it—and often unable to figure out why.

You may struggle to identify with a Persian king, a seemingly successful model and actress, an elite athlete, a popular televangelist, or a ruthless businesswoman, but you still know what I mean when I talk about people who yearn for success and significance, only to sabotage themselves time and time again. Maybe that's exactly what's happening to you. There seems to be no reason you cannot live the life you long for, yet every time you start to pursue your purpose, you get derailed. After a while, you recognize this is happening repeatedly. You are a person of dreams and destiny, but you wrestle with the reality that you simply cannot get where you want to go. Be encouraged: this chapter will help you identify, understand, and solve the problem, and break through the barriers that have blocked you from the greatness you were born to enjoy.

A King Sets Himself Up for a Fall

People have tumbled from positions of prominence to the depths of obscurity for centuries. Influential voices have been silenced because they got caught up in corruption; people of certain socio-economic status have lost their wealth; something has humbled a haughty socialite or an arrogant leader. It's what happened to the first king of the nation of Israel, a thirty-year-old man named Saul. King Saul was known early in his reign for being tall and handsome and was regarded later as a shrewd and victorious military leader. Saul preceded David, and like David, King Saul experienced remarkable success—to a point.

Soon after Samuel, the priest and prophet, anointed Saul as king, he gave Saul a series of instructions concerning things he needed to do as the nation's new leader. One of them was, "Go down ahead of me to Gilgal. I will surely come down to you to sacrifice burnt offerings and fellowship offerings, but you must wait seven days until I come to you and tell you what you are to do" (1 Sam. 10:8).

Saul partially honored Samuel's request. He did go to Gilgal, where he would fight an important battle against the Philistines, but when Samuel did not arrive seven days later, Saul took matters into his own hands.

Remember, Samuel was a prophet and the priest in Israel at the time. He was God's emissary in this situation; he alone was qualified to sacrifice the offerings. He had promised to make the offerings at Gilgal, as was fitting for him to do. The longer Saul waited for Samuel, the more frightened his army became. By the seventh day, they began abandoning him. So Saul usurped Samuel's responsibility and privilege and presented the offerings himself, instead of continuing to wait for Samuel, the proper person to offer the sacrifices.

Just as Saul finished with the offerings, Samuel arrived. Surprised that the offerings had already been made, he asked Saul, "What have you done?" (1 Sam. 13:11).

Saul told Samuel that when he realized his men were leaving

and Samuel had not shown up at the time he promised to be there and the Philistine army was gathering against his forces, he knew his army would soon be under attack. When he saw these circumstances aligning against him and did not know where Samuel was, he said he "felt compelled to offer the burnt offering" (v. 12).

Samuel's response was both stern and sad:

> "You have done a foolish thing," Samuel said. "You have not kept the command the LORD your God gave you; if you had, he would have established your kingdom over Israel for all time. But now your kingdom will not endure; the LORD has sought out a man after his own heart and appointed him ruler of his people, because you have not kept the LORD's command." (vv. 13–14)

Almost as quickly as God elevated Saul to the highest position in the land, He spoke forth his downfall through Samuel. As quickly as Saul gained God's favor, he lost it. When God chose Saul as king, he went from anonymity to royalty. With his actions at Gilgal, he forfeited everything God had for him. He basically lost his destiny, failing to maintain his position of success for the long term because he demonstrated six I-factor flaws: he had a bad habit of making excuses, he was impatient, he was disobedient, he compared himself to another and allowed himself to become jealous, he was fearful, and he was proud. Even though Saul lived centuries ago, these same weaknesses, in some form or another—sometimes alone and sometimes in conjunction with one another—comprise the basis of almost every I-factor problem that people struggle with today.

Saul's I-Factor Problems

Saul's first personal flaw was his lack of willingness to take responsibility for himself, causing him to make excuses and blame others.

We see this when Samuel confronts him after realizing he has offered the sacrifices himself, instead of waiting on Samuel. Instead of owning his offense, Saul says, basically, "Well, see, it wasn't really about me. It was my men. They were so scared of the Philistines and they started leaving."

At Gilgal, Saul had three thousand troops, but he also had God on his side. God chose him as a leader. God anointed him. God was with him. If every one of the men had left, God still would have been with him. And God plus anyone is always a majority. I would rather have God on my side and no one else than three thousand frail human beings, wouldn't you? All we have to do is think about the story of Gideon to realize that numbers are unimportant when God is with a leader (Judg. 7). But Saul did not think about that.

Based on the certainty that God was with Israel's army, Saul could have rallied his troops and inspired them by his own faith and patience to wait for Samuel, but he did not. As their leader, keeping his men calm, focused, and strong was part of his responsibility. He did not do it. He let their leaving frighten him, he allowed them to go, and then he blamed them for his sin—doing what only the priest was allowed to do.

Saul's second I-factor problem was that he lacked patience. Saul was not impatient because of a bad temper; he lost his patience in this situation because of his perspective. If we look back at 1 Samuel 10:8, we see that Samuel promised to be in Gilgal after seven days—not at noon on the seventh day, not at 4:00 p.m., not at any specific time. He told Saul which day he would arrive, not which hour. The seventh day was not complete when Saul took the inappropriate initiative of making the offerings. Samuel did come—just as Saul completed the offerings.

The third weakness in Saul's I-factor was his disobedience to God. Before I go further, let me say this: God is a God of second chances, sometimes even third and fourth chances. Whenever we fail or fall short of what He has called us to do, He is gracious to allow us to try again—because He wants us to succeed. Saul was not only irresponsible and impatient at Gilgal, he was also disobedient because he knew he was not supposed to offer the sacrifices; he knew that in God's order, only the priest could perform such rituals.

In spite of Saul's failings and foolishness at Gilgal, God gave him another chance. In 1 Samuel 15, Samuel speaks to Saul on God's behalf and tells him to execute God's punishment on the Amalekites. This army had already launched a major attack against Israel (Ex. 17), and now God was ready to deal with them. The instruction was clear and firm: "Now go, attack the Amalekites and totally destroy everything that belongs to them. Do not spare them; put to death men and women, children and infants, cattle and sheep, camels and donkeys" (1 Sam. 15:3). Based on these directions, Saul should have known exactly what to do.

But he did not do it. Instead, he spared the life of the Amalekites' king Agag "and the best of the sheep and cattle, the fat calves and lambs—everything that was good. These they were unwilling to destroy completely" (v. 9). There was no doubt about it. Saul disobeyed God's orders.

The reason God wanted the Amalekites annihilated was that He knew a remnant of the enemy would rebuild and grow and eventually return to attack Israel again, which is exactly what happened. God meant business when He directed Saul to obliterate the Amalekites, but Saul did not take Him seriously. Samuel, however, did fear the Lord and in the end, he put Agag to death because he understood the importance of obedience (vv. 32–33).

Immediately after Saul's disobedience regarding the Amalekites, God tells Samuel that He has chosen a new king (1 Sam. 16:1), a young man named David who would ultimately become Israel's best-known ruler. After Samuel anointed David king, the Bible tells us "the Spirit of the LORD came powerfully upon David" (v. 13). In the next verse, we read, "Now the Spirit of the LORD had departed from Saul, and an evil spirit from the LORD tormented him" (v. 14). Why did God send an evil spirit to harass Saul? Because of his foolishness, the sins he committed at Gilgal, and his failure to follow God's instructions about the Amalekites. But why was he foolish and sinful? Because he neglected to deal with the personal weaknesses that eventually destroyed him.

In the midst of Saul's torment, his attendants suggested they find someone who could play beautiful music to soothe him. Saul agreed, and one of the servants sent for David, calling him "a brave man and a warrior. He speaks well and is a fine-looking man. And the LORD is with him" (v. 18). Saul, of course, had no idea that God had chosen David and that Samuel had anointed David to become Israel's next king.

David's music did indeed calm Saul, and David quickly gained Saul's favor. David killed the Philistine giant, Goliath, and became a local hero for military victories that exceeded Saul's. The king promoted David to a high rank in his army and gave his daughter to David in marriage. Over time, though, Saul grew jealous of David and compared himself to him. This was his fourth I-factor flaw.

As his fifth I-factor flaw, Saul became afraid of David because he knew the presence of the Lord had left him and could tell that God's presence and favor were upon David (1 Sam. 18:12). In addition, he was too proud to acknowledge David's victories or to honor David for them—his sixth I-factor weakness. Eventually, as Saul's madness, jealousy, fear, and pride spun out of control, he tried to kill David. David fled but at one point found himself with his army in a cave, and Saul entered the cave to relieve himself (1 Sam. 24:3). David got close enough to Saul to kill him, but chose not to, saying, "The LORD forbid that I should do such a thing to my master, the

LORD's anointed, or lay my hand on him" (v. 6). David had another chance to kill Saul, and again decided against it (1 Sam. 26:6–11).

From the time he was thirty years old, Saul was destined for greatness. God saw something promising in him, or He would not have chosen him as king. Saul ascended to the highest position in Israel, and God gave him chance after chance to handle himself well. Throughout his reign, he repeatedly refused to deal with his I-factor issues—irresponsibility, impatience, disobedience, fear, jealousy, and pride. That stubbornness and lack of humility led him to years of torment and ultimately to such ongoing misery that he took his own life (1 Sam. 31:4).

One of the saddest aspects of Saul's story is that he could have succeeded. Each of Saul's faults and their consequences could have been avoided had he simply dealt with his I-factor. Had he been willing to take responsibility instead of make excuses, he could have become a strong leader instead of a tragic figure. Had he exercised patience at Gilgal, he could have been the cornerstone of a lasting reign in Israel. God told Saul that He would have "established your kingdom over Israel for all time. But now your kingdom will not endure" (1 Sam. 13:13–14).

Had Saul been obedient to wipe out the Amalekites, the nation of Israel would not have suffered subsequent attacks from them, nor would David have had to fight them (1 Sam. 27:8; 30:1–18). In addition, Saul would not have endured the personal consequences of disobedience to God. Instead of comparing himself with David and feeling inferior to him, Saul could have celebrated David as a promising young leader and shared in David's ultimate successes. Instead, he spent the last years of his life running in fear from a man who only showed him mercy and did him good. Instead of allowing his pride to destroy him, Saul could have been a humble, righteous king.

A Sad Summary of Saul's Life

In one of my favorite books, *A Tale of Three Kings*, Gene Edwards powerfully summarized Saul's strengths and weaknesses:

> What kind of man was Saul? Who was this one who made himself David's enemy? Anointed of God. Deliverer of Israel. And yet remembered mostly for his madness.
>
> Forget the bad press. Forget the stinging reviews. Forget his reputation. Look at the facts. Saul was one of the greatest figures of human history. He was a farm boy, a real country kid. He was tall, good-looking, and well-liked.
>
> He was baptized into the Spirit of God.
>
> He also came from a good family; that is, in his lineage were some of the great historical figures of all mankind. Abraham, Israel, Moses, these were his ancestors. . . .
>
> Saul united a people and founded a kingdom. Few men have ever done that. He created an army out of thin air. He won battles in the power of God, defeated the enemy again and again, as few men ever have. . . . Furthermore, he was a prophet. The Spirit came on him in power and authority. He did and said unprecedented things and it was all by the power of the Spirit resting on him.
>
> He was everything [people] today are seeking to be . . . empowered with the Holy Spirit . . . able to do the impossible . . . for God.
>
> He was also eaten with jealousy, capable of murder and willing to live in spiritual darkness. . . .
>
> There is a vast difference between the outward clothing of the Spirit's power and the inward filling of the Spirit's life. In the first, despite the power, the hidden man of the heart may remain unchanged. In the latter, that monster is dealt with.[1]

How Not to Be Like Saul

So many people today struggle with the same issues that caused Saul to lose his position and his destiny. If we are honest, I think all of us can remember times we have been irresponsible, impatient, or disobedient. We can also think of situations in which we have been afraid, compared ourselves with others and become jealous of them, and walked in pride instead of humility. Some people manage these things better than others. Some manage most of them well, but find themselves in a seemingly constant battle with another. For example, some people are not impatient, but they are irresponsible. Others are not easily jealous of others, but they do battle fear in every situation they face.

The key to sustained success is to resolve all our I-factor issues as quickly as we can, as soon as we recognize them. Otherwise, like Saul, we can be people of tremendous potential and promise, but lose everything. Thankfully, there are some ways we can begin to deal with I-factor issues we may have in common with Saul. Our stories can be accounts of increasing strength and victory, not continual weakness and defeat.

Become Responsible

Being irresponsible is easy. Taking responsibility is a bit more difficult, but it is vital to long-term success. If you struggle with irresponsibility, let me encourage you to look for areas where you can start small. For example, take responsibility for managing your time. Don't rely on a spouse or a roommate to wake you up each morning; set your own wake time on your alarm clock or electronic device. In addition, take responsibility for your health by making healthy food choices, disciplining yourself to exercise, and keeping doctor's appointments as recommended. These are simple ways to grow in your capacity to be responsible. Once you learn to take responsibility, it will become a stepping-stone to success.

Become Patient

I have seen so many people sabotage their own success simply because they were not willing to wait. When you are moving toward a new level of greatness, you can easily become excited and get ahead of yourself. But often, success is a matter of timing. Just because something does not happen when you want it to does not mean it will never happen at all. If you'll discipline yourself to be patient as your journey to success unfolds, you will learn many valuable lessons along the way. There's a reason for the old sayings, "Patience is a virtue" and "Good things come to those who wait." They're true!

Become Obedient

Saul's biggest mistake was his disobedience to the Lord. Throughout Scripture, there is a principle that says obedience leads to blessing. As long as Saul obeyed God, he enjoyed God's blessing. When he stopped, things fell apart. That same pattern is still in effect today and applies to you and me. I understand obedience is not always easy, but it's important to remember God will always lead you in the best possible way to the best possible results, even if you don't like or understand the process. Anytime He asks for your obedience, you can be sure it's for your good.

Resist Fear

The older Saul got, the more fearful he became. His fears sucked the greatness out of him. The late Nelson Mandela said, "The brave man is not he who does not feel afraid, but he who conquers that fear."[2] It's important to understand that feeling afraid is normal; it's part of life. But allowing fear to control us, to override our sensibilities, to keep us from doing what we know we should do, or to cause us to hold back when we need to move forward is a problem. Few emotions will block success and shut down a journey to greatness like fear—fear of failure, fear of the unknown, fear of what other people will think, fear of the future, or any of the other fears that so often plague humanity. In your life, fear will raise its ugly head from time to time; your job is to face it and overcome it.

Resist Comparison and Jealousy

People with a weak I-factor easily fall into comparison and jealousy. Too often, they look to see how what they are doing stacks up to what others are doing. This "doing" may be anything from people's appearances and what clothes they wear, to the cars they drive, to whether or not they are married, to their positions at work, to their athletic abilities, or to their abilities to keep a clean house. Jealousy and comparison have their roots in selfishness and pride, and there is no end to the things a jealous person will find to envy about others.

Mature people who are secure in who they are and who have strong I-factors are able to honor and enjoy the successes of others. They are able to compliment others and encourage them to go after their dreams and fulfill their potential. They can do these things without a twinge of jealousy and without comparing themselves to other people or comparing their possessions to others' belongings. This is because they know who they are, their identities are established, and they have conquered selfishness and pride. Because of their inner strength, they see things others would envy and view them as causes to celebrate those who have achieved or attained them.

Practice Humility

The English preacher Charles Spurgeon described humility this way: to be humble is "to make a right estimate of oneself."[3] I like this definition because many people have been taught that humility means not standing up for oneself, choosing weakness over strength, or becoming a doormat. None of these is true. Genuine humility requires an accurate assessment of yourself, an honest evaluation of both your strengths and your weaknesses. It also requires a respectful expression of who you really are—not a suppression of your true self in an effort to please or defer to someone else for the sake of keeping peace or being viewed as polite. To practice humility is not to refuse to act or to keep your mouth shut, but to act and speak wisely, respectfully, and truthfully whenever a situation calls for it.

A Tale of Two Kings

When I think of Saul, I also think of two modern-day men, also clearly called and anointed of God, whose outward circumstances were not like Saul's, but whose inner struggles took them down. One chose not to be like Saul, while the other unfortunately followed some of Saul's examples. These men ended up with vastly different results, which is why I call the story of these two influential Christian leaders "A Tale of Two Kings."

In the 1970s and '80s, two of the most popular and highly rated televangelists in the world were Jim Bakker and his wife, Tammy Faye. If ever there had been a Christian media king up to that point in history, Jim Bakker was it, and he and Tammy Faye epitomized everything the word *televangelist* has come to mean. They were charismatic in their personalities and anointed in their ministry, and they enjoyed the financial fruit of their calling. Jim and Tammy Faye came across as compassionate people of God with a gift for leading people to salvation.

But behind the scenes, what appeared to be a prosperous media ministry was struggling financially. As the result of an investigation by the *Charlotte Observer* newspaper, Jim faced criminal charges based on illegal fund-raising activities. In addition, he was involved in a sexual scandal at the same time his ministry was unraveling. In 1988, Jim was convicted on fifteen counts of wire fraud, eight counts of mail fraud, and one count of conspiracy. He was sentenced to forty-five years in prison and fined $500,000. In 1991, an appellate court voided the sentence and the fine and sent the case to a new hearing. Tammy Faye divorced Jim in 1992, and he was released from prison in December 1994.

Jim had nothing when he left prison, but thanks to the kindness of the Billy Graham family, he slowly began to rebuild his life—including dealing with his I-factor issues, which are clear in his book *I Was Wrong*.[4] As of this writing, Jim is happily married to his lovely wife, Lori, and they are serving God together and blessing the body of Christ in powerful ways. Jim's story could have easily ended in tragedy and degradation, but it didn't. He was humble enough to confront his weaknesses, repent of his sins, and ask God to restore his life. His story of restoration is an amazing testimony to what God can do when a person settles the I-factor issues that once ensnared him or her.

The second man I want to mention, though I will refrain from naming him, was once a leading televangelist. He also pastored a large church in one of America's biggest cities. In his world, he, too, was viewed as a ministry king at one time. He appeared to be a great man of God and preached powerfully from the pulpit. Like Jim Bakker, he accumulated wealth and influence, and built a Christian media empire. But under the surface, something was not right. He eventually settled two lawsuits that indicated serious misconduct—one based on allegations of sexual wrongdoing and one based on allegations of running a Ponzi scheme. To my knowledge, this man has never publicly taken responsibility for his actions nor repented for the damage those actions have done. To the best of my knowledge, this man now ministers to a fraction of the audience who once listened to him with such respect and operates a church that is only a shell of what it once was.

These are two men with fairly similar backgrounds, both gifted ministers trying to serve God. Both of them ran into trouble because of I-factor issues they did not confront. One eventually did confront the issues and went on to lead a beautifully restored life. The other one, well, he still preaches to a few people.

The Secret to Success Is in the Mirror

I hope the stories of Saul and the two modern-day kings have helped you understand how dangerous the failure to resolve I-factor problems can be. When a person achieves a level of success, that success is not guaranteed to last. It can only be sustained if a person is willing to work at it. While there are certain external duties that must be fulfilled in order to stay successful, the most important obligations are internal. They include stepping up to the responsibilities our roles require, managing the negative emotions mentioned in this chapter, such as impatience, fear, jealousy, and ones not specifically addressed yet, such as greed and pride. They also include being humble before God and living a lifestyle of obedience to Him.

I believe God has tremendous success in store for you—more than you could ever ask for or imagine (Eph. 3:20). Once you attain it, I believe He wants you to not only sustain it, but also grow in it. The key is to deal with the I-factor issues you currently see in yourself and the ones that you may become aware of as time goes on.

——————— Internal Building Blocks ———————

- The internal dynamics you need to achieve a certain level of success are different in some ways from those required to maintain that success long term.
- With a weak or faulty I-factor, long-term success will be a challenge, but with a strong, healthy I-factor, no matter how you define success, you can get there and stay there.
- Common I-factor problems include an inflated ego and arrogance (King Xerxes I); a hunger for attention, affirmation, wealth, or beauty (Anna Nicole Smith); the need for fame or dominance in a particular area (Lance Armstrong); the failure to manage sexuality in a healthy way (Jimmy Swaggart); and greed (Leona Helmsley).
- An I-factor weakness must be dealt with or it can lead to a person's ultimate downfall.
- The I-factor problems Saul had are still problems for people today. They include: failure to take responsibility, impatience, disobedience, fear, jealousy, and pride. You can strengthen your I-factor by dealing with these weaknesses if you recognize them in your life.

——————— Strengthening Your I-Factor ———————

1. Why are the tools needed to maintain success different from those needed to achieve success?
2. Have you noticed in yourself any of the I-factor weaknesses mentioned in this chapter? If so, which ones?
3. How can you improve in the areas where your I-factor is faulty or unhealthy?

4. Rate yourself on a scale of 1 (not good) to 10 (excellent) in the following areas:

> Responsibility
> Patience
> Obedience to God
> Courage instead of fear
> Security instead of a tendency toward jealousy
> Humility

5. Let me encourage you to dream and look ahead for a moment. When you achieve the greatness you believe you were created for, what safeguards might you need to put in place in order to sustain it?

4

Your True Self Is Your Best Self

This above all, to thine own self be true.
—WILLIAM SHAKESPEARE

WHEN I MENTION THE NAMES RICH LITTLE, DANA CARVEY, and Jim Carrey, what do you think of? They are some of the best impressionists in the world—experts at mimicking the intonations, facial expressions, gestures, and general personas of other people. If you were to close your eyes during a Rich Little imitation of John F. Kennedy, you might think you were listening to the late US president himself. But when you open your eyes, you'd know immediately that Rich Little is no John F. Kennedy. Even though Little might copy Kennedy's stance, facial expressions, and speech patterns perfectly, he wouldn't be JFK. He'd still be Rich Little.

Some people, like Little, Carvey, and Carrey have gained fame and acclaim for their impersonations of other people. But everyone knows they're just having fun. They're not actually trying to become the people they mimic. It's all in the name of good entertainment, and everyone has a laugh.

What's not so funny, and can in fact be devastating, is when people who have no interest or skill at all in impersonating others for entertainment try to become people they are not in real life. I'm sure you've seen this before, and perhaps even done it yourself a time or two. It happens when a young woman looks up to a model and then forsakes her natural beauty, trying to look like she, too, just walked off a runway; it happens when young businessmen try to emulate the dress, manner of speaking, or management style of the successful CEOs they work for. It also happens when a busy mom who has many strengths but few organizational skills tries to keep everything in place as perfectly as the organized retired woman next door, who no longer has to keep up with coats, scarves, backpacks, soccer equipment, leotards, and lunch boxes every day—and finds herself exhausted.

The same dynamic is at work when salespeople excel at selling, receive promotions to administrative jobs, and end up miserable because they're good at closing deals, not pushing papers. In these circumstances and so many others like them, a predictable pattern takes place: People are not living out of their true identities, but responding to pressures they feel to do certain things or be a certain way. They do not build their lives on the foundation of who they really are. Instead, they build their lives on an image based on what others think or want them to be, or on the persona their careers or social statuses seem to require. As a result, they are not true to themselves. I believe this is happening in epidemic proportions in the world today, and people who do it usually end up miserable. The good news, as you'll see in this chapter, is that it doesn't have to happen to you.

Asking the Right Question

Think for a minute about a man named Ron. As a little boy in school, he was fascinated by everything he learned in science class. At church, he loved hearing stories about missionaries. Tenderhearted and kind, young Ron was the type of child who stood up for children who were mocked or made fun of. Ron always tried to include the outcast and gave parts of his lunch to fellow students who had left their lunches at home.

As a teenager, Ron's internal wiring and God-given interests led him to want to be a medical missionary someday. Ron did well in college and soon after he graduated, he married his high school sweetheart Anita. Anita's parents had been missionaries in Africa, and she was eager to return to the mission field with Ron as soon as he finished medical school. During Ron's last year of medical training, he was offered a fellowship opportunity at a prestigious clinic in the United States. By this time, Ron and Anita had a young daughter, and Ron thought it was a good idea to stay in the States until she got a little older to earn more money than he would make on the mission field. Besides, Ron was rapidly gaining a reputation as a bright, promising young doctor. After talking about the situation with Anita, the two of them committed to move overseas to do mission work as soon as Ron completed the fellowship. They had prayed about the situation and felt peace about their decision.

Ron communicated his and Anita's plans to his superiors, not expecting them to be overjoyed about it. He sensed they might be interested in having him join their staff at the end of the fellowship, so he wanted them to know in advance that doing so was not an option. But the more successful Ron became, the less he talked about going to the mission field. The desire was still strong in his heart, but he grew tired of people saying, "Why would you waste a brilliant mind like yours in some foreign country, where you won't have access to the latest technology?"

Anita never lost her passion for missions, but as their daughter grew and she built relationships with other young mothers, she also realized that she enjoyed certain aspects of American life more than she ever thought she would.

During those years, Ron was extremely successful in his fellowship, and he, Anita, and their daughter were very happy. As the end of Ron's fellowship approached, he and Anita began to dream again of making a difference on the mission field. By then, a second child was on the way and they decided to postpone mission work until that baby was at least a year old. Besides, Ron was gaining national recognition as a surgeon and had recently been offered an impressive promotion at work.

Fast-forward five years: Ron was one of the foremost young physicians in his field. The pressures of his practice, speaking at conferences, and publishing in medical journals were more taxing than he ever imagined. Ron and Anita, once very much in love, could hardly make it through a day without fighting. Both children had started to exhibit behavioral problems, so Ron and Anita also felt stressed as parents. At the same time, their financial situation blew their minds; they never dreamed they would have so much money, such nice cars, or such a beautiful house.

At home, Ron was preoccupied and tired. At work, he had no time to get to know his patients or demonstrate how much he cared for them. Occasionally, he missed the opportunity to relate to them as people, but the accolades and acclaim he received from his peers seemed to compensate for the lack of personal interaction with patients. To the casual observer, everything about Ron and Anita's life *looked right*, but to them, everything *felt wrong*. They reached a point where they had to admit it: they were miserable.

One night over dinner, Ron looked at Anita and asked one of the most important questions anyone can ever ask: "Where did we go wrong?"

Anita, who had been pondering and praying about their situation for months, calmly said, "We lost sight of who we are. We gave up on the passion inside of us. We charted our own path instead of pursuing God's purpose for our lives. We failed to follow our hearts."

Ron knew Anita was right. He had reached a breaking point

under the pressures of his so-called successful career and was actually relieved to hear her diagnosis of their troubles. Before they finished their meal, they began to strategize about how to get to the mission field as quickly as possible.

Thirty years after that conversation, Ron and Anita still live in Africa. The number of physical lives saved because of Ron's skill as a doctor numbers well into the thousands. And the number of souls saved for eternity because of Ron and Anita's witness for Christ is even higher. Their marriage has been happier than they ever dreamed. Their children adjusted well to life in a new country and have grown up loving and serving God. Many aspects of life on the mission field have been difficult for Ron and Anita and their family, but they have experienced God's grace in phenomenal ways. Their journey has not been easy, but they are quick to say they would not have wanted to spend their lives any other way.

Ron represents many people in many different situations who end up unhappy because at some point on the road of life, they took a wrong turn. They once lived out of who they really were and enjoyed the benefits of it, but then something happened and their reality veered away from their identities. They found themselves in the middle of one of life's great conflicts, saying to themselves, "I know this is who I am, but this is how I'm living—and the two don't go together." They realized the realities of their lives were fighting against them instead of working for them. Almost always in situations like these, people can look back and see where they made a decision that took them away from who they were meant to be.

Until we understand and live out of our identities, we can easily become our own worst enemies and set up stumbling blocks for ourselves, often without even realizing it. We can experience difficulty or failure without knowing we created the circumstances that led to our frustration. But once we understand our identities and let that become the foundation of everything else, we can live in such a way that our reality reflects it, and we can begin to pave ourselves a pathway for success.

Universal Secrets to Success

The ancient Greek philosopher Socrates said something critically important to anyone who wants to develop a strong I-factor. He said, "The unexamined life is not worth living."[1]

When Ron and Anita sat down and asked, "Where did we go wrong?" they were examining their lives. They were no longer content to go on living the way they had lived for years. They knew something was wrong and they were determined to figure it out. They came to the same conclusion many other people have come to: the challenges and pressures of life, and the expectations of other people, had pulled them away from who they really were.

The same circumstances may be unfolding for you right now. Perhaps the need for finances is keeping you in a job that does not match your innate giftings. Or maybe you feel social pressure to engage in activities that are contrary to your values. Or perhaps your political or religious convictions are different from those of the people around you, and you feel tempted to compromise so you will not be ostracized or made fun of. All kinds of pressures and challenges threaten to draw us away from who we really are. One of the secrets of true success is to stand up to them and not allow them to do so.

The essence of living an examined life, versus an unexamined one, lies in asking the right questions. Many times, the first right question is, "Where did I go wrong?" Some people ask this question in the privacy of their own minds when life becomes frustrating or confusing. Others need to ask this question but don't know to ask it or lack the humility or wisdom to do so. In either case, asking where we've gone wrong is the first step toward taking responsibility for our lives and getting ourselves back on the path to the greatness for which we were created. Asking it can be our greatest turning point in life, putting us in position for an amazing future, while failing to ask it can be our biggest mistake, setting us up for continual disappointment and failure.

The Old Testament king Asa—David's grandson's grandson—is a good example of someone who enjoyed a season of success but allowed himself to depart from his identity and ended up in a sad situation. His story shows us what to do to enjoy success in life, but it also teaches us what not to do if we want to maintain that success.

I'll offer more details about Asa's life as this chapter unfolds, but let me simply say here that Asa definitely experienced a time when everything was going well for him. He was victorious in battle and God's favor on his life was apparent to everyone. In 2 Chronicles 14 and 15, his identity and his reality were perfectly in sync. One of the best comments that can be made about a king is made about him in 2 Chronicles 14:6, "He built up the fortified cities of Judah, since the land was at peace. No one was at war with him during those years, for the LORD gave him rest." People came from near and far to see him because they recognized that the Lord was with him (2 Chron. 15:9).

All the way through 2 Chronicles 15, all was right in Asa's world. This is because he was doing the right things from the core of who he was, never trying to impress others or imitate someone else. I doubt he referred to the things he did well as the secrets to his success, but that's exactly what they were. And they are still secrets to success today. They apply to any generation, under any circumstances, in any place on earth. What were they? Asa clearly identified the foundation of his life, which was to honor and walk with God; he made decisions and operated his life from his foundation, not from anywhere else; and he allowed everyone around him to see and know what his foundation was. Those three keys to success can be as effective for you today as they were for Asa centuries ago. Let's examine them further.

1. Identify Your Foundation

In the beginning of his reign, when Asa experienced great military victory and when people for miles around came to see him because the Lord was with him, Asa was known as a godly leader. The first comment we read about him in 2 Chronicles 14 is this: "Asa did what was good and right in the eyes of the LORD his God" (v. 2). The Bible says nothing about him before noting that he did "good and right" before God, which tells us that the foundation of his life was his relationship with the Lord. But he took his devotion to God one step further when he destroyed the objects and altars of worship to foreign gods. This publicly proved the seriousness of his dedication to the one true God.

If you read his story in 2 Chronicles 14, you'll see that the peace and rest that characterized his rule resulted from his private relationship with God and his public demonstration of that loyalty. He was living his life and leading his nation from the core of who he was, and both he and his people prospered because of it. Talking about the blessings his people enjoyed at that time, Asa said, "The land is still ours, because we have sought the LORD our God; we sought him and he has given us rest on every side" (2 Chron. 14:7). The verse goes on to say that the people "built and prospered"—one of the sure signs of a blessed nation.

Just as Asa had to identify his foundation, you and I must do the same. For Asa, his foundation was his relationship with God. For any believer, the same is true. The foundation of our lives is our walk with God. Part of that foundation may also include some things that grow out of your faith. For example, my primary foundation is my relationship with the Lord, but my commitment to my family as a loving husband and father are also foundational for me. The important thing is that once you identify your foundation, you live from it.

2. Operate from Your Foundation

The only way to find fulfillment and success is to operate every aspect of your life from your foundation and to let it guide every decision you make. When a large and mighty army came against Asa and the people of Judah, he went straight to his foundation, his walk with God, and prayed a powerful prayer of humility and trust: "LORD, there is no one like you to help the powerless against the mighty. Help us, LORD our God, for we rely on you, and in your name we have come against this vast army. LORD, you are our God; do not let mere mortals prevail against you" (v. 11).

On a practical level, this is what it looks like for a person to make decisions congruent with his or her identity. Because Asa's foundation was his relationship with God, his default in times of trouble was to say, "Okay, God. We've got a problem here and it's all on You." As a result of Asa's prayer and the way he handled the conflict, "Such a great number of Cushites fell that they could not recover; they were crushed before the LORD and his forces" (v. 13).

What does operating from your foundation look like in today's world? For example, if your foundation includes integrity in business, it could mean refusing to alter records or tamper with bookkeeping. If it includes family, it could mean skipping a social event you would really like to attend in order to support a son or daughter at a recital. If it includes being in excellent health, it could mean passing up the nachos and donuts in favor of carrots and celery sticks. I can't tell you precisely how to operate your life from your foundation, but I can guarantee that if you clearly identify your foundation, you will know when your choices align with it and when they don't. When they do, you will feel it on the inside;

it's a deep satisfaction and conviction of knowing you are doing the right thing.

3. Expose Your Foundation

If you've ever looked at the houses in a well-kept neighborhood, you'll notice that the foundations are rarely visible. The large bricks that make up the foundations are covered with well-manicured shrubs, ornamental grasses, or flowers. While hiding foundations may increase the visual appeal of a neighborhood, it's not a good idea for us to do it in our lives. We need to make sure our foundations are evident to everyone we meet.

Everyone in Asa's kingdom knew who he was and what he stood for. His identity as a man of God was so strong that it seeped into everything he did. He encouraged and led his people from his sweet spot, his relationship with God. The same should be true of us. Whatever our foundation is, we need to live in such a way that the people around us will know it.

As an example, think of someone you know who is committed to healthy living. I'm guessing that everyone who knows that person understands his or her foundation. That person makes certain lifestyle choices, eats certain foods while avoiding others, and often wears exercise clothes. In addition, he or she has a healthy glow and usually a better outlook on life. That fitness buff is living from a foundation. Everyone can tell what's important to him or her.

Sometimes, for various reasons, we present a persona that does not come from our foundations. Think back to Ron in the story at the beginning of this chapter. His colleagues knew him as a gifted surgeon, but that was not his core. At his core, he was a compassionate physician dedicated to missional living. But because of the pressures he faced, he abandoned his foundation temporarily, and while he was away from it, he developed a persona based on a skill set when he should have stayed true to his real identity and purpose.

He needed to say to his colleagues, "I appreciate the affirmation I receive in the operating room, but I really want to be on the mission field." Thankfully, Ron did not hide his foundation forever, but ultimately gained the strength to resist all the pulls and pressures of his so-called successful American medical career, leave it behind, and find true fulfillment doing what he'd always longed to do.

Failure to Ask the Question Could Be Fatal

For thirty-five years, Asa reigned over a peaceful kingdom, and we could assume based on that part of the story that he remained loyal to God throughout his lifetime. But when the thirty-sixth year of his rule rolled around, that's when the problems started. The king of Israel, Baasha, went to war against Asa and the people of Judah, and instead of seeking and relying on the Lord as he had done before, Asa tried to ensure military success by entering into a treaty with another nearby king, the king of Aram, who ruled in Damascus (2 Chron. 16:1–10). From that moment on, things spun out of control for Asa. Why? Because Asa abandoned his foundation. Just as everyone knew when he was living from his foundation, they also knew when he turned his back on it.

One day, a seer approached him and said, "Because you relied on the king of Aram and not on the LORD your God, the army of the king of Aram has escaped from your hand. . . . You have done a foolish thing, and from now on you will be at war" (vv. 7, 9). The story goes on to say that Asa was furious with the seer. Asa was "so enraged that he put him in prison. At the same time Asa brutally oppressed some of the people" (v. 10). What a shockingly different man we read about here than the good, godly king portrayed in chapters 14 and 15. When the seer visited Asa, he gave him the same opportunity Ron and Anita gave themselves when they realized their lives were headed in the wrong direction; he gave Asa a chance to reevaluate where he had come from and where he had ended up. Asa could have repented for leaving his faith and returned to the Lord. He chose not to do so and became unrecognizable compared to the man he once was.

Three years later, Asa developed a disease in his feet. The Bible says that even though his condition was severe, "even in his illness he did not seek help from the LORD, but only from the physicians" (v. 12). A person's feet are the body parts that enable us to walk. If our feet aren't healthy and working properly, we cannot move forward. Symbolically, Asa's foot disease kept him from going any further in life than he had already gone. He became immobile and ineffective once he stopped living out of his true self. Two years after his diagnosis, Asa died.

I think the greatest tragedy of Asa's life is that he did not seem to pay attention to the obvious signs that something was wrong in his life. Either he did not realize he had strayed from the core of who he was or he did not care that he had abandoned his foundation. We can surmise from his story that he never stopped to ask the vital question, "Where did I go wrong?" He just kept pushing ahead. Subsequently, his circumstances went from bad to worse.

I firmly believe Asa's life could have turned out differently than it did. Why he stopped walking with God or what caused him to seek help from human beings instead of from the Lord is a mystery. We don't know what precipitated his change of heart; we only know that it happened and the results were devastating. We can't know the details of Asa's thoughts as he transitioned from being a faithful man of God to an unfaithful, hard-hearted one, but I fully believe that somewhere along the way he could have asked, "Where did I go wrong?" He

> I think the greatest tragedy of Asa's life is that he did not seem to pay attention to the obvious signs that something was wrong in his life.

didn't, and that led to great suffering in his life and in the lives of the people in his kingdom. Failure to ask that question was fatal for him, and failing to ask it could also do significant damage to you and me.

When I hear about modern-day people with Asa's ancient problem, who once enjoyed success and then spiraled down into a season of frustration and failure, my first thought is, *God is trying to get your attention*. God wants to do something great in your life, but He needs to make some changes first. He wants to lead you to your destiny, but He sees that you took a wrong turn along the way. Maybe you went left when He was saying, "Turn right" or maybe you kept going when He said, "Stop." So He's just trying to make a loving course correction.

I definitely believe this was the case with Asa. I don't know what all God had planned for him, had he not forsaken his faith, but a foundation for lifelong greatness was established early in his reign. I am convinced that when life became difficult for him, God was trying to develop his character and redirect his path. He was trying to take Asa to greater places, but Asa was not on the same page with God.

Many of the hurdles we struggle to clear in our lives are God's way of telling us to stop and reevaluate the decisions we have made and the direction in which we are headed. A lot of the crises we find ourselves in are nothing more than wake up calls. Once God has our attention, He wants us to ask the critical question, "What did I do wrong?"

You've Got a Chance to Get It Right Again

When I hear people ask what they are doing wrong, I usually respond that the answer probably lies in what they once did right. I'm sure that would have been true for Asa. His failure to examine himself and correct his mistakes was disastrous. One of the saddest parts of his story is that for many years he did the right thing. He knew how to position himself for God's blessing. The peace that characterized the majority of his reign was not the result of an experiment. The Scriptures are clear that Asa's honor toward the Lord was the basis for the good things he and his people experienced for the first thirty-five years of his rule. We can see that Asa knew what was right; he simply didn't do it for the last five years of his life.

> Many of the hurdles we struggle to clear in our lives are God's way of telling us to stop and reevaluate the decisions we have made and the direction in which we are headed.

The redemptive and encouraging aspect of this story for you and me is that when we find ourselves in places of frustration or failure, we know what to do. We can ask the question, "Where did I go wrong?" and go back to doing what we once did right. If we've done it right before, we can do it right again. There's no better time to start than now.

If you are anything like Ron or King Asa, and you've run into a situation where the realities of your life do not reflect your identity and you've become your biggest stumbling block, here are three practical ways to get back on track and position yourself for the greatest success you've ever known.

1. Reconnect with God

I pointed out earlier in this chapter that Scripture's first mention of Asa characterized him as a man of God. It didn't talk about how smart he was or what good leadership skills he possessed. It simply said he "did what was good and right in the eyes of the LORD" (2 Chron. 14:2). When he walked away from that foundation—the core determinant of his life—everything around him crumbled.

Likewise, when Ron and Anita allowed the pressures and challenges they faced to weaken their passion for missions, they realized something was wrong in their lives. God had created them and called them for a specific purpose, and they knew it. Until they reconnected with Him, with His destiny for their lives, and with their foundational identity and calling as missionaries to help people through Ron's medical gifting, they were not truly happy.

The foundation of all identity comes from God, and who you really are starts with the Lord. In Jeremiah 1:5, God spoke to Jeremiah, saying, "Before I formed you in the womb I knew you, before you were born I set you apart; I appointed you as a prophet to the nations." The premise of that scripture holds true for you today. God is the one who formed you in your mother's womb, putting every aspect of your identity in place. He is the one who knows you and has always known you more intimately than anyone on earth. And He is the one who has set you apart, meaning that He has put a unique mantle of destiny and greatness on your life, one only you can fulfill and one that no one else would enjoy as much as you will.

2. Remember Your Passion

In the story at the beginning of this chapter, one of Ron's biggest mistakes was to let something good overshadow God's best. God had prepared Ron for years to serve Him as a medical missionary and had given him a passion to do so. But the enjoyment of success in the United States and pressures to make money to raise a family got the best of Ron for a while. Eventually, he let his passion fade.

I urge you today to reconnect with your passion. No matter how busy life has become since that dream first took root in your heart and no matter how impossible it may seem under the current circumstances of your life, let it come alive again. Begin to think about it; begin to pray about it; begin to take steps in its direction, even if they're very small. I don't know what your passion is, but I do know this: You have it for a reason. God wants to do something great in you and through you—and your passion is vital to His purpose. Even if your passion is little more than a glowing ember right now, do everything you can to cause it to burn within you like it did months or years ago.

3. Stay with It

Asa's fatal flaw was the fact that he allowed himself to become unfaithful to God, when he had spent years being faithful. That same type of flaw—turning one's back on the core of who you are—has ruined many lives since Asa's time. For centuries, people have caved in to the pressure to leave their foundations.

When Ron and Anita succumbed to a life that was not what they always wanted, they had the courage to ask, "Where did we go wrong?" and to find the answer. Asa didn't. Ron and Anita ended up with a better life than they ever dreamed of, while Asa died in pain. The difference between the two stories is that when Ron and Anita began to stray from their foundations, they reached a point where they stopped, took a hard look at their lives, recognized the choices that had led them astray, and corrected their course. Asa did not do any of those things.

Let me urge you today for the sake of your happiness both now and in the future: stay close to your core. Make the decision today that regardless of the challenges you face, you will live your life from your foundation of who you are. When you veer off course, remember Ron, Anita, and Asa. Be brave enough to evaluate where you went wrong that took you away from where you should have been, and get yourself back on the right track by making decisions that will further establish you and advance you in your foundation because that's where you will find your ultimate success.

—————————— Internal Building Blocks ——————————

- There's a lot of pressure in life to be someone you are not. The pressure comes from the desires or expectations of others, and sometimes from false expectations you may place on yourself because of various pressures you face. The best person to be is who you really are.

- To be true to yourself, it's important to keep in mind who you really are and to understand the foundation of your life.

- Socrates said, "The unexamined life is not worth living." In other words, it's important to regularly ask yourself if your life is heading in the right direction. If not, it's important to ask, "Where did I go wrong?" so you can correct your course.

- From Asa's story, you can glean three keys to success: identify your foundation, operate from your foundation, and expose your foundation.

- No matter where you've gone wrong or how you've gone wrong in life, you have a chance to make it right. You can get back on track starting today by reconnecting with God, remembering your true passion, and staying with it.

—————————— Strengthening Your I-Factor ——————————

1. Have you ever been untrue to yourself? How did that make you feel, what did you learn from it, and why is it not a good idea?

2. In this chapter, I make a point to encourage you to ask the question, "Where did I go wrong?" Now's your chance. Where have you gone wrong in life?

3. Have you identified your foundation? If so, how would you define it? Do you operate from your foundation? If so, how? Have you exposed your foundation—in other words, do the people around you know what your foundation is?

4. When you read the words "remember your passion," what comes to mind? Your first thought is probably your true passion. Define that passion on a separate sheet of paper or an electronic document.

5. Staying true to yourself is a long-term endeavor. What are some of the reasons you may have strayed from your true self in the past? How can you avoid having that happen in the future?

5

Proof of Identity

To be tested is good. The challenged
life may be the best therapist.
—GAIL SHEEHY

WHAT DO THE FOLLOWING SITUATIONS HAVE IN COMMON:
getting on an airplane, renting an apartment, and opening a bank
account? To complete these processes successfully, you have to
prove your identity. In each case, you must prove to the officials
that you are who you say you are. They won't take your word for it,
even if you have an honest face. You're required to show the proper
identifying documents.

In the natural world, the process of proving your identity to
airport security personnel, a prospective landlord, or a bank officer
is easy, as long as you have a driver's license, a passport, or some
other acceptable form of identification. In the spiritual realm, part
of developing a proper sense of identity also involves a type of proving who you are. It's not as easy as flashing your driver's license,
but it yields tremendous rewards that will benefit you for the rest of
your life. The process and purpose of proving your identity is what
this chapter is all about.

A Case of Mistaken Identity

The place was Wilmington, Delaware, and the year was 1979. The crime was armed robbery—five robberies from a bandit demanding money from store clerks to be exact. The suspect was a gunman known as the "Gentleman Bandit," a name he earned because of his nice manners during the robberies and his apologies afterward.

As usual in an investigation, the police collected information about the man's appearance from people who had seen the thief, and an artist compiled a composite sketch. A woman claiming to be the lover of one of the suspects gave them a photograph of him, which closely resembled the drawing. Police also gathered multiple anonymous tips and were shocked when they came to a conclusion about the robber's identity: Father Bernard Pagano, a popular assistant pastor at a Catholic Church in Cambridge, Maryland.[1]

On February 27, 1979, authorities charged the distinguished fifty-three-year-old with five counts of armed robbery. His church and community were dumbfounded. They could not believe this well-liked clergyman was capable of perpetrating such acts. But the police were certain they had their man. Several eyewitnesses positively identified him, convinced he was the perpetrator.

Believing he was innocent, Pagano's lawyers initiated their own investigation, looking for someone more likely to have committed the crimes. Eventually, they found a man named Roland Clouser, who once worked for the postal service in Pennsylvania. Though Pagano and Clouser were not related in any way, the two bore an uncanny physical resemblance to each other. As it turned out, Clouser was the culprit in all the burglaries. Reportedly, Clouser could not bear the thought of a priest being arrested and thrown in jail for crimes he did not commit, so he came up with a way to try to clear Pagano without incriminating himself. He staged additional robberies, hoping to cast a reasonable doubt about Pagano in the authorities' minds.

In the end, Clouser confessed to three of the robberies. Though some authorities still thought Pagano was guilty of at least two of the crimes, his name was ultimately cleared, the charges against him were dismissed, and he received a formal apology from the prosecuting attorneys, while Clouser went to jail.[2]

The Accuser Is at Large

Father Pagano had his accusers in early 1979. You and I have ours today—the enemy of our souls who bombards our minds with negative thoughts and lies, and sometimes the people around us who operate under his influence. The enemy often attacks us with false accusations about who we are. He knows that if he can only get us to question or doubt our identity in Christ—such as making us believe we are defeated and hopeless instead of victorious and filled with faith—the chances are high that he will eventually be able to ruin us. He uses this tactic against believers in all kinds of ways today, and he tried to use it against Jesus centuries ago.

When John the Baptist baptized Jesus in the Jordan River, God the Father spoke a powerful declaration of Jesus' identity: "This is my Son, whom I love; with him I am well pleased" (Matt. 3:17). Another translation renders the verse this way: "This is my dearly loved Son, who brings me great joy" (NLT). *The Message* renders the sentence, "This is my Son, chosen and marked by my love, delight of my life."

We need to realize that when God made these strong statements, Jesus had not yet begun His ministry. He had not healed anyone, walked on water, fed five thousand people with only a few fish and several loaves of bread, or performed any other miracles. God's love and joy were entirely based on who Jesus was, not on what He did. Because you are in Christ, that same intense affection and acceptance from God belongs to you.

Only a few verses after God's great declaration of love for His Son, things seem to go in a negative direction. The celebration soon turns to temptation and frustration—and God orchestrates it all. This is important to understand because so often we credit God with the situations we view as good in our lives and we blame the devil or other people for the ones we think are bad. It's just not that simple. Sometimes God does lead us into hard situations; the good news is He also leads us out of them, just as He did when Jesus went into the wilderness.

The Synoptic Gospel writers report that the Holy Spirit led Jesus into the wilderness (Matt. 4:1; Mark 1:12; Luke 4:1). He didn't wander into it on His own and the enemy did not lead him. However, the enemy did meet Him there. Every taunting word the enemy spoke to Jesus was an attack on His identity; he began the first two temptations with the phrase, "If you are the Son of God . . ." (Matt. 4:3, 6). Keep in mind that right before Jesus went into the wilderness, God had spoken strongly, "This is my Son." Jesus knew His identity; He simply had to prove it. He did and, according to Matthew 4:11, "the devil left him."

Ever Wonder Why You're in the Wilderness?

In 2014, General Motors (GM) had to recall more than thirty-nine million vehicles. The reason for the recall was that the cars, trucks, and sport utility vehicles had not been thoroughly tested. A number of deaths were linked to faulty ignition switches, and GM ended up paying hefty settlements to the families of those who lost their lives. In addition, the company sustained serious damage to their credibility as people who trusted GM lost faith in the once-reputable car company. The tragic loss of life could have been avoided had GM simply put their vehicles through a proper testing process.

This story about GM proves how vitally important a good testing process is. It's true for the car manufacturers and it's true for you. God is so committed to His will for your life that He will not release you to your next step of destiny until He knows you are ready and until you have proven your readiness to yourself. That only happens in the wilderness.

> God is so committed to His will for your life that He will not release you to your next step of destiny until He knows you are ready and until you have proven your readiness to yourself.

I would venture to say that everyone who wants to grow in God has a wilderness experience. It's usually not a vast outdoor space, as we might imagine. It's almost always an internal place, a location in our hearts and minds. It may be a time of illness or grief; it may be a season when a son or daughter brings heartache and concern instead of joy; it may be the loss of a job for some reason you think is wrong and unfair. Your wilderness could be any number of circumstances.

While I cannot describe the specifics of your personal wilderness, when you're in it, you know it. It's a lonely, frustrating place and in the midst of it, the voices of doubt and the devil are often easier to hear than the voice of God. You find yourself confused and wondering how to get out, while also saying, "God, I thought You led me into this." Many times, He does lead us into our wilderness encounters, and I want to explain why.

From God's perspective, the wilderness is the proving ground of our identities; it's the place where we pass or fail the test of knowing who we really are. The destiny to which you are appointed demands you know who you are, and identity that has not been tested is not identity at all. Your identity is not determined by what you say or what others say about you. It has to be confirmed and sealed in your heart. There's no better place for that to happen than the wilderness.

God has been proving identities in the wilderness for ages. When He took His people Israel through the wilderness in what turned an eleven-day journey into one that lasted forty years, Moses explained God's motive this way: "Remember how the LORD your God led you all the way in the wilderness these forty years, *to humble you and test you* in order *to know what was in your heart*, whether or not you would keep his commands" (Deut. 8:2, emphasis added).

When you go through a really difficult experience, when you feel lost and alone and God seems far away, you're in the wilderness for sure. But more than that, you are in the place God has chosen as your testing ground. This is the place where God wants to strengthen you and solidify your sense of identity so you will have the internal resources you need for the good future He has planned for you.

The wilderness may look desolate, but be encouraged: it's designed to help you grow, and on the other side of this growth process, God has something great for your life. How can I be so sure? Because Deuteronomy 6:23 says, "Then He brought us out from there, that He might bring us in, to give us the land of which He swore to our fathers" (NKJV). God brought the Israelites *out* of Egypt, *through* the wilderness, and *into* the promised land.

> When you go through a really difficult experience, when you feel lost and alone and God seems far away, you're in the wilderness for sure. But more than that, you are in the place God has chosen as your testing ground.

That's the same pattern He uses in our lives today when He wants to lead us into something wonderful.

How God Grows People

When we think about how God leads us through the process of spiritual and personal growth, which certainly includes getting us firmly established in our identities, the three words we need to know are: *out, through,* and *in.* This is exactly what He did for the nation of Israel and it is a picture of what He does for us in modern times.

Israel was enslaved in Egypt, a geographical location in Old Testament times just as it is today. But in biblical symbolism, Egypt is more than a country; it's a metaphor for bondage, difficulty, and oppression. It represents any type of bondage or bad situation you might find yourself in today. God called Israel out of that hard place because He had something better for them; the same is true for you. God led the Israelites through the wilderness in order to do what we read in Deuteronomy 8:2, to test them and humble them so they would trust Him fully and to know what was in their hearts. Only after their testing and proving in the wilderness was God ready to fulfill His word to them and lead them into the promised land.

The problem with many of us today, and perhaps with the ancient Israelites, too, is that we want out of the wilderness *now*! Given the choice, most of us would probably skip the wilderness altogether and go straight from our negative situations into the things God has promised us. When we face obstacles or difficulties, we want God to turn them around overnight, to move us quickly from our hard places into the promised land. But God doesn't work that way.

God has applied the same pattern of *out, through,* and *in* for generations. If we look at the biblical accounts alone, we see that

He did it for Abraham, Joseph, David, and Job, in addition to the nation of Israel. And He does it in the life of anyone who commits to living for Him.

Trust That God Knows What He Is Doing, Even If You Don't Like It

Most people understand that the wilderness is not designed to be a happy place. When you're in it, chances are you won't like it. It's hard, and the difficulties are what help strengthen our sense of identity. Sometimes, God's point in taking us into the wilderness is simply to help us grow. At other times, we get through our wilderness experiences and realize that what we thought was bad was actually good for us. Both of these results took place for the Old Testament character named Jacob.

If his story is not familiar to you, you can read it in its entirety in Genesis 29–30.

Jacob fell in love with a beautiful young woman named Rachel (Gen. 29:18). When I say he fell in love, I mean he fell *hard* for her. The first time he kissed her, he was so overcome with emotion that he began to weep (v. 11). He agreed to work for her father, Laban, for seven years in exchange for having Rachel as his bride. During that time, his love for her intensified, and I'm sure that by the end of seven years, he was ecstatic when their wedding day finally arrived.

In those days, weddings were much different than they are in Western culture today. Part of the wedding celebration included a feast, after which the bride entered the wedding chamber, where her groom was waiting for her. Given the darkness of the wedding chamber and the fact that the bride was veiled, the groom could not see his bride.

I'm sure by then Jacob had Rachel's face memorized. He had

waited seven years to spend this night with her and consummate their marriage. We can only imagine what happened as these two lovers finally entered into the intimacy they had waited so long to enjoy.

The next morning, as Jacob awakened next to his bride, "there was Leah!" (v. 25). Jacob was expecting Rachel, but he woke up next to her older sister instead! What a disappointment that was to him, and what a cruel joke it was for Laban to play. Furious and feeling deceived, I'm sure, Jacob asked Laban what was going on. Laban responded that Leah had to be married first because she was the oldest. I can almost imagine the smirk on his face as he told Jacob about this custom, perhaps in a condescending manner, with a look that said, *You should have known that.* He told Jacob he could also wed Rachel, but he had to work another seven years. Because Rachel was the woman Jacob loved with all his heart, he agreed.

Jacob found himself in a wilderness through no fault of his own, married to a wife he did not want, and he had to work fourteen years for his father-in-law to fully pay for Rachel, the wife he truly loved.

What to Do When Your Rachel Turns Out to Be Leah

Most of us have experienced similar wilderness experiences—times of surprising and significant disappointments, moments when we end up with Leah when we thought we were destined for Rachel. Maybe that has happened to you. It can cause you to feel insignificant, devalued, and unloved. When you have invested much prayer and faith into what you were so looking forward to, you may even feel that God has let you down, that He does not care about what's important to you. This kind of frustration is normal at times, and

as you will see in subsequent pages, it is often a painful but necessary part of strengthening your I-factor and becoming who God
wants you to be. But that does not mean it doesn't hurt when you
feel God or someone close to you has played a trick on you.

Your Rachel may have been a romantic interest, but it also
could have been what you've always considered your dream job,
or your dream home, or something else you longed for and finally
got, only to realize it was not at all what you thought it would be.
And I don't mean that it was better than you ever imagined. Those
situations do happen and I will address them in the next section of
this chapter. I'm talking about situations in which your heart sinks
because something for which you held such high hopes turns out to
be worse than you ever thought it could be. I'm talking about when
your dream becomes your nightmare.

Ordinary disappointments in life are bad enough, but when
you thought you were going to be living on cloud nine and you
suddenly find yourself living in the wilderness because a major
disappointment catches you off guard, those circumstances are
particularly hard to deal with. But they don't have to cripple you;
they can become stepping-stones to greatness. Let me share four
ways you can allow those heartbreaks to strengthen you and root
you even more firmly in your identity.

1. Grieve Your Loss

Any loss or disappointment is real and needs to be grieved in a
healthy, appropriate way. Many good grief resources are available,
and I encourage you to seek them if you need them.

Perhaps the best-known model of the grieving process is the
one developed by the late Swiss psychiatrist Elisabeth Kübler-Ross.
While I don't agree with everything Kübler-Ross believed in, this
model does summarize five emotions most people go through as
they process loss. They are denial, anger, bargaining, depression

(which I prefer to refer to as "deep sadness"), and ultimately, acceptance. I mention this grief model to point out that negative emotions such as anger and profound sadness are normal parts of the grieving process. When people feel angry or deeply saddened, and their faith or their culture tells them these emotions are wrong, they may deny themselves the chance to deal with these feelings in a healthy manner.

If you have suffered a loss, or if something you hoped for did not turn out well, let me encourage you to allow the grieving process to run its course in your life. Getting through it may not be easy and it may take a while, but it's the first step toward eventually being able to move on with your life in a positive, productive way.

2. Keep Your Dream Alive

Whenever you hold a dream or a promise of God in your heart and you work to bring it to pass only to find out it's not anything like you expected, you can feel tempted to give up. But once the raw emotion of the disappointment subsides and you get your intense feelings sorted out, the chances are high that your dream simply will not die. It's likely to keep making itself known to you, whether you want it to or not. My best advice is to stoke the fire of that dream, even if it's nothing more than embers. Even if you ended up disappointed once, you may not be disappointed again. It may be that the timing was not right or the circumstances were not optimal. You've invested so much in it for so long. Don't let a disappointment cause you to let go of it now.

One redemptive aspect of disappointment is that something good can come from it. People who sustain losses in their lives often change their values, priorities, and perspectives on life as a result of what they have suffered. Many times, they find themselves wanting to help others or impact the world in ways they are equipped to do only because of what they have endured. For example, sometimes young people who lose a loved one to cancer become passionate research scientists, dedicating their lives to finding a cure. Or people who lose a teenage child to drug abuse become champions for drug education in high schools. Or those who are impacted by sexual assault work to strengthen laws against offenders. There are lots of good things happening in the world today because people who once endured great pain allow themselves to dream again.

3. Find the Good in a Bad Situation

For Jacob, the good in the bad situation was that Leah was fertile and bore him six sons. She was the primary vessel through which his legacy lived on. I understand that Jacob's sons could be real rascals at times; they did not always behave. But I also believe there were times when they brought him great joy, and they became the fathers of the twelve tribes of Israel, God's chosen people. After a good bit of drama over the course of Jacob's life as a father, his sons settled down and reconciled, and Jacob died at peace. He was blessed, and the world was blessed, through Leah—a woman once at the center of Jacob's bad situation.

4. Capitalize on the Lessons a Surprising and Significant Disappointment Can Teach You

When you're struggling with a major disappointment, you have a unique opportunity to learn some important lessons about yourself. For example, you may learn that you are stronger, braver, smarter, or more compassionate than you once thought you were. You may also discover that your dream means even more to you than you previously realized. Working your way through this challenge may also adjust your priorities and your perspective on life. In addition, it may inspire you to get creative in ways you never thought to be creative before. As a result of disappointment, you may find just the right avenue to help you reach your dream, one you never knew existed until a letdown led you to look for it.

Life's wilderness experiences, its challenges and difficulties, have a way of never being 100 percent negative. One of the best blessings they hold for us is the way they help us grow, strengthen us in our identities, and prepare us for the future.

How to Get Out of the Wilderness

God never intends for anyone to take up permanent residence in the wilderness. Any time He leads you into it, His goal is to get you out. What can you do to facilitate that? I have two pieces of advice. First, look in the right direction, and second, learn the lessons of maturity.

1. Look in the Right Direction

Anyone stuck in a natural wilderness would be tempted to look around, trying to find the quickest way out. He or she would want to know what kind of trees were nearby, what kind of animals to guard against, and how far the nearest water source would be. But when we're in the kind of wilderness I've been talking about in this chapter, looking outward won't help. We have to look inward. The enemy is trying to take advantage of our God-given position in the wilderness and question our identities based on those circumstances. He might say things like, "You thank God you are blessed and highly favored because of your relationship with Him? If that's true, why are you unemployed and broke?" or "You believe you are strong and walking in divine health so you can serve God like never before? So why are you constantly struggling with your weight and with one minor illness after another?"

The enemy will point to your circumstances to undermine your identity. He wants us to question our identities based on what's happening around us. The fact is, identity has nothing to do with what's going on around us; identity is about what's happening within us. If we allow the circumstances around us to motivate us and determine how we live our lives, we will never tap into the greatness God has put inside of us. The pressures of a wilderness experience force us to dig deep into our internal resources and draw out strength we never knew we had, strength that comes from knowing who we are in God.

2. Learn the Lessons of Maturity

If you've ever been through a wilderness experience or a hard time, you know those seasons of life often force people to grow. Sometimes they are the turning points that not only push us to grow, but make us grow up. For people who are seriously walking with God, it's almost impossible to go through the wilderness without gaining a new level of growth and maturity.

The fundamentals of your identity do not change, but they do mature. And you mature in the way you live out of the identity God has put inside of you. In order for maturity to be developed and revealed in a person's life, it has to have a demand placed on it. A wilderness experience certainly places that demand.

God wants mature sons and daughters—and I think everyone could agree that the world desperately needs them. Let me share some characteristics of maturity, because if you are in a wilderness season, this is part of what God is building in you. These qualities will serve you well for the rest of your life.

- **Maturity enables us to see beyond circumstances and emotions.** A wilderness season lets us practice doing this because it forces us to look at what's inside of us instead of what's going on around us. Immature people allow their circumstances to determine whether they have a good day or a bad day, but mature people can stay steady and positive, no matter what they have to deal with.

- **Maturity recognizes the value and necessity of hard work.** In contrast, immaturity expects to get something for nothing. Jacob knew that he would have to work for Rachel, the woman he really wanted, for a total of fourteen years. He got busy and did it. Immaturity seeks the place of comfort, ease, and the path of least resistance.
- **Maturity empowers us to focus on others, rather than on ourselves.** An immature person is self-centered and seeks to meet personal needs at the expense of others, while a mature individual will make personal sacrifices in order to help or bless other people.
- **Maturity values growth, strength, and a firm sense of identity over compliments, flattery, or affirmation.** Immaturity is self-centered, self-consuming, and self-reverential, while maturity values one's identity without becoming self-absorbed. Mature people do not require affirmation from others to grow in their understanding of who God made them to be.
- **Maturity values other people because of who they are, not because of what they can do.** A mature person treats others honorably and well, while an immature individual uses and manipulates people—consciously or unconsciously—to meet their needs.
- **Maturity is flexible and adaptable, always willing to change in order to benefit a group or help a greater cause.** Mature people are team players, but immature ones demand their own way, refuse to listen to others' opinions, and often decline to participate when they do not get what they want.

- **Maturity looks to give, while immaturity looks to get.** A mature person asks, "How can I benefit the world around me?" Immature people ask, "How can this benefit me?" Immature people's choices are influenced by what they can gain, but mature individuals make decisions based on what they can contribute.

Forty Days or Forty Years?

In this chapter, I have shared two stories of the wilderness. Jesus entered into the wilderness, made good choices, demonstrated maturity, honored God, and came out after forty days. The Israelites went into the wilderness, made bad choices, showed immaturity, dishonored God, and did not come out for forty years. Most of the people who left Egypt headed toward the promised land never reached that place God had promised them. They died in the wilderness. To put in I-factor terms the contrast between these two situations, Jesus had a strong sense of identity and a strong I-factor, while the nation of Israel did not. Unresolved identity is a major I-factor problem, and it can hinder people from fulfilling their destinies. Those who stand firm in their identity in Christ and have a healthy I-factor usually find themselves on the fast track to reaching their potential.

I trust you have seen the value of the tests God puts people through in the wilderness. The next time you realize He is leading you into the wilderness, I trust you will welcome it as a perhaps uncomfortable but definitely important time of personal growth, strength, and maturity. How eager are you to fulfill your destiny and to enjoy the success God has planned for you? Are you eager enough to embrace your wilderness seasons as purposeful gifts from God, designed to test you and establish you more and more fully in your identity? Are you eager enough for your destiny that you will look inside yourself instead of at your circumstances? Will you allow a whole new level of maturity to rise up in you so God can use you and bless you to the greatest possible degree in the days to come? I pray you are!

Internal Building Blocks

- No one gets through life without having his or her identity tested. This is good because your strength as a person is directly related to the strength of your sense of identity.
- Difficulties and disappointments can ultimately work for your good. It's important to take the following steps in order for these situations to strengthen you instead of weaken you: acknowledge and grieve your losses, refuse to let your dream die, find the good in a bad situation, and make the most of the lessons your hardship has taught you.
- When you're stuck in the wilderness, your natural inclination will be to look around you and see how you can escape it. The secret to getting out is to look within yourself and draw your strength from knowing who you are in God.
- The way you handle your wilderness experiences determines how long they will last.
- There are many lessons of maturity. Learning them well and putting them into practice will strengthen your I-factor and position you for new levels of greatness and success.

Strengthening Your I-Factor

1. What valuable life lessons have you learned from past wilderness experiences you have been through? How have some of your difficulties turned out to be blessings in disguise?
2. If you are going through a wilderness experience right now, can you identify any reasons you may be in the midst of it?

3. Why is the secret to getting out of the wilderness inside of you and not around you?
4. Both Jesus and the Israelites went through wilderness experiences. Because of the way they handled these experiences internally (mentally, emotionally, and spiritually), one came out in forty days while the other remained for forty years. What lessons can you learn from these two extreme examples about what to do and what not to do when you are going through hard times?
5. As you think about the lessons of maturity, which one or ones do you most need to work on in your life? How do you think growth in these areas will benefit you in the future?

The Journey to Significance

*I love the paparazzi. They take pictures and
I just smile away. I've always liked attention.
I didn't get it very much growing up, and I
always wanted to be, you know, noticed.*

—ANNA NICOLE SMITH

WHEN PEOPLE HAVE A WEAK OR FAULTY I-FACTOR, THEY almost always also have a craving for attention. Sometimes their attempts to get attention are annoying and sometimes they are downright foolish or dangerous. My first thought when I read Anna Nicole's comment about her need for attention was, *At least she could admit it.* In that regard, she was a step ahead of many people who seek attention in all kinds of ways, not realizing that what they are really after is the fulfillment of their basic human need for significance. Most of the time, because they don't understand their need and do not know how to meet it properly, their efforts fail. Unfortunately, that proved to be true for Anna Nicole Smith. It was also true for Leah, the Old Testament woman I mentioned in the previous chapter.

Though Leah and Anna Nicole Smith were two vastly different people, they had one thing in common: the legitimate, God-given need for significance. They both wanted to be noticed and loved. The need for significance is genuine. It only becomes a problem when people try to meet it in unhealthy or destructive ways. It's completely different from a hunger for attention. People with troubled I-factors clamor to be noticed; people with strong I-factors embark on a healthy search for the significance only God can give.

Leah must have felt rejected, as she was married to Jacob only because we assume her father was afraid no one would ever choose her. Jacob did not love Leah; he was crazy about her beautiful sister, Rachel, and Leah knew it. We can only imagine how painful that must have been, because despite his obvious lack of interest in her, she clearly loved him.

> People with troubled I-factors clamor to be noticed; people with strong I-factors embark on a healthy search for the significance only God can give.

Thus far, we have looked at the story of Jacob, Rachel, and Leah from Jacob's perspective. Often, people read it and feel a combination of pity and respect for Jacob—pity because what happened to him is so heartbreaking, and respect because he loved Rachel so much that he agreed to work an additional seven years for her to become his wife. They also feel outrage on his behalf. Sometimes, people read this story and feel compassion for Rachel, since she was just as much in love with Jacob as he was with her. We can only guess how much disappointment and anger she must have felt knowing her sister had been given to the man she loved.

Rarely have I heard of anyone who reads this story from Leah's perspective. But when we fail to do so, we miss the depths of the pain, the complexity of the problems, and the powerful message from God this story contains. In order to hear what God wants to communicate for people in search of significance, we have to see this story through Leah's eyes.

The Weak-Eyed Perspective

"Leah had weak eyes" (Gen. 29:17), and she knew Jacob did not want her. I cannot explain why she did not speak up and identify herself to Jacob once she was alone with him in the wedding chamber, but I wonder if somewhere, deep inside, she wanted to know what it felt like to be the object of a man's unbridled affection. She knew her father thought the only way she would ever marry was for him to trick someone into becoming her husband, so we can conclude that she lived with a profound sense of rejection. She knew Jacob would eventually discover who she was, but maybe she realized that under cover of darkness, she would have one night to feel truly loved, even though it would be under false pretenses. So she took her one chance at feeling loved.

One of the biggest problems in this story is that Leah fell in love with Jacob, but he never fell in love with her. We know this because the New International Version of Genesis 29:31 says, "When the LORD saw that Leah was not loved . . ." The King James Version puts it more strongly: "When the LORD saw that Leah was hated . . ." Compared to the love Jacob felt toward Rachel, his feelings toward Leah felt like hatred to her. That complete lack of love and absence of affection from her husband, I believe, more than anything that happened previously, set Leah on an often-futile search for significance that lasted for years.

As a direct result of the fact that Jacob did not love Leah, Genesis 29:31 goes on to say that God opened her womb. She began to bear children. Her search for significance is evident in the names she chose for each one.

"I Want to Be Seen"

I often wonder if Leah had children because she felt she could become significant in Jacob's life if she did. After all, in her culture, having children was the right thing to do. It was the way to please a husband and hopefully capture his attention. The reason I came to this conclusion is that Leah named her first son Reuben, which in Hebrew means "see a son." According to the note in my NIV *Thinline Bible*, when the word *Reuben* is pronounced in Hebrew, it sounds like a person is saying, "He has seen me."[1]

I believe Leah named her first son Reuben because what she wanted with her whole heart was to be seen. She wanted to be noticed and to matter to her husband. She wanted to be significant. I would not be surprised if Leah said to herself, "I am doing everything I can do for Jacob. I am a good wife. I keep a good house and I cook delicious meals. I am ready for intimacy at a moment's notice. Whatever he wants me to do, I am there. But he does not see me. He does not pay me any attention. All he does is pine for Rachel."

Feeling invisible is painful for anyone. If you have ever hoped someone would notice you, but he or she didn't, you can understand how Leah felt. In some cases, people are oversensitive and they feel rejected when really they are not being rejected at all. But in Leah's situation, Jacob really did overlook and ignore her most of the time. That hurt. It hurt Leah centuries ago and it hurts everyone who feels it today.

"I Want to Be Heard"

Leah named her second son Simeon (Gen. 29:33), which gives us as much insight into her personal struggles as Reuben's name did. *Simeon* means "to hear."[2] Symbolically, this indicates to me that Leah had been talking about her pain and discouragement—and no one had been willing to listen to her. To feel that no one is listening is to feel ignored and devalued. We can't blame Leah for sending a powerful message through Simeon's name. She wanted to be heard.

Have you ever tried to communicate something to someone and felt the person was not even listening to you? Most of us have had that experience, and it's frustrating and painful. When you risk sharing your heart with someone or mentioning your needs to people who are in positions to care about you and they are not paying attention, it's easy to feel devalued. The truth is we are not invaluable or insignificant. Not being heard contributes to an unmet need for significance, and it is a painful experience whenever it happens.

"I Want to Be Connected"

I have mentioned that the name of Leah's first son, Reuben, sounds like "he has seen me," and her second son's name, Simeon, means "to hear." Now I want to call your attention to her third son. She named him Levi, which means "joined" or "connected."[3] In addition to wanting to be seen and heard, Leah also wanted to be connected. She wanted to feel that she was not alone. Leah even said, "Now at last my husband will become attached to me, because I have borne him three sons" (Gen. 29:34). In other words, she wasn't successful when she said she wanted to be seen. She got no results when she sent the message that she wanted to be heard. But now that she'd had another son, now that she'd done something else right, she hoped the connection she longed for would finally fall into place.

I expect mothers can readily identify with Leah's attempts to get attention, though the message is for everyone. Mothers understand what twenty-seven months of pregnancy is like. They know the physical toll of bearing three children. They have dealt firsthand with having their bodies stretched and disfigured for a season and experiencing painful labors and deliveries. They can relate to Leah's thinking, *I have been through all this to give my husband strong, healthy sons. The least he can do is connect with me and appreciate it.*

Maybe you have never been through Leah's precise circumstances, but you have had your life disfigured. Things have been turned inside out and stretched out of shape because of your longing to be joined with a certain individual or group. Maybe your finances have been stretched too thin because you thought wearing the right clothes or driving the right car would finally cause someone to notice you. Maybe your identity has been challenged or threatened in a situation because you wanted a meaningful connection with someone or something and you pretended to be someone you aren't.

The connections you really long for are not going to happen because you work hard enough, spend enough, adjust your personality enough, or do enough right things. From a spiritual perspective, your connection with God is already established. It's a matter of turning your focus onto Him in a fresh way and away from the people who aren't paying attention anyway. From a human relationship perspective, the divine connections God has for you don't require the kind of effort you've been putting in to connect with others. When God wants to join your life with someone else's, there is a grace, an ease, a peace, and a deep sense of rightness about it. You don't have to bend over backward struggling to make it happen. God makes it happen for you.

Are You Tired Yet?

Leah's name comes from a Hebrew word meaning "weary."[4] This is both interesting and sad because there seems to be no doubt that Leah grew weary wanting to be seen, heard, and connected in intimate relationship. For years, she worked hard to get herself noticed and to gain a sense of community and relationship. But it did not work. No matter how hard she tried, every effort left her alone, ignored, disregarded, and devalued. Exerting that kind of emotional and relational energy is often much more draining than running several miles, moving boxes, or making any other physical effort. Those activities leave our bodies tired, and a good night's sleep can fix that. The kinds of efforts Leah made—and so many people today make—leave a person's soul depleted. Physical rest will not solve the problem of an empty, barren soul. That takes a supernatural healing touch.

How many times have you struggled to be seen or heard, or to connect with people in a meaningful way—and wound up weary? Let's face it. The search for significance can be exhausting. It *can* be, but it does not have to be. When we look for value in the wrong places, we end up weary like Leah. But when our search takes us in the right direction, we find ourselves rested, restored, and renewed.

If you have worn yourself out trying to feel significant, you do not have to stay tired and frustrated. A wonderful verse in the book of Acts offers the key to the most meaningful rest you will ever know. It says that "times of refreshing" come from the presence of the Lord (Acts 3:19) when we repent of our sins. The word *repent* means "to change one's mind" and applies especially "to acceptance of the will of God."[5]

I believe God's will for us as His sons and daughters is to find our significance in Him alone—to allow Him to create in us a strong sense of identity. We need to build on that identity a robust awareness of our intrinsic value and worth, not based on anything we can do for ourselves, but on what His Son has already done for us (2 Cor. 5:21). He has saved us, redeemed us, healed us, set us free, and made us more than conquerors. He has good plans for us that will lead us to the significance we long for. All we have to do is stop looking for value in the things around us and realize our search ends in His great love.

Leah Got It Right

There's a big difference between seeking attention and searching for significance. Erma Bombeck, the popular, now deceased, newspaper columnist understood the difference, though she did not specifically use the word *significance.* "Don't confuse fame with success," she said. "Madonna is one; Helen Keller is the other."[6] No doubt Helen Keller lived a successful life. Her success was inseparable from her significance; those two dynamics worked together.

Helen Keller is well known now, but she is not famous in the sense that Madonna is famous or Anna Nicole Smith was famous. No one followed Helen around because of her good looks; her singing, dancing, or acting ability; or her fine figure. The paparazzi never ran after her the way they chase countless celebrities today. No one wanted a photograph of her leaving the gym or climbing out of a black SUV. Her everyday life did not capture people's attention; her contributions to humanity did. People were curious about her ability to lead a meaningful, productive life despite substantial obstacles. In a nutshell, that's the difference between fame and success, attention and significance.

For those who seek true significance in life, attention alone is never enough. The right kind of attention from the right people can go a long way toward helping people feel significant and begin to understand their value, but it can't completely fill a significance gap in a person's heart. Only God can do that. Thankfully, it seems that Leah finally learned that lesson.

Leah gave birth to a fourth son in Genesis 29:35. When she did, she said, "This time I will praise the LORD," and she named that son Judah, meaning "praise" (Gen. 29:35). After Judah was born, she stopped having children for a time. Reaching this point in the story makes a person want to clap for Leah because after so many years of trying to do the right thing, she finally did the right thing. She looked to God and worshipped Him.

I think Leah had a revelation of truth. She finally understood some things she had been missing all along. It's as though she said, "You know what? I don't know what's up with Jacob and I can't be sure he will ever love me. But I do know that God is paying attention to me. God loved me before Jacob ever came into my life and He loves me now that I am Jacob's wife. He loved me before I had children and He will love me when I stop having them. I don't have to perform to get His love. I am finished trying to be seen, I am finished trying to be heard, and I am finished trying to be connected. I realize that I am seen; I am heard; I am connected. So I will praise the God who sees me, hears me, and has joined me to Himself."

Prior to the birth of her youngest son, Leah represents people who feel they must earn their right standing before God. They believe they can earn His love if they perform well enough, so they wear themselves out trying. This is why we need to understand Ephesians 2:8–9: "For it is by grace you have been saved, through faith—and this is not from yourselves, it is the gift of God—not by works, so that no one can boast." In other words, no one can do anything to earn God's love. It's a gift. We can't work for it; we simply receive it—and then we praise the Lord out of grateful hearts that finally know the truth.

Things Are Not Always As They Seem

If you have ever felt like Leah—tired, frustrated, and confused because you thought you did everything right, but everything still went wrong—I want to submit a perspective for your consideration. I'd like to suggest that perhaps the best thing God has done in your life is to close certain doors of opportunity, to keep you away from certain relationships, or to say "no" or "not yet" to dreams you were bursting in anticipation to see come true. It's possible, even likely, that the greatest thing God has done for you is to allow people to ignore you. Even though it made you sad and angry at the time, the fact that God isolated you for a season can be your greatest blessing.

Think of it this way. When all those disappointments came your way, when you sat by yourself with tears running down your face, maybe you were not isolated for a season, but isolated for a reason. Only when a person reaches that point of desperation can he or she say, "God, I realize that You are my only hope. This time, I will praise the Lord."

Are you finished trying to impress people? Have you had enough of trying to make people like or appreciate you? Have you reached the point where you understand that if all you ever have in life is Jesus, He is enough? Are you convinced that you and God are a majority and you will be just fine? Has your statement of faith become "This time I will praise the Lord"? This is the place where you live for God and God alone. You know you really only have an audience of One. This is where Scripture takes root in you and begins to nourish you and come to life in you; this is where you can say, "If God is for me, who can be against me?" (Rom. 8:31, author's paraphrase).

What to Do When You Feel Like Leah

Looking at this story from Leah's perspective leads to a crucial I-factor question for you. What do you do when you are Leah—when you have hopes and dreams, but you are not the chosen one? When you want to be loved, but are rejected instead? How do you handle the pain when you feel, like Leah, that you have done all the right things and the people you hope will notice you still don't see you?

Maybe you are currently in a relationship in which you long to be loved, but your spouse's affections are going in a different direction. I do not necessarily mean your spouse is interested in another man or another woman, but that he or she has become engrossed in work or enamored with some kind of hobby or activity outside the home. Maybe you have worked for years to advance in your career, taking on extra projects, refilling the coffeepot and wiping the puddles on the bathroom counter, gaining new skills so you could be more effective—yet you get passed over for every promotion that becomes available. That's a painful situation; being overlooked and rejected stings. No human being can heal you from it, and you cannot heal yourself. It's a job for God.

When you find yourself feeling like Leah, the most important thing you can do is remember God sees you. That's the most important point I hope you'll take away from this chapter: no matter how other people treat you, God sees you and God loves you.

Think about what happened to Leah. When God saw she was not loved (Gen. 29:31), He opened her womb. This tells us God was paying attention to Leah when no one else was. It shows us He had compassion for her and knew the pain she felt from being ignored and rejected. This is exactly the way He feels about you. He knows what you long for, He knows when you're not getting it, and He has compassion on you.

Before I go on, let me say what has been said many times in Christian circles: God is not Santa Claus. He is not a big gift-dispenser in the sky who will drop down a present every time a person feels sad about a certain circumstance. Jesus Himself said we will face hard times in this world (John 16:33), and we know that suffering at times is part of the Christian life. But there are also times when God sees the pain in a person's heart and reaches into his or her life to bring comfort, hope,

> When you find yourself feeling like Leah, the most important thing you can do is remember God sees you.

encouragement, and strength, as He did for Leah. That's what I am praying for you.

A similar situation to Leah's is described in Ezekiel 16:3–5, except that it happens with an entire city instead of one individual:

> This is what the Sovereign LORD says to Jerusalem: Your ancestry and birth were in the land of the Canaanites; your father was an Amorite and your mother a Hittite. On the day you were born your cord was not cut, nor were you washed with water to make you clean, nor were you rubbed with salt or wrapped in cloths. No one looked on you with pity or had compassion enough to do any of these things for you.

God was saying to the people of Jerusalem, "I saw how they neglected you. I saw how they ignored you. I saw that they did not even acknowledge you had been born." He went on to say, "Rather, you were thrown out into the open field, for on the day you were born you were despised" (Ezek. 16:5). This is a bleak and tragic picture, yet we know that while God was talking about a city in these verses, the same situations occur in people's lives. Not being noticed, not being accepted, and not being valued happen to people all the time.

But once God finished His poignant observations on Jerusalem's sad state, everything changed. He then said, "I came by and saw you there, helplessly kicking about in your own blood. As you lay there, I said, 'Live!' And I helped you to thrive like a plant in the field. You grew up and became a beautiful jewel" (vv. 6–7 NLT).

The message in this passage for anyone who feels like Leah is this: God knows you have spent so much time looking for acknowledgment, acceptance, and approval from other people. He knows they have not seen you, have not cared for you, and have not given you a chance. Everything they failed to do for you, He will do for you. Every time they turned their heads when you walked by,

God turned His head in your direction. When other people don't see you, God does. He is the One who will do for you much more than they ever will. Paul praised God and described Him this way: "Now to him *who is able to do immeasurably more than all we ask or imagine*, according to his power that is at work within us, to him be glory . . . for ever and ever!" (Eph. 3:20–21, emphasis added). God's eye is on you, and not only can He meet your deepest needs and desires, He can do even more than you can imagine.

It's Time to Get Some Things Out of Your Life

I want us to take another look at Judah's name because it tells us what to do once we've reached the point where we can praise the Lord, stop performing, and receive His unconditional love. I mentioned that Judah's name means "praise," but it means a certain kind of praise. It comes from the Hebrew word *yadah*, which means "to lift one's hands" and "to throw something away."[7] When Leah named her fourth son Judah and said, "This time I will praise the LORD" (Gen. 29:35), she was saying, "I am going to throw some things away and get them out of my life because of what I now know about God. I finally understand that He loves and accepts me, so I can throw away the need for Jacob to see, hear, and connect with me. I can stop having babies out of my need to be significant. I can stop wearing myself out trying to feel loved. I'm going to throw away the pain and the frustration, the heartache and disappointment I have known for so long. I'm letting it go, and I'm stepping into a whole new life of love and acceptance."

As we close this chapter, the most important question I can ask is this: What do you need to throw away?

What have you tried to make happen for yourself, but were never able to make work? What emotional burdens have you carried because of the way people treated you? Have you been searching for significance for so long that it has left you weary? These are some of the things it's time to throw away:

- The need to be liked
- The need to feel better about yourself
- The need to be loved by people of your choosing, rather than letting God lead you into relationships of His choosing
- The idea that you have to earn God's love
- The idea that there is anything you can achieve or purchase that will increase your true worth and value
- The desire to impress certain people
- The fear that you are not accepted
- The fear that you are not valuable
- The worry about what people think of you
- The fear of the future

What else can you think of? What is it specifically that has felt like an emotional tyrant to you, driving you to seek significance everywhere but the one place you will truly find it, which is in God? I encourage you to take a look at your life and determine what thought patterns and emotional tendencies are good and right for you, and which ones you need to get out of your life. This won't be an easy exercise, but if you will do it, I'm certain you will end up happier, more fulfilled, and more excited about the future God has planned for you.

—————— Internal Building Blocks ——————

- The search for significance is completely different than a hunger for attention. People with troubled I-factors clamor to be noticed; people with strong I-factors embark on healthy journeys toward the significance only God can give.

- Wanting to be seen, heard, and connected to others in meaningful ways is a God-given desire and need. Some people try to meet it in unhealthy ways, but people with a strong I-factor learn to meet it in healthy, appropriate ways.
- You can't control how other people treat you or relate to you, and you are not responsible for them. You are only responsible to develop a healthy, growing relationship with God.
- God sees your pain and your struggles, and He wants to help you through them.
- To move forward in life, some things from the past must be thrown away.

———— Strengthening Your I-Factor ————

1. What does significance mean to you? How would you describe your need for it?
2. On a scale of one to ten, with one being "not at all" and ten being "completely," how well do you feel seen? How well do you feel heard? How connected are you with people who are important in your life?
3. What needs, desires, or fears have driven you to search for significance in places where you ultimately will not find it? How will you throw them away?
4. Why do you think God wants to meet your need for significance, and how can He meet it in ways nothing or no one else has been able to?
5. How can you stop trying to look for acceptance in all the wrong places and accept God's unconditional love for you?

A Training Ground
for Greatness

*Failures, repeated failures, are finger
posts on the road to achievement. One
fails forward toward success.*

—C. S. Lewis

WHILE I WAS WRITING THIS BOOK, A SCHOOL OF THOUGHT became extremely popular in the Christian world. Its main tenets assert that God does not see the sins people commit, that confession is unnecessary, and that repentance is a form of legalism. Its goal, apparently, is to make Christianity easy. It allows for behaviors and excesses that traditional orthodoxy views as unbiblical, and it portrays God only as a supreme being who wants life to be fun and free from any kind of discipline or difficulty.

Although I realize many people are attracted to this movement, its theology focuses too much on certain aspects of the gospel message, such as God's great grace and abundant mercy, while completely ignoring others, such as the need for acknowledgment, confession, and repentance of sin. This kind of thinking results in an unbalanced view of God and a faulty view of what a healthy, thriving relationship with God ought to be.

I mention this because any time people view God as a cosmic feel-good machine, they miss out on a rich and vital aspect of His love. You may be thinking, *What? Isn't God's love all about helping me feel better?* Not really. God's love is about helping you *be* better—helping you become a stronger, wiser, more compassionate, more whole person equipped to fulfill His great plans for your life.

People do not grow stronger while everything in life is going well. The better we understand and embrace this, the stronger our I-factors become. We grow when we have to develop new mental and emotional muscles, and that only happens when we face challenges and hardships. Walt Disney once said, "All the adversity I've had in my life, all my troubles and obstacles, have strengthened me. . . . You may not realize it when it happens, but a kick in the teeth may be the best thing in the world for you."[1]

Disney was right. Sometimes the best thing that can happen to us is something we would describe as painful or difficult. This is because problems and crises are often God's chosen tools to develop character in us. When He allows these situations in our lives, it's not only to build our character, but also to equip us for the next level of destiny and greatness He has for us.

I'm convinced your best days are ahead of you, not behind you. I know this because 1 Corinthians 2:9 says, "No eye has seen, no ear has heard, and no mind has imagined

> We grow when we have to develop new mental and emotional muscles, and that only happens when we face challenges and hardships.

what God has prepared for those who love him" (NLT). You can be sure God has prepared great things for you, things so good you cannot even imagine them. Those things are prepared for you, so the question becomes: Are you prepared for them? In other words, are you ready to handle the wonderful opportunities that are in store for your life? Do you have the wisdom, the maturity, and the character you need to steward them well?

The Crucible of Character Development

When God wants to do something significant through people's lives, He often takes them through a crisis designed to prepare them for promotion. The true essence of who we are is developed and determined in the crises of our lives.

All the way through the Bible, God led people through crises before He elevated them to greater significance.

- Abraham waited in faith for years to have a son, even when it seemed naturally impossible (Gen. 18:10–11; 21:1–2). Then, in obedience to God, he endured the agony of knowing he had to sacrifice that son. In the end, his son was spared, but that situation was a crisis indeed (Gen. 22).
- Joseph was mocked, ridiculed, and sold into slavery by his brothers (Gen. 37:3–28).
- Moses was treated badly by the people he was called to lead (Ex. 32:1–7; Num. 14:1–2; 16:41).
- Joshua had to wait and wander in the wilderness for forty years before finally fulfilling God's purpose for his life, which was to lead the Israelites into the promised land (Deut. 1:38; 31:7).
- David was not affirmed by his father (1 Sam. 16:11) or liked by his brothers (1 Sam. 17:28). He was also anointed in obscurity (1 Sam. 16:12–13) and then had to serve King Saul even though Saul tried to kill him every time he had a chance (1 Sam. 18:8–11; 19:2).

- Job lost his family, his health, and his possessions (Job 1:13–22; 2:3–7). His so-called friends blamed him for his troubles (Job 4; 5; 8; 11; 15; 18; 20; 22; 25), instead of realizing God had orchestrated a test of faith in Job's life.
- Paul had a dramatic conversion experience that involved temporary blindness (Acts 9:1–9) and suffered with an unspecified ailment he called "a thorn in my flesh" (2 Cor. 12:7).

Each of these people, who eventually became highly significant in God's story, went through one or more major crises as part of God's plan for his life. He knew He wanted to use them in powerful ways, but He knew they first had to go through experiences that would strengthen their characters.

Even Jesus went through the ultimate crisis of being betrayed by His own people and abandoned by His disciples. He was beaten, spat upon, and subjected to a crown of thorns, then He suffered the cruelest death imaginable—crucifixion—for crimes and sins He did not commit.

Plenty of people who lived much later than biblical times also experienced problems and setbacks on their journeys to prominence.

- Bill Gates's first business venture was a total failure. He and a partner developed a device to read and process traffic data. When they tried to sell it, they could not even get it to work well enough to finish the sales presentation.[2]
- Benjamin Franklin's parents were so poor they could not afford to pay for his education past age ten. Determined to learn, Franklin continued his learning through independent study and prolific reading.[3]

- Marie Curie was not allowed to attend the all-male university in her hometown of Warsaw, Poland, so she studied at an informal, unofficial university. Her family could not afford to educate both Marie and her sister, so Marie supported her sister while her sister went to school, and then her sister supported her as Marie pursued her studies. Her work made possible the science of radiology and the X-ray machine, which has helped millions and millions of people. She is the only woman ever to win two Nobel prizes—one in chemistry and the other in physics.[4]

- Steven Spielberg wanted to pursue his college education at the University of Southern California, but the school rejected him—twice. Not to be deterred, he went on to hone his filmmaking craft and became one of the most brilliant filmmakers of modern times. The university later acknowledged Spielberg's genius, awarding him an honorary doctorate and inviting him to sit on the school's board of trustees.[5]

- Ludwig van Beethoven wrote some of the world's greatest symphonies, but he never heard them. He went deaf at the age of twenty-six. He also battled depression, perhaps as a result of his difficult childhood and repeated disappointments throughout his life.[6]

- Rosa Parks spent years silently enduring racial prejudice and mistreatment. One day, she had had enough, so she took the risk of standing up for herself and sparked the Civil Rights movement.

These types of character-building experiences are not limited to biblical or historical figures. They are also prerequisites for promotion in our lives today, and they are necessary building blocks for a strong I-factor. The path to our destinies almost always leads through crisis and takes us through what I call "dying places," situations we find extremely difficult or painful, but that are necessary for our personal growth and strength.

How to Hang In There and Handle a Crisis

Every road to success takes a detour through a dying place—a place of failure—sometimes more than once. When that happens, the temptation is to want to give up. When we find ourselves in crises, we often want to walk away from those hard situations and find something easier. But we must understand character is tested by commitment. Commitment that wavers because of our circumstances indicates that our character needs to be strengthened, and that's the very reason for the crises. If we give up in the heat of the battle, we will never taste the victory God has for us.

> When we find ourselves in crises, we often want to walk away from those hard situations and find something easier. But we must understand character is tested by commitment.

Learning how to deal with the crises that come our way is crucial. I've found three successful ways to do that. First, we acknowledge our pain; second, we recognize that the pain is one part of a larger process; and third, we understand that the process leads to the fulfillment of our potential.

1. Acknowledge the Pain

The great poet and writer Maya Angelou said, "There is no greater agony than bearing an untold story inside of you."[7] Angelou should know. When she was young, her parents divorced and sent her and her brother to live with their grandmother in Arkansas, where they endured racial discrimination. While visiting her mother when Maya was about seven, her mother's boyfriend raped Maya. When her uncles found out what he had done, they killed the perpetrator. This situation was so traumatic that Maya's speech basically shut down. For years, she barely spoke a word.[8] But no doubt, the horrors of her story continued to replay themselves in her mind day after day. Even though people around her knew what happened, for a long time she obviously could not verbalize its effect on her or share with others in such a way that they could help her heal. So when she wrote of the agony of an untold story, she knew firsthand what she was talking about.

Someone else who understood pain was the writer of Psalm 137, someone who knew the agony of exile to Babylon.

> *By the rivers of Babylon we sat and wept*
> *when we remembered Zion.*
> *There on the poplars*
> *we hung our harps,*
> *for there our captors asked us for songs,*
> *our tormentors demanded songs of joy;*
> *they said, "Sing us one of the songs of Zion!"*
>
> *How can we sing the songs of the* LORD
> *while in a foreign land?*
> *If I forget you, Jerusalem,*
> *may my right hand forget its skill.*
> *May my tongue cling to the roof of my mouth*
> *if I do not remember you,*
> *if I do not consider Jerusalem*
> *my highest joy. (Ps. 137:1–6)*

These words describe the innermost feelings of the children of Israel during the days of their Babylonian captivity. They sat by the river and wept for their homeland. In the midst of the crisis, the Babylonians ask them to sing. We can imagine that the Babylonians might have heard about how passionately the Israelites worshipped their God. Perhaps they had heard about worship experiences so powerful the priests in the tabernacle were not able to perform their service (2 Chron. 5:14). They wanted to hear the songs of Zion, but the Israelites did not feel like singing.

Then they asked an important question: "How can we sing the songs of the Lord while in a foreign land?" In other words, they were in a strange, new place. The environment in which they had always worshipped was now only a memory. It strikes me that their response is transparent and sincere. They don't do what so many people in crises today do, which is to deny the pain or ignore the situation, hoping it will go away. They did not go through the motions other people expected of them. They just said, "How could we even think about worshipping right now?"

Maybe you can relate to the Israelites. Perhaps you have lost your job, received an unsettling medical report, fallen back into an old addiction, or are going through a terrible situation with one of your children. All these situations and so many more constitute a crisis. And in the midst of a crisis, people are often simply trying to survive. They may not want to smile, joke around, give others a high five, or watch a ballgame and cheer for their team. In such circumstances, the healthy course of action is to admit to God how painful the situation is.

During a crisis, you could feel alone and abandoned. Acknowledging your pain to God reminds you that He is there. When you know He is there, you remember that He cares for you and He will bring you through your situation. This is why the psalmist's conversation changed in Psalm 137:5. He said, "If I forget you, Jerusalem, may my right hand forget its skill." This is his remembrance of better days. When he thought of his past in

Jerusalem, he remembered all that God did for His people there. And when that happened, his disposition changed completely; he ended up talking about his highest joy.

When you are in the midst of a crisis, it's a big mistake to focus only on what you are going through at the moment. If you fix your eyes on the present circumstances, you'll get stuck in them. While *living* in the past can create real problems, *remembering* what God has done in the past can help you pull yourself out of the sadness, confusion, fear, anger, or heartbreak a crisis can cause.

The next time you go through a crisis, it's okay to feel down and discouraged at first, but don't let yourself stay there. Remember all the good things God has done for you in the past and all the doors that have opened for you when it looked like every avenue to success was blocked.

Recognize That Pain Is Part of a Process

Napoleon Hill was one of the first authors to contribute to the field of personal success literature. His 1937 book, *Think and Grow Rich*, is a classic and a perennial bestseller in its category. He said: "Every adversity, every failure, every heartache carries with it the seed of an equal or greater benefit."

One of the most important things to understand about pain is it never happens in a vacuum; it's always part of a bigger picture. Putting it into context and seeing it as one portion of the larger journey of your life will help you deal with it from a holistic perspective and in a healthy way.

"Blessed are those whose strength is in you, whose hearts are set on pilgrimage. As they pass through the Valley of Baka, they make it a place of springs; the autumn rains also cover it with pools. They go from strength to strength . . ." (Ps. 84:5–7). This passage is talking about people who are dealing with a crisis. We know this because they are walking through the Valley of Baka, and *Baka* means "weeping."[9] These people, much like people today, wanted out of their bad situation. They wanted their circumstances to change; they wanted someone to fix their problem for them.

But that wasn't happening, so they did something that would be wise for all of us to emulate. They set their hearts on pilgrimage. This means they refused to let their crisis paralyze them; they were determined to keep moving until they got all the way to the other side of it. They realized they were on a journey and that while their difficulties were part of their present, they would not be part of their future. They would be able to use the lessons of the crisis to strengthen and prepare them for the future, but they would not be living in the situation long term.

Your journey through life will likely lead you through some difficult places. At times, you may feel you are in a valley of weeping because of the sadness or frustration you experience. The key to getting through a crisis successfully is not to give up in the midst of it. Instead, recognize your crisis is part of a process that will teach you lessons you need for the future. The hard seasons of life are not a waste of your time. They are incredibly valuable, and they are necessary for your success in the days to come. You are going *through* something bad in order to get *to* something good. Keep going and set your mind on making it all the way through your challenges, reaping as many benefits from them as you possibly can.

Understand That the Process Leads to the Fulfillment of Your Potential

Anytime you go through a period of suffering or hardship, keeping in mind that the process is leading to something greater is imperative. In Psalm 84, the people going through crisis "make it a place of springs." This is an old-fashioned way of saying they make the best of a bad situation. They don't sit around, hoping something good will come to them; they get proactive and make it happen.

If you are trying to work your way through difficult circumstances right now, their example is a good one to follow. You can make your point of crisis a place of springs in several ways. First, keep a hopeful, optimistic attitude. Second, look for the lessons and positive aspects of your negative situation, because every negative does have a positive. Third, refuse to become overly self-focused. Even when life is hard, it's usually easy to find someone who has a greater need or a more difficult situation than you do. Doing something to help someone else, even if it seems minor to you, can be tremendously beneficial to that person. In addition, it will put your problems in perspective and provide the joy that comes from helping others. These are a few examples of ways you can take initiative to make your hard place a place of springs.

The second part of Psalm 84:6 makes a point we could easily misunderstand in our modern, non-agrarian culture. After noting that the people make their valley of weeping "a place of springs," it says, "the autumn rains also cover it with pools." The psalmist is talking about the difference between the spring rains, which are also called the "former" rains, and the autumn rains, also called the "latter" rains. Let's look at this from a farmer's perspective.

The former rains fell in the springtime for a specific purpose—to soften the ground for planting. After a cold winter, the ground was hard and dry, so the spring rains provided the moisture needed for the ground to be able to receive and begin to nurture the seeds the farmers planted as the weather became warmer. The latter rains, which the psalmist mentioned in Psalm 84, did not come until fall, just before harvest time. Their purpose was to provide a burst of nutrients near the end of the growing season to ensure the best quality harvest.

You may be wondering how this applies to your life. The seed represents your potential promise—something you believe with your whole heart that you can achieve. Perhaps it's a promise you have made to yourself or something you have felt destined for, or something that seems like a promise from God for your life. The reason you face times of crisis and go through valleys of weeping is that your tears are the autumn rains that nourish the promises you long to see manifest in your life. You may not realize it, but your tears are watering the promise or the dream you want to fulfill. If you are living in a difficult season right now, it may indicate that your harvest is about to come in. Your challenges are strengthening you, maturing you, and preparing you for a new level of greatness.

From "Troublemaker" to Peacemaker

On July 18, 1918, a little boy was born in Transkei, South Africa. His parents named him Rolihlahla, which translates literally as "pulling the branch of a tree," but is understood to mean "trouble-maker."[10] Little did they know that day their child was destined to become one of the greatest peacemakers the world has ever known. I'm talking about Nelson Mandela.

Named Nelson by a schoolteacher during his early years, Mandela grew up in a small village called Qunu. His father was once wealthy and destined to be a tribal chief, but lost his status and his financial resources over a legal dispute with another local leader. The elder Mandela died of lung disease when Nelson was only nine years old.[11] This early loss changed Nelson's life forever.

As a favor to Nelson's father, a friend named Chief Jongintaba Dalindyebo, leader of the Thembo tribe, adopted Nelson after his father's death and moved him from Qunu to the capital of Thembuland. While there, Mandela began to hear about how the coming of white people to Africa had disrupted the typically peaceful lives of black Africans and how the whites oppressed and took advantage of the blacks.

At age sixteen, Mandela came to understand that white land

ownership in South Africa meant that black citizens had lost their influence and authority in their home country and would never be able to govern themselves.[12] He began to realize that his people had become slaves in their own homeland.

Mandela spent his college years preparing to work in some type of civil service job, perhaps as a clerk. For a black man in that day, such a job was the best he could hope for. While in school, Mandela participated in one of his earliest expressions of activism—a boycott against the administration over lack of food and their unwillingness to allow the student council to participate adequately in decisions affecting the student body. As a result, school officials expelled him, but the chief who raised him forced him to go back to school, even though that meant Mandela would have to suppress his feelings.[13]

Ultimately, Mandela finished college by taking correspondence courses and then moved to Johannesburg, where he eventually opened a law firm committed to providing legal services to black people for little to no cost. At the same time, Mandela led nonviolent protests against the South African government's racially unfair policies.[14]

By 1961, Mandela realized that peaceful resistance was ineffective against the government and cofounded an anti-apartheid group that practiced armed, guerilla warfare tactics. He also organized and led a three-day strike of the nation's workforce, and later found himself under arrest and sentenced to five years in prison for that initiative. In 1963, with ten of his like-minded colleagues, Mandela was charged with political offenses and sentenced to life in prison. He spent the next twenty-seven years behind bars.[15]

Mandela's imprisonment could not change his convictions, stifle his influence, or silence his voice. The Nobel Prize website says of Mandela: "During his years in prison, Mandela's reputation grew steadily. He was widely accepted as the most significant black leader in South Africa and became a potent symbol of resistance as the anti-apartheid movement gathered strength. He consistently refused to compromise his political position to obtain his freedom."[16]

On February 11, 1990, after being held captive for twenty-seven years, Mandela was released from prison. He won the Nobel Peace Prize with South African president F. W. de Klerk in 1993, and in 1994, he became South Africa's first black president, skillfully and effectively leading a deeply divided nation into peace and reconciliation during his time in office. Mandela died in 2013 at the age of ninety-five, leaving a powerful legacy of wise leadership, reconciliation, and social justice.

In recent years, plenty of photographs and videos of Mandela's cramped prison cells have been made public. People have been able to see firsthand the conditions under which he lived for twenty-seven years, but no one could truly know the full measure of the hardships he endured.

I believe Mandela did exactly what Psalm 84 teaches. He acknowledged and accepted his pain—both the pain of apartheid and the oppression and pain of being in prison—never trying to get out of it by compromising his principles. He recognized that his pain was part of a greater process, and he allowed the process to unfold, even while he was behind bars, by continuing to speak for social change. Finally, he understood that the process, even though it included prison, would lead to the fulfillment of his potential— the potential to heal a nation and change the world.

I hope Mandela's story inspires you to dig deep for the greatness within you. In many ways and for many years, he was an ordinary guy with a passion for justice who was willing to fight and suffer for what he believed in. Ultimately he experienced tremendous success as a political leader, fulfilled his destiny, and saw his dream of peace and reconciliation come true.

Whatever your destiny, whatever your dream, and whatever you have to endure to see these things come to pass, it will be worth it. If you are willing to embrace the journey to significance, even with its difficulties, you *will* achieve the greatness you were created for.

Internal Building Blocks

- God is love and God is kind, compassionate, and merciful. But God's ultimate goal in your life is not to help you feel better when life gets difficult. His goal is to make you *be* better.
- Pain, disappointment, heartache, crisis, and difficulty are necessary elements on anyone's journey to greatness. The key to achieving greatness is learning to handle them well.
- Here's a recap on how to handle a crisis: acknowledge the pain, recognize that pain is part of a process, and understand that the process leads to the fulfillment of your potential.
- Nelson Mandela underwent a transformation from a man whose name meant "troublemaker" to a leader who became one of the world's great peacemakers. You, too, can be transformed and become someone or something you have never been before. If you have made mistakes in your past, let his story give you hope.

Strengthening Your I-Factor

1. Why is it important to understand that God's goal for your life is not to help you feel better when you are struggling?
2. What is God's ultimate goal for your life? How does understanding His goal change your perspective on challenges or suffering?
3. Of the people mentioned in this chapter, which one most inspires you to overcome challenges or failure on the path to greatness? Why?

4. Have you acknowledged your pain, failure, or challenge in a healthy way? If you have had trouble doing that, would you consider allowing a qualified minister or counselor to help you and make plans to confide in this person?

5. Pain is part of a process leading to the fulfillment of your potential. As you look back on your life, what painful experience led to something greater in your life? In your current situation, how can you adjust your perspective to anticipate fulfillment of a hope or dream that has yet to be realized?

8

The Biggest Favor You Can Do Yourself

The weak can never forgive. Forgiveness
is the attribute of the strong.

—MAHATMA GANDHI

ONE OF MY RELATIVES IS A MAJOR FAN OF THE REALITY show *Duck Dynasty*, which stars some of the men of the Robertson family from West Monroe, Louisiana. One of the most powerful stories I have ever heard involves a husband and wife from that family who do not appear on the show as often as some of their family members. Al, who is Willie, Jase, and Jep's older brother, is known as "the pastor" and his personal story is amazing. He has endured deep pain and come through it with faith as solid as gold.

Al and his wife, Lisa, write about their lives in the book *A New Season*, and the story they tell is better than anything any scriptwriter could come up with.[1] In a nutshell, Al and Lisa seemed happily married for several years and had two young daughters when Lisa had a nonsexual, emotional affair with a local businessman. When Al confronted her about it, she admitted it and they began to work on their marriage as best they could. Al, of course, was deeply hurt, but he was a committed Christian, doing his best to live his life according to God's Word. At the same time, he admitted he really did not know how to deal with his pain, so he basically ignored it while he and Lisa continued with their lives. By then the man in the affair had moved out of town, so Al and Lisa thought he was no longer a threat to their marriage. They didn't realize that his absence would not solve their problems.

Several years later, Lisa had another affair, and that one did become sexual. While that affair was taking place, Lisa was also embezzling money from Al's family business, Duck Commander. When Al found out about it, he was understandably furious and devastated. As he thought and prayed about what to do, he came across a book on forgiveness and read it, though he found it overwhelming and struggled to get through it. While he really did not want to forgive Lisa at times, he ultimately did—fully and freely.

But Al was not the only one who had to forgive. On their journey of healing and restoration, Lisa realized much of her behavior was rooted in abuse she suffered as a little girl at the hands of a relative. For various reasons, Lisa was not able to receive the help she needed. Her emotional wounds never had a chance to heal; they festered and grew until she made some hurtful decisions that nearly destroyed her marriage.

As Al and Lisa worked through their issues, she had a life-changing encounter with Jesus Christ and realized how much she needed to forgive her abuser. Once she did, the healing and wholeness that eventually resulted in her life have been astounding. Today, Al and Lisa are a happy husband and wife, joyful parents and grandparents, and wise, trusted advisors to married couples who find themselves in deep trouble. They are also bringing hope to thousands and thousands of hurting people who have been inspired by their journey from abuse, abandonment, foolish decisions, deceit, guilt, shame, and heartache to faith, peace, truth, joy, and love. None of the goodness and the influence Al and Lisa now enjoy would have been possible had they not opened themselves up to God's transformative grace and healing power through their willingness to forgive.

Unforgiveness Cripples, Forgiveness Sets You Free

I mention Al and Lisa Robertson's story because the pain they suffered helped build the foundation for their lives today. Had they never struggled with the things they had to deal with, they would never have learned the lessons necessary to develop the strength, wisdom, and unshakable faith they have today. They learned the unchangeable truth that unforgiveness binds us to the past, while forgiveness frees us for the future. While some people do not have to fight battles as intense as Al and Lisa's, almost everyone suffers some kind of pain or loss—something deeply hurtful that needs to be forgiven—at some point in his or her life.

Unforgiveness pierces our souls when we are hurt, offended, or disappointed and we do not handle those feelings properly. Instead of assuming the best about people, giving them grace, and moving on with our lives, we feel pain. Because we don't like pain, we feel badly toward the person who caused it. If the pain is deep enough, we can fall into ongoing anger, bitterness, resentment, or full-blown unforgiveness. When that happens, we often cripple ourselves on the journey toward a bright, fulfilling future. The moment we choose not to forgive is the moment we bind ourselves to the past.

> The moment we choose not to forgive is the moment we bind ourselves to the past.

One of the biggest reasons people live in bondage to past failures, past mistakes, past relationships, or past opportunities is that they do not forgive the people who have hurt them or held them back. This may happen as a result of stubbornness or pride, or it may take place because they do not understand the importance of forgiveness. Regardless of the reasons they choose not to forgive, the unforgiveness keeps them from moving forward in life. Once they understand that forgiveness is vital to success and they learn how to forgive those who have done damage to their lives, they will soar to new heights of greatness.

When someone hurts, offends, or disappoints us, we naturally feel justified in being angry and holding a grudge. Especially in situations that result in deep pain, gross injustice, or significant loss, we rarely even think about forgiving the people who caused the problem; we want the bad situation to somehow turn out for our good. And sometimes we want revenge, we want to get even, or we think the offender should pay for the offense. We almost always think that unforgiveness is the "right" way to feel. But harboring unforgiveness ends up hurting us much more than it will ever hurt anyone else.

Unforgiveness keeps people trapped in their pasts and unable to move forward because it prevents them from assessing the present appropriately and from seeing the future clearly. Think about this: If you want to drive from your house to the grocery store, you put your car into gear and drive forward. To get there safely, you have to keep your eyes on the road in front of you. If you try to make the trip looking in the rearview mirror, you will probably have an accident. The same principle applies to life. If you keep looking backward, you can't move forward without a problem.

That's as true for your life as it is for your driving. You cannot move into the new relationships, new opportunities, and new sources of provision that are ahead of you if you will not look in their direction. The good plans God has for your future are in front of you, not behind you. I understand the situations that have happened in your past may feel more tangible to you than what is yet to materialize in the future. I concede that past things are easier to see with your natural eyes. That's why faith and vision are so important. Those two dynamics aren't needed when people only want to look backward. They only work in the forward dimension and they create the ability to see internally what you cannot yet perceive externally.

Faith and vision empower you to look ahead of you, not behind you. Unforgiveness puts a block on your capacity for faith and vision because it keeps you looking at the past, not toward the future. Forgiveness removes that block and enables you to dream of better days to come, to envision good things before they happen, and to believe that blessings are coming your way. As Bishop T. D. Jakes says: "So then, forgiveness is essential if we are to grow into the fullness of who God created us to be . . . Forgiveness isn't about weakening you but strengthening you to live again and love again, performing at your highest capacity, unencumbered by yesterday's maladies."[2]

> Unforgiveness puts a block on your capacity for faith and vision because it keeps you looking at the past, not toward the future.

In order to develop a strong I-factor, people *must* learn to forgive. It's non-negotiable because part of a healthy I-factor is the ability to break free from the pain of the past and move beyond life's obstacles—not only external obstacles such as mistakes and failures, but also internal obstacles such as the pain of betrayal or personal offense. Unforgiveness is one of the greatest possible deterrents to a robust I-factor because it prohibits a person's journey into the amazing future God has planned, but forgiveness brings inner strength and opens the door to destiny.

What Forgiveness Is—and Isn't

Sometimes it's helpful to define what something is by first explaining what it is not. That's true for forgiveness, which may be one of the most frequently misunderstood concepts in the world. If you understand what forgiveness is not, then you can better understand what forgiveness really is. The most common misperceptions I have heard about forgiveness fall into four categories. I want to dismantle each of these myths about forgiveness so I can then help you understand what it really means.

Forgiveness Does Not Mean Minimizing an Offense

When you forgive someone who has hurt or wronged you, you are not saying the offense is no big deal or that it didn't really hurt. No, it did hurt and it is a big deal. I know this may come across as overly simplistic, but think about it. Wrong words and behaviors cause pain, and pain tells you there is something or someone you need to forgive.

When you choose to forgive, you are making an intentional choice not to hang on to the hurtful situation because if you do, it will rob you of your freedom. I'm not talking about freedom in some idealistic or esoteric sense; I'm talking about it in the most practical terms possible. Unless you forgive, you will forever feel an invisible bond with the person who hurt you. To harbor unforgiveness is to hold the offender in an invisible prison. Unfortunately, that prison is not off campus from your life. It's in your heart, so it is always with you.

No matter how hard you try to forget what happened to you or how much it hurt, memories of the event or the perpetrator will hover over you until you forgive. To try to forgive without acknowledging the depth of the pain you suffered or the extent of the loss you sustained is not healthy. People can be brutal, and when someone is brutal toward you, let yourself feel the pain and grieve the loss. That's an important step toward healing, and it's a vital step toward forgiveness and freedom.

Forgiveness Does Not Always Lead to Reconciliation

Forgiving someone and letting go of what they have done to you does not mean that you have to reconcile with them. That's a common misconception, and I have no idea where it came from because it certainly is not biblical. This faulty thinking may be the single biggest deterrent to forgiveness. I can't prove that with statistical data, but when I think about the many situations involving unforgiveness that I have been aware of as a pastor through the years, I would say the biggest hindrance to people's willingness to forgive is they think forgiveness demands a restored relationship. It doesn't.

"If it is possible, as far as it depends on you, live at peace with everyone" (Rom. 12:18). This brief verse makes two important points. First, it acknowledges that living at peace with all people is not always possible. Second, it says "as far as it depends on you," which means sometimes there is nothing you can do to get along with someone. I fully believe God understands that sometimes reconciliation is not the best choice. He knows that some people are much better off without each other.

In order for a relationship to be restored, three dynamics need to take place. First, the offender must sincerely repent. This means not only being sorry, but also stopping the hurtful behavior. Second, some type of restitution, repayment, or making things right needs to happen, depending on what is appropriate under the circumstances. Third, the rebuilding of trust is necessary and happens as the person who did wrong proves himself or herself through words and actions. I view these things as non-negotiables for reconciliation, but even if they do not happen, you can still forgive—because forgiveness is not the same as reconciliation. Reconciliation takes two people, but forgiveness is a one-player game.

People often say, "When so-and-so apologizes, then I will forgive." Individuals who have that attitude become hostages to the very person who wronged them in the first place because they have made their freedom contingent on someone else's behavior.

Let me encourage you not to wait on an apology before you choose to forgive and not to delay forgiving someone because you think forgiveness means you have to re-engage with that person. Forgiveness is a step toward reconciliation, but it is not equal to reconciliation. You can forgive someone and never have a relationship with that person again.

Forgiving Is Not the Same As Forgetting

We often think that to forgive someone, we must forget what has happened and deny the pain of it. People even say, "Forgive and forget," but that's not good advice. The truth is, when something painful happens, we may never forget it. In some cases, not being able to forget it keeps us from getting into the same situation again.

Forgiveness and forgetting are two completely separate issues, and I think that's okay. We do need to move beyond what has happened to us and we certainly should not obsess over it, but I'm not sure we always need to forget it altogether because we can learn so much from those circumstances. Often those same circumstances position us to help others in ways we could not have done otherwise. The scope of our lives and the future that lies ahead of us are bigger than any one incident, so forgiving those who offend us is important. Forgiving others allows God to heal our hearts and remove the pain of the offense, so that when we do remember what happened to us, we don't have to relive the heartache associated with it.

Forgiveness Is Not a Feeling

One reason people fail to forgive is that they say they are still angry with their offenders, they are still hurt by what happened, or they simply do not want to forgive. This comes from a fundamental misunderstanding that forgiveness is rooted in the emotions when it's not; it's rooted in the mind. Forgiveness is a choice, not a feeling. It's something we decide to do, not always something we want to do. The beloved author and speaker Corrie ten Boom said, "Forgiveness is an act of the will, and the will can function regardless of the temperature of the heart."[3]

Forgiveness is also something we do because God asks us to. He doesn't want us to forgive so we can be noble or so we can suffer to obey Him; He wants us to do it because our forgiveness toward others opens the door for His forgiveness toward us. He knows we fail and need to be forgiven. He is eager to forgive us; He just wants us to put ourselves in position to receive it.

"O Lord, you are so good, so ready to forgive, so full of unfailing love for all who ask for your help" (Ps. 86:5 NLT).

"[God] does not punish us for all our sins; he does not deal harshly with us, as we deserve. For his unfailing love toward those who fear him is as great as the height of the heavens above the earth" (Ps. 103:10–11 NLT).

These Old Testament verses assure us of God's eagerness to forgive. Let's also look at Christ's New Testament teachings about forgiveness. He said, "If you forgive those who sin against you, your heavenly Father will forgive you. But if you refuse to forgive others, your Father will not forgive your sins" (Matt. 6:14–15 NLT). He also said, "And when you stand praying, if you hold anything against anyone, forgive them, so that your Father in heaven may forgive you your sins" (Mark 11:25).

Also in the New Testament, Paul wrote: "Be kind and compassionate to one another, forgiving each other, just as in Christ God forgave you" (Eph. 4:32). And John wrote, "If we confess our sins, he is faithful and just and will forgive us our sins and purify us from all unrighteousness" (1 John 1:9).

The scriptures I have mentioned are only a few of many throughout the Bible that emphasize God's desire to forgive us and the necessity of our forgiving others. When we read them, we can see that forgiveness really is an act of the will, as Corrie ten Boom said, not a product of the emotions.

When a person makes the choice—sometimes a very difficult choice—to forgive, something amazing happens. The feelings begin to follow. Once a person decides to forgive, the anger begins to wane and hurt begins to sting a little less. Bitterness and resentment lessen over time. Eventually, the one who forgives can think about the offender without pain. And that is an incredibly liberating feeling.

If you need to forgive someone and have been waiting to feel like doing it, let me encourage you not to put it off any longer. Go ahead and make the decision to forgive, and I guarantee you, the feelings will follow. Forgiveness is not a favor to the offender; it's one of the biggest favors you can do for yourself.

Now that I've explained what forgiveness is not, I'd like to elaborate on what forgiveness is. It is the intentional choice to refuse to hold another person hostage for the pain he or she caused in your life. Forgiveness acknowledges the wound the other person inflicted, but says, "I am not going to hold you accountable for this. I know you did it, but I am going to release you from the responsibility for it. I will not allow you or your past actions to control my present or dictate my future." In setting the other person free from the offense, you set yourself free from it. When you can live free from the people who have hurt or hindered you, you can take bold steps into a new life of destiny, purpose, and fulfillment.

Forgiveness Isn't Fair—Thankfully

Sometimes when I speak to people about forgiveness, they mentally grasp what it is and what it is not. But when all is said and done, and they really do understand it, they object to forgiving someone because they say it's just not fair. They feel that because the other person hurt them, he or she should hurt too. They know the other person does not deserve to get a free pass for the offense, and they focus on the fact that he or she needs to make it right.

Sometimes people also view letting an offender off the hook as weak or wimpy. They're right that forgiveness is not fair but wrong about its being weak. It takes a person of strength and wisdom to forgive someone else and to participate in a dynamic that from many earthly perspectives is not fair at all.

I'd like to submit that we should be very grateful forgiveness isn't fair. The reason forgiveness isn't fair is that God is not fair. When He looks at us, it's not through the lens of what we deserve; it's through the filter of mercy and grace. Christ took all our sin on Himself and died an agonizing death for it—in our place. There's nothing fair about that. It's the best thing that ever happened to humanity.

Before Jesus' crucifixion, the disciple Peter had a question about forgiveness. The nature of his inquiry makes me wonder if someone had offended him repeatedly and had worn out his patience. He asked, "Lord, how many times shall I forgive my brother or sister who sins against me? Up to seven times?" (Matt. 18:21).

Jesus' answer may have been shocking, because Peter seemed to think forgiving someone seven times would be a lot. Jesus said, "I tell you, not seven times, but seventy-seven times" (v. 22). Seventy-seven is not to be taken literally; it represents "times without number."[4] In other words, there is no limit to how often we should forgive. This is exactly how God deals with us. He forgives time and time and time and time again.

Yes, You Can

I once spent hours in my office talking with some people stuck in unforgiveness. They wanted to escape the misery of the bad feeling that comes with refusing to forgive someone, but they wanted to do it without forgiving. To put it in the words of an old saying, they wanted to have their cake and eat it too. This hardly ever works, especially in situations where forgiveness is needed. There's no way to get around doing it.

By the time I had explained what forgiveness is and what it isn't and admitted that it really is not fair, they were closer than ever to being ready to forgive. But then they raised one final exasperated protest: "I just can't do it." They understood correctly that extending forgiveness is not easy. They knew it would take lots of work emotionally and mentally, and they said, "I just don't have it in me."

Then they rehashed a story I had already heard, maybe more than once, emphasizing the depth of the pain they felt as a result of the appalling wrongdoing against them. When they said, "I just can't do it," they didn't mean they were powerless; they weren't powerless. They really meant, "I *won't* do it." But people with a healthy I-factor are people who are willing to make the difficult choices in life. Making the choice to forgive can be grueling, but it can also lead to unprecedented personal strength and empowerment.

As a pastor, my job is to help people believe they can forgive and to lead them toward doing it. That's the only way they can break the stranglehold the offender has on them and the only way they can set themselves free from pain to enter into the future that awaits them. That new level of freedom is what I want for everyone I encounter, including you. If you have ever said, "I just can't forgive," let me share a few insights that will help you finally reach the point where you can—the point of your greatest freedom.

The Idea That You Can't Forgive Is a Lie

We live in a world in which a spiritual battle rages 24/7. The enemy, also known as the devil or Satan, continually opposes God's plan. This does not only happen on a cosmic level; it takes place on the battlefield of the minds of people who seek to follow God's way for living. Jesus said about the devil, "He was a murderer from the beginning, not holding to the truth, for there is no truth in him. When he lies, he speaks his native language, for he is a liar and the father of lies" (John 8:44). One of the primary ways the devil opposes God's people is to lie to them, and one of the lies he tells is, "You can't forgive. The offense was too great and the pain is too deep. You can't let that person off the hook."

The truth is that whenever God asks us to obey Him, as He asks us to forgive those who hurt us, He gives us the power and grace to do it.

You're Stronger than You Think

In our human strength, many things seem overwhelming or impossible. Forgiving someone after a serious offense can be one of them. As long as we feel we have to accomplish a difficult task all by ourselves, we will be tempted to think we cannot do it because we don't have the strength. This is why we have to learn to take our focus off ourselves and our abilities and look to God and His power. We need to lean on Him, not on ourselves.

Centuries ago, the apostle Paul wrote to a group of believers, "I can do all things through Christ who strengthens me" (Phil. 4:13 NKJV). This is as true for you today as it was for Paul so long ago. In Christ, you *do* have the strength to forgive. The more you tap into God's resources and draw from the well of all He offers you, the stronger your I-factor becomes.

God Will Give You the Grace to Get Free

Freedom is vitally important to God. He sacrificed His only Son to a brutal death on the cross so we could be free not only from sin, but also from sickness, eternal torment, and every form of bondage. "It is for freedom that Christ has set us free" (Gal. 5:1). We can be confident that God wants us free because He has already gone to the greatest possible limits to secure our freedom through His Son. All we have to do is choose to walk in the freedom He has made available to us. Part of experiencing the fullness of the freedom He offers us is to free ourselves from the prison of unforgiveness.

God's grace is abundant toward those who want to walk in freedom. He is always ready to help us more than we deserve. Paul wrote, "He [the Lord] said to me, 'My grace is sufficient for you, for my power is made perfect in weakness.' Therefore I will boast all the more gladly about my weaknesses, so that Christ's power may rest on me" (2 Cor. 12:9).

If you feel weak and unable to forgive a certain person, remember that thinking you can't do it is a lie from the enemy. Remember in Christ you are stronger than you think and God's grace is always available to help you embrace the freedom He has for you.

The Most Important Person to Forgive

Over the course of your lifetime, who has done you more harm than anyone else? You may immediately think of a former friend or romantic interest, a boss or professional colleague, or a family member. You may also have to admit that as much as other people have wounded you in the past, you have also hurt yourself. If this is true for you, you are not alone. For many people, the person they most need to forgive is the one they see in the mirror every day.

Living with unforgiveness toward ourselves is just as damaging as living with unforgiveness toward others. For most of us, the reasons we cannot forgive ourselves fall into two general categories: we can't forgive ourselves for doing something we should not have done, or for failing to do something we should have done. Sometimes we live in guilt, shame, and condemnation for years on end, and we sabotage our own destinies because we cannot forgive ourselves.

I have met with many people who struggle with self-unforgiveness and have become aware of frequently mentioned circumstances that cause people to feel so guilty they cannot forgive themselves. I would like to mention some of them now, in case you can identify with them. I don't think I need to elaborate on these because if you feel guilty about any of them, you will know it, and you will be painfully aware of the specific circumstances and people involved. So let me ask you, do you need to forgive yourself for

- losing your temper and speaking words you now regret?
- misunderstanding someone's motives and judging that person?
- taking a risk you thought would pay off big and then losing everything, causing hardship for your family?
- being so selfish as a spouse that your partner left you?
- being unduly harsh or critical toward someone?
- failing to resist when someone asked you to compromise your integrity?
- an honest, innocent mistake that resulted in harm or injury to someone else?
- not embracing the opportunity of a lifetime when it came along?

- misunderstanding someone's struggle and not helping him or her through it?
- sacrificing a potentially wonderful relationship on the altar of busyness?
- allowing yourself to be so stressed that you are not kind enough or attentive enough to the people you love?

No doubt there are countless other situations for which we need to forgive ourselves. This list simply represents some of the most common reasons. If any of these, or something similar, applies to you, I have good news. You can forgive yourself, break out of the self-imposed prison the situation has built around your life, leave the pain behind you, and move forward into better days ahead.

How to Forgive Someone

The freedom that comes from forgiving those who have wounded us is so important to God that He made sure Jesus gave three simple, specific instructions on how to do it during His ministry on earth. God's way of forgiveness is nothing like the world's way, and in my experience, it works much better. If you do it, it will change your life.

As I mentioned earlier, forgiveness is a choice, not a feeling. After we decide to forgive someone, we have the opportunity to make three more choices that put forgiveness into practice. They are: pray, bless, and do good.

Pray for Those Who Have Hurt You

The people who followed Jesus during His time on earth were people just like you and me. While they lived two thousand years ago in a country and culture not familiar to most Westerners, they don't seem to have been any more eager to forgive their offenders than we are today. They needed to be taught the way to freedom, just as you and I do. Jesus said to them:

> You have heard the law that says, "Love your neighbor" and hate your enemy.
> But I say, love your enemies! Pray for those who persecute you! In that way, you will be acting as true children of your Father in heaven. . . . If you love only those who love you, what reward is there for that? Even corrupt tax collectors do that much. If you are kind only to your friends, how are you different from anyone else? Even pagans do that. (Matt. 5:43–47 NLT)

Bless Those Who Have Wounded You

Paul wrote, "Bless those who persecute you; bless and do not curse" (Rom. 12:14). This instruction applies to our thoughts and our words. In our minds, we are to wish good things on those who have wounded us instead of hoping, even privately, that bad will come to them because of the pain they brought to us. With our mouths, we are to speak well of them instead of talking negatively about them.

Do Good to Those Who Have Offended You

Jesus said, "Love your enemies, do good to those who hate you, bless those who curse you, pray for those who mistreat you" (Luke 6:27–28). I've already commented on blessing and praying for those who have offended you, but it is also important to actively do good to the people who have done you wrong. When you have a chance to express kindness to them, don't let it pass by.

These steps to forgiveness are your keys to freedom. Whether you put them into practice toward someone who has hurt you or toward yourself, they will liberate you from the pain of your past and position you for the greatness that can only come to those who are free to experience it.

Internal Building Blocks

- Unforgiveness binds you to your past, while forgiveness frees you for your future.
- One of the main reasons people live in bondage to past failures, past mistakes, past relationships, or past opportunities is they do not forgive the people who have hurt them or held them back.
- To foster a strong, healthy I-factor, people must learn to practice forgiveness. Part of a healthy I-factor is the ability to break free from the pain of the past and move beyond life's obstacles.
- Lots of people misunderstand forgiveness. Forgiveness does not mean minimizing an offense; forgiveness does not always lead to reconciliation; forgiveness is not the same as forgetting; forgiveness is not a feeling, it's a choice.
- Yes, you can forgive. Why? Because the idea that you can't forgive is a lie, because you're stronger than you think, and because God will give you the grace to get free.
- The most important person you can ever forgive is yourself. Doing this is vital to your freedom and well-being.
- Three steps to forgive: pray for the people who have hurt you, bless those who have wounded you, and do good to the ones who have offended you.

Strengthening Your I-Factor

1. What is forgiveness, and what is it not? What misunderstandings about forgiveness became clear as you read this chapter?
2. The idea that you cannot forgive is a lie. Why?
3. Who is it in your life that you need to forgive? How is unforgiveness keeping you in bondage? How will forgiving this person set you free?

4. Is there anything for which you need to forgive yourself? What is it? Will you choose to take this important step?

5. How will forgiving yourself set you free? Once you do it, what will you do with the newfound freedom forgiveness will bring to your life?

6. Specifically, how will you pray for, bless, and do good to someone who has hurt you?

9

Success Is an Inside Job

A head full of fears has no space for dreams.
—Author unknown

COURAGE. IT'S A POWERFUL WORD, ISN'T IT? IT'S POWER-
ful not only because it evokes images of bravery and boldness, but
also because it's something most of us wish we had more of. Deep
inside, we long to be more courageous than we are. We know that
one quality, that one emotional dynamic, could be the key to living
our dreams. Deep inside, if we had to give a succinct answer for the
real reason we don't always go after our dreams with as much passion as we would like or we keep putting them off, it would not be
that we don't have the time or the money; it would be that on some
level we are afraid we might fail.

We have one-sided conversations with ourselves that go something like this:

"I really want to go after that dream of starting my own business. Sometimes I can hardly wait. Sometimes I feel confident and
sometimes I think I'm crazy. What will my family think if I try it
and it doesn't work out? What will we do if I lose the money we
keep trying to save to start the company?"

"I've been wanting to go to college for years. Everyone thinks
I'm too old, but I don't think my age should limit me. It's not that

I'm in my thirties [or forties or fifties or beyond] that bothers me. It's that I've been out of school so long I might not be able to keep up. I'm not sure I can do the work. And then people will say I just had a big head about going to college and I'm not as smart as I thought I was."

Both of these conversations, and lots of variations on them, are common. You could interchange any dreams and any excuses with the ones I've mentioned. People come up with all kinds of reasons to talk themselves out of pursuing their dreams, but at the end of the day these "reasons" are nothing more than fears—fear of failure, fear of inadequacy, fear of what other people will think about us, fear of lack, fear that the future will not be what we had hoped, or fear of countless other things. We want to be strong, both in the way we present ourselves to other people and the way we think about ourselves. And society tells us admitting our fears is not a strong thing to do. So we suppress them, talk around them, and put other labels on them.

We avoid at all costs saying, "I'm afraid. . . ." But the truth is, as difficult as it is to admit, the reason many of us live only *wishing* we could do certain things instead of *doing* them is that we lack courage. This is because we do not know what to do with the fears and doubts that arise when we think about pursuing the dreams and great things we want to do. The difference between people who only wish for greatness and those who go on to achieve and sustain it is that the people who reach it are able to manage well the internal issues they face along the way. These issues are often fear-based, so courage becomes a non-negotiable for anyone who wants to follow a dream or go after greatness.

Courage is an ancient word with roots going back to French and Latin words that mean "heart." A modern definition of the word is "mental or moral strength to venture, persevere, and withstand danger, fear or difficulty."[1] An older and fuller definition, from the

1913 edition of Webster's dictionary, is this: "that quality of mind which enables one to encounter dangers and difficulty with firmness, or without fear, or fainting of heart; valor, boldness, resolution."[2] We can see from these definitions that courage is an intensely personal quality. It's an I-factor issue—something that exists or doesn't exist within a person's heart, not in external things.

> The difference between people who only wish for greatness and those who go on to achieve and sustain it is that the people who reach it are able to manage well the internal issues they face along the way.

While people can certainly encourage us, they can't force us to be courageous. We have to do that for ourselves, and the sooner we do, the sooner we will find ourselves living the lives we once only imagined.

Steve Jobs said this about courage: "Your time is limited, so don't waste it living someone else's life. Don't be trapped by dogma—which is living with the results of other people's thinking. Don't let the noise of other's opinions drown out your own inner voice. And most important, have the courage to follow your heart and intuition."[3] That is my hope for you, and it comes from a strong I-factor.

The Connection Between Identity and Courage

Courage comes from within a person and it can't be faked. There are times in life when people say, "I have to put my game face on," meaning they want to appear focused, determined, and poised for victory in some situation. It may be a ball game or some other type of competition, but I also hear this term when people go into business meetings or other negotiations and they want to emerge feeling they have won something for themselves, their clients, or their companies. While a game face may fool or intimidate an opponent, it's only skin deep. People who have true courage that's rooted deep in who they are don't need a game face they can put on when the occasion calls for it. They live with confidence and boldness every day, in every situation because it's part of who they are, an integral aspect of their I-factors.

The only way to be truly courageous is to live your life based on your identity. Trying to drum up courage any other way simply will not work. I learned this lesson years ago when I realized many people around me were dealing with fear. Fear was keeping them from applying for better jobs than they had at the time, it was holding them back from relationships that probably would have been good for them, and it was keeping them from making decisions that could have improved their lives significantly. Worst of all, it was keeping them stagnant in life, stuck in the same old situations when they really wanted more; they just didn't have the courage to go after it. They were afraid. I knew courage was the opposite of fear and was what they really needed, but in order to help them find it, I first had to understand and help them deal with their fears. One of the most important results of this experience is it taught me that fear is the fruit of misplaced identity. When we become established in our identities, fear will flee and courage will come.

Only when we are firmly grounded in our knowledge of who we are can we take a strong stand for something or go after our destiny. Think about it. Let's say a young man dreams of becoming an attorney some day, but no one in his family has ever been to college. His siblings and cousins have little ambition and are content with part-time jobs, as long as those jobs allow them enough time to play video games. The young man's parents can see that he's different and they

> When we become established in our identities, fear will flee and courage will come.

know he's smart, but they tell him his dreams are foolish. They tell him that he needs to do something more like other people in the family do—maybe go to a vocational or technical school like his father did. His family and friends accuse him of being "uppity" and thinking he's better than the rest of them; they mock his desire to study and excel in school, and they call him names. But that's not the case at all. He simply has a different dream—and he hopes to someday earn enough money as a lawyer to make life a little easier for his mom and dad.

This young man needs courage to stand up to the people around him and go after his dreams despite their negative comments. If he is insecure in his identity, constantly telling himself, "These people have known me all my life. Maybe they're right," he will not have the strength to stand against them. If he is afraid of what they think of him, or if he fears they will abandon him because they do not understand his heart, that fear could become so big it leads him to live exactly as they do, never doing what he feels he was created for. But if embedded in his I-factor is the knowledge of who he is and the understanding that he has value and potential apart from the environment and the players of his past, he can move forward and reach his goals. The same is true for you.

Pursuing a Promise

In the Old Testament, God promised the Israelites a land of their own after they left Egypt, a good, rich land flowing with milk and honey. For many of these people, this promise was their dream. After years of backbreaking labor as slaves to the Egyptians, they looked forward to happier times.

When the nation's travels took them close to the promised land and they needed to know how to approach it, their leader, Moses, appointed twelve spies to go into the land, explore it, and find out about the people who lived there. "See what the land is like," he told them, "and whether the people who live there are strong or weak, few or many" (Num. 13:18). He also wanted to know whether the land was good or bad, whether the cities were walled or not, and whether the soil was fertile or poor (vv. 19–20). He expected the spies to come back with a comprehensive report on all these things and asked them to bring back some of the fruit from this country God had promised.

After a forty-day expedition, they reported:

> We went into the land to which you sent us, and it does flow with milk and honey! Here is its fruit. But the people who live there are powerful, and the cities are fortified and very large. We even saw descendents of Anak there. The Amalekites live in the Negev; the Hittites, Jebusites and Amorites live in the hill country; and the Canaanites live near the sea and along the Jordan. (Num. 13:27–29)

All in all, it was not a very good report. While the men acknowledged the milk and honey, they had more to say about the enemies who inhabited the land than about anything else.

Then one brave spy named Caleb spoke up and said, "We should go up and take possession of the land, for we can certainly do it" (v. 30).

The other spies were not convinced. In fact, they objected, saying, "We can't attack those people; they are stronger than we are" (v. 31). From that moment on, a bad report about the land began to circulate among all the people of Israel (v. 32).

Then, in what seems to be a bit of an exaggeration, the spies began to pile more negativity on top of what they had already said: "The land we explored devours those living in it. All the people we saw there are of great size. . . . We seemed like grasshoppers in our own eyes, and we looked the same to them" (vv. 32–33). As a result of this report, fear and drama spread like wildfire through the nation of Israel, and the people decided they did not want to pursue the land God had given them. They began to doubt His character, asking why He would bring them through the hardships they endured in Egypt only to let them be killed or defeated by the people currently living in the promised land (Num. 14:2–3).

It's important to understand that none of the perceived enemies in the promised land lifted a finger or uttered a threat against the Israelites. The ten spies were not afraid because of anything that happened to them, but because of what they saw. The mere appearance of difficulty caused fear to overwhelm these men, and once it took hold of them, it was contagious.

The bad reports from only ten men basically inspired fear in an entire nation and caused them to turn on their dream. The people gave it up quickly and completely, just because some nervous, pessimistic guys said they should not pursue it. They had not even seen the land for themselves; they simply took someone else's word for what it was like.

I can only imagine how exasperated Moses and his brother Aaron, who helped him lead the Israelites as high priest, must have been when this happened. Thankfully, Joshua spoke up at that point, and he and Caleb together said:

> The land we passed through and explored is exceedingly good. If the Lord is pleased with us, he will lead us into that land, a land flowing with milk and honey, and will give it to us. Only do not rebel against the Lord. And do not be afraid of the people of the land, because we will devour them. Their protection is gone, but the Lord is with us. Do not be afraid of them. (Num. 14:7–9)

In response, the people, still infected with negativity from what the ten spies had said earlier, decided to stone Joshua and Caleb (v. 10). God intervened and kept them from killing these two brave men, but the people did end up wandering around in the wilderness for forty years instead of going straight into the promised land in a matter of days. Ultimately, after Moses' death and the deaths of the adults who believed the ten spies, Joshua led the next generation of Israelites into the promised land. Even though they eventually got there, the process could have been quicker and easier, had the ten spies not given such a bad report and had the people not believed them and grown fearful as a result.

Joshua and Caleb were on the same exploratory venture the other ten spies were on. They all saw the very same things, but Joshua and Caleb interpreted those things differently and drew a vastly different conclusion than the other men. One of the biggest problems that separated the ten spies from Joshua and Caleb had to do with the spies' thinking. All twelve spies had heard the promised land was flowing with milk and honey, but ten of them did not stop to think about everything involved in milk and honey. They did not expect any difficulty during the pursuit of their dream. They thought because God promised them the land, getting into it would be easy. Joshua and Caleb clearly recognized the challenges, but they also had the courage to look beyond those obstacles.

The fact is, if people are going to get milk, they will have to get close to some cows, and that probably means stepping in some manure. If they're going to get honey, they will have to risk some bee stings. The different mind-set Joshua and Caleb had on the promised land is what gave them the courage to believe the Israelites could take it. They knew that with hard work and a willingness to overcome their enemies, the entire nation of Israel could enter into their dream of life in the promised land. In the end, that's exactly what happened.

You Can Live Your Dream Too

I trust you have a dream in your heart—something you want to experience or become. The very thought of this dream makes you feel awesome. You know it's huge and you know you'll have to work for it, but something deep within you keeps whispering, "You were made for this." You may view this dream as your destiny, your purpose for living, or as a promise from God. However you frame it, you know you must go for it.

American philosopher Henry David Thoreau offered some great advice: "Go confidently in the direction of your dreams. Live the life you've imagined." I wonder: What is the life that you've imagined for yourself? When you really think about what you want out of life, what do you see? Many people can answer these questions quickly and definitively. If you are not one of those people and you are not yet certain what your dream is, these questions are worth pondering. Give them some thought, and I'm pretty sure you will end up with a dream.

Once you have a dream in your heart, are you moving toward it with confidence, or have you let disappointments and delays cause you to believe it will never come true? Have you, like the Israelites, allowed negative people to try to talk you out of going after it? There's no shame or condemnation at all if this has happened to you. It happens to the best of dreamers. Everyone encounters naysayers and discouragers. Sometimes these people are the ones we would least expect, and that's painful. It takes courage to stand up to them.

Whether you are just now starting to think about your dream or whether you need to commit afresh to your pursuit of it, it's time to move toward it. Your promise or dream is worth pursuing. As Thoreau urged, "Go confidently" in its direction.

For years, I have studied and spoken to people about the process of pursuing their promises and dreams. I'd like to share some of the most helpful insights and pointers with you.

No Dream Is Too Big

I once read, "No dreamer is ever too small; no dream is ever too big" (anonymous). No matter who you are or what your circumstances are, you can be a dreamer. Your dream can never be too big, especially when it's a dream God has placed in your heart. Whatever your mind can envision, you can achieve. I want to challenge you to come up with the biggest dream you can think of, removing every limitation from your thinking as you explore possibilities.

Joshua and Caleb were able to adopt God's big dream for Israel as their own, and they understood something that's important for you to understand as you go after the big dream in your heart. It won't come easily. Challenges are to be expected. If you know that ahead of time, you can be prepared to deal with your challenges, and once you've overcome them, the fulfillment of your dream will be even sweeter. I hope you'll be willing to work at your dream, to be innovative as you pursue it, and to be patient as it comes to pass, but dream as big as you can dream. Difficulties don't invalidate your dream.

You'll Become What You Dream

I like to say, "Whatever you move toward, moves toward you." With that comment in mind, let me ask: What do you want to become? This time next year, or this time ten years from now, who do you want to be and what do you want to be doing with your life? As you consider these questions in the context of your life, I would encourage you not to think about the reasons your dream can't happen or the obstacles that stand in your way. Think about ways you can make your dream happen and about all the potential that dwells within you. You won't ever become your job or your house or your car; *you will become your dreams.*

Your Dream Is Worth Protecting

In the movie *The Pursuit of Happyness,* Will Smith plays a character named Chris Gardner, who says, "You got a dream? You gotta protect it. You want something? You go get it. Period."[4] Gardner is absolutely right. What are you protecting it from? From dying. From being forgotten and never coming true.

A dream can be fragile, and one way to protect it is to keep it in the forefront of your mind every day. Whether that means putting a photo that represents the dream on your screensaver or a note about it on your mirror, make sure you stay mentally aware of it and take steps toward it on a regular basis. The steps don't have to be big or dramatic; they just need to be intentional. For example, you may decide to skip your daily latte one day and put the money aside to help finance your dream. That won't fund the whole thing, but it'll be one small, deliberate step that will remind you of what your dream is and will move you in the right direction.

The best way to protect your dream is to share it wisely. When you have a dream, no matter what it is, the temptation is to tell everyone about it. You're excited, so you naturally expect the people around you to be excited too. But some people simply are not mature enough to support other people's dreams and aspirations. Because of their own insecurities, they become jealous or critical. When you have a dream, share it only with people who have proven themselves to be on your side, people who will encourage you, affirm you, and help your dream come true.

Dreams Require Discipline

As you can see from Joshua and Caleb's story, dreams don't come true overnight. Because dreams rarely come true easily, a person must have the discipline to fight for them. On the way to becoming realities, most dreams get tested. As you go after the dream in your heart, you will face obstacles and times of confusion and frustration. The important thing is not to be like the ten spies and let those things discourage you or make you want to give up. Instead, be like Joshua and Caleb and allow those challenges to inspire you to pursue your dream even more intensely.

Be disciplined with your time, your energy, and your finances, and realize that prioritizing your dream may require sacrifice. For example, you only have a limited amount of time away from work and a finite amount of energy. Will you use your free time and extra energy sitting on the couch watching movies, or will you take concrete steps that will get you to your dreams? Along the same lines, you also have only a certain amount of money each month. Will you spend it on designer clothes or the latest electronics, or will you save it until you have enough to invest in your dream?

I hope these insights and inspirations on dreams are helpful to you. The better you understand your dreams and the process required to make them come true, the better you can engage in pursuing them.

Overcoming Hindrances to Your Dreams

Just as Joshua and Caleb understood they would have to endure manure and bee stings as they worked toward their dream of the promised land, you will have to overcome some obstacles and enemies on the way to your dream. If you are going after a great and worthy dream, I can almost guarantee that you will face challenges—maybe big ones—and opposition. That's the way dreams work. I'd like to mention a few of those challenges and offer some advice on how to break through them so you can keep moving in the right direction.

Ignore the Naysayers

One main reason people abandon their dreams is that others mock or discourage them. Maybe you shared your dream with people and they ridiculed your idea or told you that you could never do such a thing. This kind of situation is extremely discouraging; it can cause you to doubt yourself and wonder about your dream. Here's what you do: Ignore every negative, discouraging word. If you have thoroughly thought through your dream and been willing to accept wise counsel when offered, then there is no need to be open to unwise input. Don't give those comments any space in your brain. Forget them. And start dreaming again.

Break Through Past Disappointments

Disappointments can be extremely painful and cause us to stop moving toward our dreams because we don't want to be disappointed again. Let me try to take hurt and disappointment out of the perspective of pain and put them in a different light: Hurts and disappointments are the bridges that will take you from vision to reality, from the dream you hold in your heart to its fulfillment. Many times, disappointment is the risk you take for being courageous enough to go after a dream. It can be the fare you pay to move from expectation to manifestation.

When you get hurt or face disappointment, learn the lessons those situations can teach you. Look at them, analyze them, and milk them for all they're worth. The way to maximize a disappointment is to use it for your good by allowing it to make you stronger and smarter as you try again to fulfill your dream.

Resist the Temptation to Settle for Mediocrity

One reason some people fail to follow their dreams is they become willing to settle for mediocrity. Once they realize how many hindrances can stand in the way of their dreams and see how hard they may have to work to break through them, they become willing to accept average. When average becomes acceptable, people tend to stop pursuing the greater dreams in their hearts. Some people settle for mediocrity because it's comfortable or familiar. Others settle simply because they don't want to do the work necessary to change their circumstances. Here's the truth: The minute you settle for less than you deserve, you get even less than you settle for. You cannot dream big dreams and remain safely mediocre at the same time. People with a strong I-factor are better than average.

Get Creative About Resources

Have you ever had a dream in your heart, something you *really* wanted to do, but you gave up on it because you didn't have the resources for it? Maybe you didn't have the money to pay for it or couldn't take enough time off work to make any progress toward it. Maybe you lacked the resource of the support you needed from family and friends.

I am always sad when I meet people with great dreams who are not willing to start pursuing them because they know they do not have what they need to make the dreams come true. I'm reminded of the old adage, "You never know until you try." Today, sources for funding abound more than in any other time in history. People can even get total strangers to help pay for their dreams via the Internet!

Whatever your shortage is, you can change it. You may need to rearrange your schedule to create time to work toward your dream, find another source of income, or get a few new friends who will encourage you instead of discourage you, but it will be worth it to pursue that dream.

Breaking Free from Fear

Perhaps the number one reason people do not go after their dreams is that they are afraid. That's certainly the biggest hindrance I know. Some people fear they will make mistakes or look silly or stupid, some are afraid of what other people will think of them if their dreams are particularly big or considered unusual in some way, and many are afraid of failure. Because fear is such a deterrent to doing something to make progress toward our dreams, we must overcome it. That's where courage comes in. As I mentioned earlier, the major difference between people who see their dreams become realities and those who don't is the ones who succeed handle the fears and doubts that stand in their way.

Let me share with you a few facts about fear because I believe that understanding these truths will help you realize how much damage fear can do to your dreams and help you recognize when fear is holding you back. Once you recognize fear, you can do something about it.

Fear Skews Your Perspective

Fear never represents any circumstance as it truly is. It blows things out of proportion as nothing else can. It has an unfailing tendency to make bad situations seem worse than they may really be. For example, the fear of failing as you go after a dream may cause you to think the consequences of failing are more severe than they actually would be. Let's say your dream requires a financial risk. You may feel afraid you will lose everything, monetarily speaking, if you fail. That's not necessarily true. If you plan well and keep certain assets protected, you can effectively limit what you will lose if things don't work out.

Next time you find yourself feeling fearful when you think about going after your dream, step back from the situation and put it in its proper perspective. When you see it for what it really is, you'll be better able to calm down, deal with it effectively, and keep moving toward what your heart longs for.

Fear Steals the Present and Sabotages the Future

When we think about the fear that keeps us from going after our dreams, we are rarely talking about current fears. We are usually talking about some type of fear of the future—fear that if or when we step out in the direction of our dreams, such-and-such *will* happen. (Notice that *will* is a future word.) These fears steal the joy and power of present moments from us and jeopardize the future. We can't focus on the present and enjoy it if we are trapped in the fear of what might happen tomorrow or next week.

Any time you feel afraid to do something to move toward your dream, fight that fear by focusing on what is good, secure, and pleasant about your life in the present moment; choose to believe that the future will be good too. This kind of positive attitude will give you the courage to go after what you really want to pursue.

Fear Wants to Paralyze You

It's important to understand something about fear: It paralyzes us. It gets us stuck in a rut, unable to move ahead in life and certainly unable to work toward our dreams. It can keep us from doing the very things we need to do in order to become all we are created to be or experience what we dream of doing.

When you're afraid to take the next step toward your destiny, it's important to ask yourself if the best response is to plow through the fear and keep moving forward in spite of it—because often, it is.

If Fear Can't Paralyze You, It Will
Keep You Running in Circles

Because the Israelites allowed the ten spies to evoke fear in their hearts, they wandered around in the wilderness for forty years, trying to make an eleven-day journey. Most of them died before they ever got to the edge of the promised land. I think about what these people missed because they never got to enter into God's dream for their lives. And I pray that you will not allow fear to hold you back from anything He has for you.

Embracing the Courage to Help
Your Dreams Come True

I trust this chapter has inspired and equipped you to go after your dreams with fresh passion and courage. I encourage you to remember the lesson of the Israelites, which is not to allow anyone to discourage you from your dream or convince you not to pursue it. I also hope you'll remember the lesson of the ten spies; no matter how good a dream sounds, even if it's flowing with milk and honey, seeing it come to pass will involve hard work, determination, and at times, getting dirty or getting hurt. Finally, I want you to carry the lesson of Joshua and Caleb with you through the rest of your life. This lesson says that when it comes to going after a dream or a promise from God, you can be right even when everyone else is wrong.

If you have the courage to pursue your dream, regardless of the obstacles or messes you may go through, you will end up in a rich place. Wise King Solomon said, "A dream comes with much business and painful effort" (Eccl. 5:3 AMP). That business (which is also translated "activity" [NLT, NKJV]) and effort require courage. I believe you have the courage you need in order to do everything necessary to live the life you've always dreamed of.

Internal Building Blocks

- Most people have dreams they would love to pursue. Fear is the primary reason they don't. One of the keys to going after your dreams is learning to manage the internal issues that would hinder you, especially fear.
- Never assume that difficulties or hindrances mean you should not continue to pursue your dream. They do not; they simply mean you'll have to work a little harder for it.
- Four key points about your dreams are: no dream is too big, you'll become what you dream, your dream is worth protecting, and dreams require discipline.
- People with healthy I-factors are able to break free from fear. To do that, ignore the negative comments people make about you and your dreams, break through past disappointments, refuse to settle for mediocrity, and find creative resources to help you achieve your dreams.
- To break free from fear, it's important to understand that fear skews your perspective, steals your present, and sabotages your future, and either paralyzes you or keeps you running in circles.

Strengthening Your I-Factor

1. What is your dream and how has fear hindered your pursuit of it?
2. How can difficulties and challenges make the ultimate realization of your dream even sweeter?
3. What are some specific ways you can protect your dream and keep it safe as you go after it?
4. How can you get creative about finding resources to help you achieve your dream?

5. In the section "Breaking Free from Fear" I mentioned several ways fear could impact a person. How has fear impacted you, and how can you keep that from happening in the future?

Don't Stop Now

It does not matter how slowly you
go as long as you do not stop.
—Confucius

HAVE YOU EVER HAD TO WAIT FOR SOMETHING? I'M NOT talking about waiting in a long line for a hamburger at a drive-through. I'm talking about a serious wait for something that is important, a deep desire, a passionate pursuit, or a goal you're convinced you are destined to reach. It is the kind of thing that keeps you up at night and occupies your thoughts throughout the day. And I'm talking about waiting months, years, or even decades.

Perhaps you know people who have struggled financially for *so long,* or men and women who have been single while longing for a spouse for *so long,* or individuals who have wrestled with health problems for *so long,* or families that have dealt with the same arguments and disappointments for *so long.* These longtime difficulties can wear on a person. Maybe one of these situations, or something similar, is wearing on you.

Unlike postage stamps, fine wine, or antique furniture, waiting does not seem to get better with time; it gets worse. Waiting does teach us certain lessons and strengthen us in specific ways, and we know that. We've been told time and time again to embrace the process and find the good things in it. While most of us understand the importance of valuing the process of going after a goal or working toward a dream, we want the process to ultimately produce something.

We don't work toward the opportunities we want in life for the sake of working; we work for the sake of finally experiencing the fruit of our efforts. When we invest our time, energy, and hearts in pursuing something important to us and always seem to come up short, we start to wonder if we will ever achieve it. After months or years, when we do not see the change we hope for or experience the breakthrough we feel we need, we can easily begin to think, *This will never happen.*

Many times, there is a pattern to reaching a goal or fulfilling a dream. First, you have a dream or a goal and you can hardly contain your excitement. You feel you have finally found the one objective that will make your life wonderful if you can reach it. Second, the dream does not come true overnight. In fact, it doesn't come true over weeks and months. Sometimes, you feel your life is moving farther from it instead of closer to it as you face various challenges. Then, you decide to take the pursuit of your goal more seriously and you put an unprecedented amount of effort into it. After you've waited and waited and tried and tried, you begin to wonder if it's ever going to happen. Once that question surfaces, a train of thought begins to chug in your mind: *If I can't see results, why would I even hold on to this desire? Wanting and working for something isn't any fun if I'm constantly chasing a moving target. The obstacles no longer feel like beatable challenges designed to strengthen me. It looks like there will be no reward at the end of them.*

The most dangerous aspect of a dream that seems denied or destiny that feels delayed is after we have done all we can do to bring it to pass, we can be tempted to give up on it altogether.

Once the idea of quitting gets a grasp on us, apathy begins to creep into our attitudes. We begin to disconnect from our dreams emotionally. We simply don't care anymore because caring is painful and frustrating if it will not ultimately take us where we want to go.

Apathy can overwhelm the best-intentioned person, and I understand why it happens. But I also believe apathy left to run its course in our lives leaves behind nothing but disappointment and failure. It cuts us off from our destinies. That does not have to happen. When we first begin to hear in our minds the words, *I'm so tired of waiting that I just don't care anymore*, we do not have to allow them to make us negative and jaded. They do not have to lead us to give up. As we grow in our I-factors, we learn to deal with our negative thoughts and neutralize their threats to our future success.

> The most dangerous aspect of a dream that seems denied or destiny that feels delayed is after we have done all we can do to bring it to pass, we can be tempted to give up on it altogether.

Do You Want Things to Change?

Some people have been stressed, disappointed, hurt, or frustrated for so long that they have stopped believing in the breakthroughs they need. One of the most inspiring stories I know for those people took place centuries ago. There was a man in Jerusalem who had been unable to walk for thirty-eight years (John 5:5). Now *that's* a long time.

In Jerusalem was a pool called the pool of Bethesda. From time to time, the waters in the pool began to stir mysteriously and whoever entered the pool first after the waters moved received healing. For this reason, lots of sick and disabled people visited the pool each day, hoping that day would be their day for a miracle.

One day, Jesus went to the pool and noticed the lame man. The Scripture says, "When Jesus saw him lying there *and learned that he had been in this condition for a long time*, he asked him, 'Do you want to get well?'" (John 5:6, emphasis added).

When Christ asked this question, the man did not even answer it. He simply offered an excuse, "I have no one to help me into the pool when the water is stirred. While I am trying to get in, someone else goes down ahead of me" (v. 7).

This man totally missed the power of the moment, when Jesus the Miracle Worker singled him out and said, "Do you want to get well?" He missed it because he was so stuck in his past that he could not see how vastly different this present moment was from every other moment he had ever known. Things had stayed the same for him for so long that he did not even recognize his breakthrough when it showed up right in front of him. This miracle is unlike any other in the Bible because this man had the same problem for so long that he did not even get excited when Jesus the Healer arrived. Apathy had so overtaken him that he did not ask Jesus for help; Jesus had to ask him if he wanted to be healed.

As sad as this situation was, it teaches a valuable lesson: No matter what you have been through, how long you have suffered, or how many times you have been desperate for things to change and they didn't, every day is new. Every day is the day your situation could change. Every time you get up in the morning is a day you just might see your breakthrough before you go to bed that night. When you have a strong I-factor, you never give up. You never stop hoping, never stop dreaming, never stop trying, and never stop believing that life's very best can be yours.

This is why allowing your heart to heal from the pain and disappointment of the past is so vital. You will never be able to see yourself for who you really are if you look at your present through the lens of your past. Unless you process well the pain you have suffered, you will squander every present moment of opportunity for change because you will be stuck in days, weeks, or years that are long gone. A healed heart can remember the past without reliving the pain.

The man at the pool of Bethesda was stuck in his pain and his past, and he almost missed his miracle because of it. Jesus never asked him why he was still lame after thirty-eight years; He was not interested in excuses. He asked the man, "Do you want to get well?"

You may wonder why God would allow this man to be in a situation in which his breakthrough depended on something he did not have the ability to do. Physically, he could not move himself to the pool. Some people read his story and think the whole scenario was unfair to him. It wasn't unfair. God knew the day would come when the man would experience something far better than getting into the water. He knew the man would have a healing encounter with Jesus Christ.

Do you have an area of your life that feels weak or hopeless, especially something that has caused you heartache and struggle for a long time? In that struggle, do you feel you are powerless to help yourself? If this is you, let me share three lessons from the story of the man at the pool that will help you on your healing journey.

1. Life Is Probably Better Than You Think

The man at the pool of Bethesda was surrounded by goodness; he just didn't realize it. The word *Bethesda* means "mercy"[1] and the five porches around the pool represent grace.[2] Once Jesus showed up, the man had immediate access to everything he needed, but he didn't see it. Yes, the man was infirm; he definitely had physical limitations and had struggled with them for a long time, but he was in a good place. Although his focus was on what he did not have, the truth is that everything around him was mercy and grace. When Jesus, the incarnation of mercy and grace, walked into this man's life, his longtime focus on his infirmity prevented him from seeing his best-ever opportunity for healing and restoration.

Likewise, when we wait so long for something or suffer so much in a situation that never changes, we can also develop tunnel vision. We focus so excessively on what is wrong in our lives that we fail to recognize and value what is good and right. Difficulties have a way of taking over our fields of vision and causing us to believe every aspect of our lives is negative and hopeless, when that is not true. Learning to value where we are in life and what we do have is vital to our success and well-being. Most of the time, we may struggle with one or two hard situations, but other circumstances are positive.

Think of a person who has a broken leg. She may be unhappy that she can no longer engage in certain activities and sad about being sedentary for a period of time. She may complain about the pain and discomfort of a cast and crutches, and she may not want the scar that resulted from the surgery necessary to heal her leg. All this is unfortunate because she has much to be thankful for. The surgery, cast, and crutches will help her leg heal properly. She has people to help take care of her, even though temporarily she cannot get around well. If she will focus on the positives of her situation instead of the negatives, she will be much happier and be better able to recognize the good things that come her way. If she does not focus on the good things, she will likely stay stuck in what she does not like about her circumstances.

You may be in a situation you find painful or difficult. Regardless of how negative it is, I hope you will begin to look for the good in it, because that's what people with a healthy I-factor do. For example, be thankful for friends and family who care about you, be glad you have access to medical care, or appreciate that you are able to work. Chances are, your circumstances could be much worse than they are. Finding the positive aspects of them and appreciating them will help you get through this season in your life.

2. The People Around You Affect the Way You See Yourself and Influence Your Perspective on Your Life

The man at the pool not only struggled because he thought too much about what was wrong with him and not enough about what was right, he also suffered because he was surrounded by people who kept him discouraged, not encouraged.

John 5:3 tells us that "a great number of disabled people" who were blind, lame, and paralyzed came to the pool of Bethesda. As I see it, these descriptions metaphorically represent blind people, those who have no vision; lame people, those who have no strength; and paralyzed people, those who are unable to work. Every day at the pool, the man encountered people with problems when what he really needed was to encounter people with solutions. He was surrounded by the same types of weakness he struggled with, when he needed to be encircled with strength. Too many people around him were living in conditions similar to his, when he needed some role models who could inspire him to want to live differently.

I sometimes wonder about the conversations that took place around the pool. I'd like to know if the people sat around talking about their troubles instead of sharing words of hope. If they were anything like some people in our modern society, they did. Today, you can walk into many restaurants, coffee shops, workout facilities, break rooms, and social events and notice that people with similar struggles seem drawn to one another. I have seen this happen repeatedly among people who have been through disappointing romantic relationships or suffered broken marriages. They get together and talk about the therapists they have seen; they talk about how difficult their lives are now that they are alone; they bash members of the opposite sex; and they tell each other they are so glad to find someone who understands, because hardly anyone ever does. Rarely do these people offer each other hope. More often, they feed on one another's negativity and bitterness.

I understand that some people suffer real tragedies and heartbreaks in life. That's not what I'm talking about here. I'm talking about people who have some fairly common hard knocks in life and refuse to let themselves heal. They often surround themselves with people who feed their negativity instead of people who will draw them out of it.

I believe the man at the pool of Bethesda had negative influences everywhere he looked. Most of the people around him supported, instead of challenged, the way he saw himself—as an invalid who had been at the pool for thirty-eight years while nothing ever changed.

An important question to ask yourself when you go through hard times is, "Who do I have around me?" Think about what kinds of influences your friends, family members, and colleagues are exerting on you. If you are in a situation that tempts you to hopelessness, don't put yourself around people who will reinforce that. Find some friends who will speak words of hope and help you see the good in your life instead of the bad, some people who have strong I-factors that will rub off on you. You will become like the people you spend your time with (Prov. 13:20), so make sure those people are taking you in a positive direction.

3. Chances Are, Life Would Be Much More Enjoyable If You Could Change Your Point of View

During one of my trips to Durban, South Africa, I noticed a curious phenomenon. I saw a number of supercars and other obvious displays of wealth. I also noticed that based on what I could see, the wealthiest people were not Africans, but people of Indian descent. This was interesting because I was familiar with the history of people from India who came to South Africa during the late 1800s. They started out as farm workers, but their humble beginnings are not evident today in the current population of

Durban. When I asked myself how people who had roots as laborers could appear to be the wealthiest and most privileged, the answer that came to my mind was, "No one ever told them they couldn't succeed."

As I became acquainted with some of these people, I realized they have great faith. They believe that with God, all things are possible (Matt. 19:26). They do not view themselves through the lens of their pasts or who their forebears were, but through the lens of the present and who they are. They see themselves full of promise and potential, and they are fulfilling their potential every day.

I wonder, what is it that needs a new perspective in your life? How could you change your life by simply adjusting your point of view? Had the man at the pool seen himself as a miracle in the making, he would have been ready when Jesus asked, "Do you want to get well?" Instead of making excuses, he would have shouted, "Yes, I do!" If you need a change in your life, let me encourage you to begin to believe it is on its way. Then, when you find yourself in the moment you realize life is asking you, "Do you want things to be better?" you can say yes, be strengthened and healed, and start your journey toward the best life you have ever known.

He Never Gave Up

A man who had to have been tempted to give up on his dream, but never did, was Abraham Lincoln, who became the sixteenth president of the United States in 1861. Born in Kentucky in 1809, Lincoln spent many of his formative years in Indiana, having moved there with his family in 1816 or 1817. Though his family had a tiny log cabin in Kentucky, when they moved to Indiana, they became squatters on public property and struggled to make ends meet.[3] For many years, life remained difficult for Lincoln. He suffered many painful losses, both personal and professional. While he is known for being depressed at times, he never allowed his despair to get the best of him. As a young adult, he became aware of the negative impact of slavery on the United States, an awareness that ultimately led to the White House and empowered Lincoln to bring an end to the practice of slavery in America.

> What is it that needs a new perspective in your life? How could you change your life by simply adjusting your point of view?

Lincoln's journey to the presidency was not easy. He did not have the pedigree of a Roosevelt, the wealth of George Washington, or the military accomplishments of Eisenhower. Known as a hard worker and a self-made man, Lincoln worked his way from humble beginnings to the pinnacle of greatness. He had many opportunities to give up on his political ambitions, due to the hardships he endured, but he never did. Take a look at some of the things he suffered.

- In 1818, his mother died of a disease called milk sickness, which comes from drinking milk from cows that ingested the poisonous snakeroot plant.
- His family could not afford to send him to school. His formal education is estimated to have lasted only eighteen months. Other than that brief period of schooling, he was self-taught, often walking miles to borrow books to read.[4]
- His only living sibling, a beloved older sister named Sarah, died in childbirth in 1828.
- Lincoln lost his first election for the Illinois General Assembly in 1832, finishing eighth of thirteen candidates.
- His first girlfriend died in 1835 before he was able to ask her to marry him.

- Lincoln's first business, a general store with a partner in New Salem, Illinois, struggled so much that he sold his share.
- In 1849, after serving in the Illinois state legislature, Lincoln lost his bid for United States senator.[5]
- Lincoln's second son, Edward, died at the age of four in 1850.
- In 1853, Lincoln's fourth son, Tad, was born. He suffered with a speech impediment, perhaps due to a cleft palate, and was a high-spirited, often difficult child with little interest in education and little respect for discipline.[6]
- In 1858, Lincoln participated in the most famous debate series in American history, his debates with Stephen Douglas. The winner would be elected as US senator from Illinois. Lincoln lost, but this bitter defeat gave him the national exposure and acclaim he would later need when running for president.
- Lincoln's third son, Willie, died in 1862, at the age of eleven.
- After being reelected as president of the United States in November 1864, Lincoln was assassinated April 14, 1865.

On April 12, 1861, just weeks after Lincoln's first inauguration, the Civil War broke out, making Lincoln the leader of a deeply divided, angry nation. On January 1, 1863, Lincoln announced the Emancipation Proclamation, which declared that "all persons held as slaves within any State or designated part of a State, . . . shall be then, thenceforward, and forever free."[7] On November 19 of that same year, Lincoln gave one of the most stirring and memorable speeches in American history, the Gettysburg

Address. Before his untimely death at the hands of an assassin, Lincoln had transformed the United States of America and set the nation on a course toward peace and unity. His accomplishments cannot be underestimated, and none of them would have happened had he chosen to give up when he had opportunities to do so.

If At First You Don't Succeed . . .

You may remember the old proverb traced back to American educator Thomas Palmer, "If at first you don't succeed, try, try again." But are you familiar with the second part of it? It goes like this: "Don't give up too easily, persistence pays off in the end."[8] Most people understand, theoretically, the importance of not giving up. But in the midst of repeated failure or continuous opposition to a dream or a goal, knowing exactly *how* to keep going can be a challenge. I'd like to offer some suggestions.

Reaffirm Your Commitment

Commitment is more than simply telling yourself you will do something; it's promising yourself you will do it *no matter what*. When you have tried and tried to accomplish something and it has not worked, it's easy to get discouraged and be tempted to give up. That's when it's important to reaffirm your commitment to your goal or your destiny. If you truly believe your dream is meant to happen, there is no substitute for committing to it in a fresh way and renewing your determination not to be denied. When you are committed, you keep going regardless of the obstacles you face or the naysayers who may try to talk you out of pursuing your goal. Reaffirming your commitment will give you the mind-set and mental energy you need to persevere until you get where you ultimately want to be.

Reevaluate Your Strategy

Often, when people set out to accomplish a goal or realize a dream, they think they know exactly how to go about it. Sometimes, the path seems so obvious that they head down it without considering other ways to reach their destinations. When their efforts are not productive, they feel they have failed and they may want to quit. But quitting will never get them where they want to go.

If you have ever been frustrated in trying to reach a goal, I would encourage you not to give up, but to reevaluate your strategy. As a simple example of this, let's think about a married couple who are in debt and want to be financially free. It may seem obvious to both of them that they need to spend less money each month in order to start paying off their bills. But with rising costs on so many consumer necessities, they may find themselves struggling and frustrated as they try to find extra money for bills by reducing expenses. If they were to reevaluate their strategy, they would realize they could get extra money through other means. They could have a garage sale to sell items they no longer want or need, renegotiate interest rates, take advantage of coupons and sales, or take part-time jobs until they eliminate their debt.

Whatever your objective is, if you find yourself frustrated as you pursue it, I would encourage you to consider rethinking your approach to it. Experiment with some new and different ways to reach your goal, and you'll probably land on just the right one.

Focus on Your Strengths

When you have encountered so many obstacles and so much opposition that you want to give up, you have two choices: give in to discouragement or fight it. One of the best ways to fight it is to focus on your strengths. Look at what you do well instead of worrying about what you may not be good at. Think about what has helped you succeed in the past, and find ways to apply those abilities and character traits to your current situation. When you focus on your strengths, you feel strong and capable instead of weak and insecure. When you feel strong, you begin to believe you can overcome any obstacle that stands in your way. That feeling of strength gives you the mental, physical, and emotional energy to keep moving forward, even in the face of resistance. That will eventually lead to the breakthrough you need.

Shore Up Your Weaknesses

Everyone has both strengths and weaknesses. Weaknesses can be liabilities, so finding ways to deal with them well will help you move toward your goals more easily. There are at least two key ways to shore up your weaknesses. The first is to recognize and acknowledge them. The second is to find appropriate help. For example, let's say you want to start a business, but you have never been good with numbers. Many talented, creative people have failed in business because they did not realize the importance of good bookkeeping. If you know you have a weakness in this area, then finding a good bookkeeper is vital to your success. Sure, this professional service will cost you money in the short term, but in the end, it could save your business. Whatever your specific weaknesses are, know them, don't be afraid or ashamed to admit them, and find qualified people who can keep those weaknesses from slowing you down or even stopping you altogether on your journey to success.

Stay Positive

Certain circumstances do make you want to give up in your pursuit of your goals and dreams. Those are times to dig in and keep going forward, not to back off or consider abandoning your cause. Often, if you'll persevere a little more, you will find your breakthrough is closer than you thought. One of the best ways to do this is to remain positive. Staying positive motivates you to move forward because you believe something better is ahead.

One attitude that keeps people positive is the simple practice of gratitude. It's a powerful force that will train your mind to focus on and appreciate the things that are good in your life. The more you acknowledge your blessings and benefits, the less you'll think about your struggles. The more you think about the positive experiences you've already had, the easier it is to believe more good things lie ahead. When you can look forward with anticipation and excitement, you can easily break free from the desire to quit and move ahead with confidence.

Acknowledge and Celebrate Every Milestone

I have never heard of anyone who reached a major goal all at once. Most significant objectives must be accomplished one step at a time. One of the best ways I know to keep yourself motivated and not to give up is to recognize and celebrate every completed step on the way to where you want to go in life. For some people, a celebration means dinner at a nice restaurant, while for others it means pizza and a movie at home or a picnic in the park. For still others it means taking a day off to do something enjoyable or to go to the spa. Whatever a celebration means to you, plan to do something to acknowledge each successful step on the path to your dreams.

Don't Mistake Delay for Denial

I'm sure you have realized at this point in your life that sometimes the best things in life take a while. They don't happen overnight; and yet, if you're like most people, you don't like to wait. If you think you have to wait too long in certain situations, you may be tempted to give up on them altogether.

If you give up, you could miss something tremendous. Just because things take a while does not mean they will never happen.

Delay does not always equal denial. I hope you will not give up on a person, an opportunity, or a situation just because it isn't happening as fast as you'd like. Learn to practice patience and remember the time-tested saying, "Good things come to those who wait."

Never Give Up

I trust this chapter has encouraged you to stay the course as you pursue your dreams and your destiny, regardless of the obstacles you may face. The story of the man at the pool of Bethesda could be your story. Perhaps you, too, have wanted something for so long and found many reasons you could never get it. As you think about that man and the outcome of his situation, let me remind you that when Jesus asked the man if he wanted to get well, the man said he had no one to put him in the pool. But let me also share with you what Jesus said to him in reply to that excuse: "Get up! Pick up your mat and walk" (John 5:8). The story goes on to say, "At once the man was cured; he picked up his mat and walked" (v. 9).

For the man at the pool, his mat was his place of ease, but it was also his place of infirmity. He was comfortable with it, but it held him back from better things and kept him stuck in his disease. Jesus had little patience with that. He told the man to get up and get moving. That's what I want to encourage you to do as we close this chapter. Whatever is holding you back, even if it's comfortable, have the courage to pick it up and move forward. Any journey to greatness includes challenges and disappointments, but I hope you will view them as stepping-stones, not stumbling blocks. I believe the best days of your life are ahead of you, as long as you never give up.

———————— Internal Building Blocks ————————

- Often, the pursuit of a dream, a passion, or a goal follows a pattern: you identify a dream; you pursue it, but it doesn't come true, even after months or years; you put unprecedented effort into the dream, but it still doesn't come to pass; you wonder whether you should completely give up on the dream.
- Look on the bright side. Chances are, you are surrounded by goodness and life is probably better than you think.
- The people around you have a powerful influence on the way you see yourself and on your life perspective. That's why it's so important to surround yourself with the right people.
- Many times, if you can simply change your point of view on a situation, life becomes much more enjoyable. People with strong I-factors are people with positive attitudes.
- If at first you don't succeed: reaffirm your commitment, reevaluate your strategy, focus on your strengths, shore up your weaknesses, stay positive, acknowledge and celebrate every milestone, and don't mistake delay for denial.

———————— Strengthening Your I-Factor ————————

1. What are you waiting for right now? If you have ever been tempted to give up on the possibility that it could become a reality, how can you reverse that thinking?
2. As you pursue your dream, take time to reaffirm your commitment and reevaluate your strategy. What specific strategy could you try to change?
3. As you go after the dream in your heart, what strengths can you focus on? What weaknesses do you need to shore up? Develop a plan for doing that.

4. If the pursuit of your dream is taking longer than you would like, what steps can you take to stay positive and celebrate your milestones as you wait?

5. Have you ever mistaken delay for denial? If you are in the midst of a delay right now, how can you make the most of it, believing that your dream will come true when the timing is right?

Head First

We can't solve problems by using the same kind
of thinking we used when we created them.

—ALBERT EINSTEIN

IF YOU'VE EVER BEEN SHOPPING AT MACY'S DEPARTMENT
store, you may appreciate the selection it offers, the quality of its
goods, or that it sometimes has great sales. But do you know anything about the history of this nationwide retail giant? I think you'll
find it interesting and learn some important lessons from it.

Rowland Hussey Macy, known to his friends as R. H., was born
August 30, 1822, in Nantucket, Massachusetts. As a young man,
Macy put in long, hard hours working on a whaling ship. During
that time, he had a red star tattooed on his hand, a symbol that still
is an element of the Macy's logo.[1]

Disappointed in his meager wages for such difficult work on
the whaling ship, Macy came ashore at the age of nineteen and in
an effort to follow in the successful footsteps of Benjamin Franklin,
took a job in Boston as an apprentice to a printer. The printing
business did not work out for Macy, so in 1843, he opened his first
retail store, with his brother as his partner.[2]

Between 1843 and 1855, Macy opened four dry goods stores. Not
a single one, including the original Macy's that opened in Haverhill,

Massachusetts, in 1851, was successful. I can only imagine how discouraging this was, but Macy would not be deterred by his repeated business failures. No doubt having thought about how to do things differently next time, Macy moved to New York City and opened a store in Manhattan in 1858.

By that time, he had learned a lot. Each of his failed business ventures had taught him lessons, perhaps more lessons about what not to do instead of what to do in order to succeed. He also had his printing background, which would serve him well when he needed to advertise. In addition, he benefited from the experience he gained working in real estate speculation in California during the Gold Rush.

In his new Manhattan location, Macy refused to accept credit, insisting that all sales be completed on a cash basis.[3] Over the years, Macy's became perhaps America's best-known department store and R. H. Macy is a true American success story. According to MacysInc.com, the store has long been known for its creativity and willingness to break new ground:

> Always the innovator, Macy's is known for several firsts that changed the retail industry. Macy's was the first retailer to promote a woman, Margaret Getchell, to an executive position, making business history. Macy's pioneered such revolutionary business practices as the one-price system, in which the same item was sold to every customer at one price, and quoting specific prices for goods in newspaper advertising. Known for its creative merchandising, Macy's was the first to introduce such products as the tea bag, the Idaho baked potato and colored bath towels.[4]

All the firsts mentioned on Macy's website affirm the spirit of innovation in R. H. Macy. Some people succeed by the sheer power of determination, while others succeed because of innovation. To be innovative is to use one's mind to formulate a fresh approach to an old problem. In Macy's case, the old problem was his struggle to build a thriving retail business. Because he was open-minded and eager to learn skills that ultimately lead to success, Macy revised his business approach over the years. When the New York store rose to prominence, he never rested on his accomplishments and profits, but remained an innovative thinker for the rest of his life.

The key lesson from Macy's story is this: when we change our thinking, we can change our lives. Do you need a change in your life? It begins in your mind. People who have healthy, growing I-factors are always willing to entertain new ideas, look at problems from different angles, and approach life from fresh perspectives.

I believe the reason R. H. Macy finally succeeded—and succeeded in such a big way after failing four times—is he learned to think differently about his retail endeavors every time he opened a store. I am sure Macy's secret to success was not in working harder but in working smarter. Many people would give up after failing once, or certainly after failing twice. But not Macy; he kept fine-tuning his mental approach to business until it worked like no one else's business had worked before. When he opened his store in New York, had he done so with the same mind-sets he had used previously, the store would likely have failed as the four before it did. Because he thought differently about that store, it thrived and laid the foundation for one of the biggest and best-known department store chains in history.

It's All in Your Head

When babies are born as nature intends, they leave the womb headfirst. This is the normal, healthy way for babies to make their entrances into the world. If they exit feet first, they are considered breech, and this condition is abnormal. Anatomically, a headfirst birth makes sense. When a baby's head comes out first and after the shoulders are also out, the rest of the baby's body leaves the mother quite easily. We can understand why it's best for both the mother and the baby. I also like to look at it metaphorically, believing that entering into life headfirst is a powerful picture of the way we need to live every day. What I mean is the head represents the mind. When we have strong healthy minds and we meet the circumstances of life with right thought patterns and mind-sets, everything that follows tends to emerge and fall into place fairly easily.

The ancient Roman emperor Marcus Aurelius made a point we all need to remember: "You have power over your mind—not outside events. Realize this and you will find strength." Indeed, one of the greatest powers we have is the ability to choose our thoughts and discipline our minds.

> When we have strong healthy minds and we meet the circumstances of life with right thought patterns and mind-sets, everything that follows tends to emerge and fall into place fairly easily.

Many people face problems in life, sometimes the same problems over and over, and never seem to be able to figure out why. They wonder: *Why do I always get passed over for promotions at work? Why can't I get a breakthrough in my marriage? Why do I never have enough money, even though my job pays me decently? Why do I seem to be sick all the time? Why do my children cause so much trouble and heartache?*

Most of the time, people remain stuck in cycles of the same problems, like a hamster on a wheel, until they finally realize that the trouble is not with their bosses, their spouses, their bank accounts, their health, or their sons and daughters. The trouble is more personal than that; it's in their minds. Once they realize they can change their lives if they will change their thinking, then they are finally headed toward a breakthrough. This is exactly what happened to R. H. Macy.

One way I like to talk about the power of the mind is to say this: "In some ways, you're always right." This comes from Proverbs 23:7, which teaches whatever people think in their hearts, that's who they are. In other words, you are what you think you are. That's why whatever you think is usually correct on some level. When I think about this biblical principle, it reminds me of an airplane. On a plane, there is a captain and a crew, along with the vessel itself. Using this metaphor, this verse teaches that your mind is the captain, your emotions are the crew, and your body is the airplane. Your mind is in charge of your life, your emotions support what's in your head, and your body follows along.

Many people fail to understand this truth. They allow their physical desires or their feelings to sit in the cockpit of their lives, while their minds are back in the galley somewhere. As an example, people addicted to drugs and alcohol frequently live this way. Their bodies crave certain substances and their emotions tell them the substances will make them feel good, so they sniff, smoke, inject, or drink. The mental realities of substance abuse never occur to them. They don't think about the fact that they could harm themselves or others, nor do they consider the long-term physical or psychological damage these strong substances could do to them. When people's minds are set on drugs or alcohol consistently for a long enough period of time, they eventually become druggies or alcoholics. That's because as a person "thinks in his heart, so is he" (Prov. 23:7 NKJV).

> Your mind is in charge of your life, your emotions support what's in your head, and your body follows along.

The same is true for people who cannot control their emotions. People who are controlled by anger or jealousy often do and say things they later regret; people controlled by fear often make decisions primarily based on that fear instead of more reasonable factors. For example, to draw another illustration from air travel, I once heard about a smart businesswoman in Florida who was qualified and eager for a promotion. In order to receive it, she had to interview at her corporate headquarters in Idaho. Because of time constraints, she could not make the long trip by car, but she was terrified of flying, even though commercial air flights are generally considered the safest form of travel. In the end, she could not overcome her fear. Although her superiors agreed that she was the most qualified candidate for the job and knew she would get it if the executive leaders could meet her face-to-face, the job went to someone else— someone who was not afraid to hop on an airplane and show up for the interview.

In simplest terms, what Proverbs 23:7 means is that many times whatever you think, you're right. If you think you can succeed in a certain area, you can. If you think you're destined to fail, then failure is likely right around the corner. That's how powerful the mind is, and because it's so powerful, it needs to take the lead over our emotions and our physical desires. Part of having a strong I-factor means understanding the power of thinking the right thoughts and being willing to do so.

If you are desperate for something about your life to change, it's important to understand that a change of mind precedes a change of circumstances. The willingness and ability to take responsibility for having good, healthy thoughts that will move you forward in life is necessary for a strong I-factor. Otherwise, the same thought patterns that sabotaged you in the past will lead to failure in the future. If you don't know how to think differently, you won't know how to act differently or how to make different decisions than you've made previously. But once you realize you can choose to think new thoughts and you begin to do it, you will be amazed at how much different and how much better your life will be.

Breaking Free from the Prison of Your Mind

Thought patterns that lead people to take the same actions and make the same decisions year after year become like mental prisons. Once certain mind-sets have been in place long enough, they become second nature to us and we find them difficult to break free from. Eventually, we become comfortable in these well-established ways of thinking, and our thoughts keep us stuck in the sameness of our lives instead of setting us free to grow and change so we can fulfill our destinies.

One of the most powerful stories I know about breaking free from mental entrapments comes from a story about a man who found himself in a Middle Eastern jail centuries ago. He was the apostle Peter, known for his intense devotion to Christ and his fiery temper. Peter found himself locked up and in line for decapitation (Acts 12). His fellow disciple, James, had been beheaded not long before his imprisonment, so Peter knew that King Herod and the opponents of the gospel he preached were serious about silencing him.

Not only was Peter in prison; he was also in chains and confined to a cramped cell with sixteen soldiers standing guard around it. In addition, to his right and to his left, he was chained to soldiers assigned to guard him, just in case he somehow tried to break free. All this happened on the eve of a trial, which would no doubt end in a death sentence. Everything in Peter's environment was bad for him; it was designed to keep him confined, keep him still, and keep him alive until the executioners were ready to kill him. In the midst of this misery and anguish, Peter went to sleep.

As he slept, the story took a dramatic turn. "Suddenly an angel of the Lord appeared and a light shone in the cell. He struck Peter on the side and woke him up. 'Quick, get up!' he said, and the chains fell off Peter's wrists" (Acts 12:7).

I want to call your attention to the fascinating three-step process the angel took Peter through as he set him free from prison. People trapped in mind-sets that are not working or thoughts that prevent them from reaching their full potential can go through the same process in order to find freedom and start living better lives.

1. Revelation

First a light shone into Peter's cell as the angel appeared. If you've ever unlocked a hotel room door and stumbled over a piece of furniture while fumbling for a light switch, then you understand how powerful light can be. It lets you know exactly where you're going, and it helps you get around safely. When you turn on a light in a hotel room, the light does not make the furniture, art, and draperies suddenly appear; it simply lets you know they are already there. The same principle applies when light begins to shine in your mind in a certain situation. Some people may call this illumination; I call it revelation, especially when God orchestrates it and when the insights that result from it could only come from the Spirit of the One who knows everything.

I believe any change in a person's life begins with revelation. It starts with realizing something needs to be different. For example, that moment happens when a person steps on a scale and finally says, "That's enough. I am overweight and unhealthy. Starting today, the number on this scale is going to go down instead of up." That moment happens when a person logs in to an online banking account and thinks, *I will never be able to save any money if I keep spending at this rate. I need to stop overspending.* Whatever the situation, the revelation moment has to come.

What happens in our minds in moments like the ones I've just described is exactly like what happens when we flip the light switch in a dark hotel room. We suddenly recognize a problem that has been there all along; we just didn't see it before. Once we see it and understand that it is not good for us, we can begin to change it. This kind of insight and understanding always precedes personal breakthrough.

2. Affliction

Next, in an action that may seem odd for an angel, he struck Peter on the side, causing him to wake up. Wake-up calls, especially when God orchestrates them in our lives, come in many shapes and sizes. Most of the time, they are difficult or painful, but they are necessary. The wake-up calls may feel like some type of burden or affliction, but they are motivated by love and intended to help us go beyond the limitations of our current conditions and move into something better.

In R. H. Macy's case, his wake-up call was a series of business failures. Once four small-town stores had fallen apart, he knew he had to think differently than ever before in order to succeed on his fifth try. When he did succeed, his success in New York City, the shopping capital of the Western hemisphere, far outweighed the success he could have had in other cities. Something much bigger and more significant was waiting for him on the other side of his failures.

If you are in the midst of a wake-up call right now, let me share a secret about it. Whatever it is, it is not designed to cause you pain. It's intended to send you this message: You are better than this. You were never meant to get comfortable in this limited situation. It's time to wake up and move on because God has something so much better for your future than you are experiencing in the present.

3. Resurrection

After the angel brought revelation and affliction to Peter, he then brought Peter to a moment of resurrection, a time when Peter could rise up and walk out of his prison cell. The angel told Peter to put on his clothes, his shoes, and his coat. Once Peter had done that, the angel said, "Follow me" (Acts 12:8).

Notice that until this point, the angel had acted independently. Peter had no choice about what was happening to him. But when the angel told him to get dressed and follow him, Peter had a decision to make. If he was going to participate in the miracle that was unfolding, he had to stand up and start walking. I don't believe God sent the angel to Peter in prison simply to bring revelation to his situation, and I don't think He sent him just to awaken Peter and afflict him momentarily for a good reason. I'm convinced the point of God's sending the angel was to give Peter an opportunity to arise and walk out of his bondage.

Notice this is Peter's first chance to make his own decision about his circumstances. The revelation and the affliction came from an outside source. In the wake of these things, Peter had an I-factor decision to make: Would he stand up, get dressed, and follow the angel to freedom, or would he stay in the confining cell that probably felt familiar to him by then?

I can imagine the angel saying, "Stand up, Peter! I know you're in prison, but stand up. I know you're in a bad situation, but stand to your feet and get ready to go. I know you didn't do anything to create the mess you're in, but stand up. Everything is about to change for you."

That's the same message I hope you will hear in the midst of any circumstance that makes you feel confined, restricted, held back, or in bondage. Beyond the story and the words of Acts 12, the message of the passage is that anyone entangled in any situation can be set free. Whatever you are going through, you don't have to crumble under the weight of the burden. You don't have to be overwhelmed by the size of the problem. You don't have to give up or give in due to the nature of the circumstances. You can plant your feet, firm up your backbone, square your shoulders, and stand up to it.

Peter's story is not about escaping an actual prison. Rather, it illustrates the process of breaking free from the thought patterns and mind-sets that keep us from being all we can be and from fulfilling our destinies.

How to Stand Up

I want to dig a little deeper into the practical ways you can stand up in order to position yourself to break free from any mental constructs that are holding you back from your best life. First, it's important to acknowledge your situation and be honest about the ways it restricts you. Second, it's vital to recognize and resist the temptation to become too much at ease in a restricted environment. Third, I cannot overemphasize how completely certain circumstances can paralyze you and how critical it is not to allow that to happen. Fourth, once you have done the work to break free from any form of mental prison, your destiny requires that you leave the past behind and move on, full speed ahead.

Acknowledge Your Situation and Its Limits

Most people either currently live or have lived in some type of mental prison. Some of them understand that about themselves; others don't. Some are willing to talk about it, others will not. The best way to begin to break free from thought patterns that limit us is to acknowledge our circumstances and be honest about their negative impact on our lives. I have heard several sad stories about husbands and fathers who lost their jobs but kept getting dressed and leaving home at the same time every morning so their children would not know the truth. I have to wonder if these people really were trying to protect their children (who rarely understand the impact of job loss until it affects their living conditions) or if they were trying to protect themselves from the pain of being let go. Whatever your situation is, denial won't help anyone. Admitting it and acknowledging how it affects you will position you to take the next step toward freedom.

Resist the Temptation to Become Comfortable in Confinement

What I find so interesting about the angel striking Peter to awaken him is that Peter was able to sleep on the night before his trial, chained between two soldiers. Could it be that Peter was way too comfortable in his dysfunctional situation?

I have seen many people who find themselves in dysfunctional environments and instead of working to free themselves, they settle in and make a nest. They go to sleep, figuratively speaking, as they quit noticing the little freedom they have and how bad their situations are.

Have you ever become so familiar with the negativity around you—so comfortable in dysfunction, so tired of trying to do better for yourself, or so afraid that if you try to escape your circumstances, they will only suck you back in—that you simply sigh and close your eyes? Have you ever allowed yourself to put up with something that holds you back because staying in that situation is easier than fighting to be free? Maybe you are in an abusive marriage and you have learned to do your makeup so well that no one seems to notice the bruises anymore. Maybe you are so deeply in debt that you don't notice how quickly the balance and interest go up each time you whip out a piece of plastic to pay for something you really don't need and definitely can't afford. If any of these situations or the many others that result in similar bondage applies to you, I have good news. You do not have to stay in those chains forever. Keep reading; I'm going to help you find your way free.

Don't Let Your Circumstances Paralyze You

A woman named Hagar and her son, Ishmael, were asked to leave their home because Hagar's mistress, Sarah, became jealous of Hagar when Sarah should not have been jealous at all. It's a long story, and you can read it all in Genesis 16 and Genesis 21:1–19. What's important for our purposes in this chapter is that when Hagar and Ishmael ran out of food and water, Hagar walked away from her son and sat down in agony, knowing she could not save him (Gen. 21:16).

Her sitting down represents her allowing her circumstances to paralyze her. When she realized that she could do nothing to make her desperate situation better, she sat down and gave up. Her sitting down was perhaps worse than Peter's confinement in prison. He was severely restricted against his will, but she *chose* to limit her movements because of the circumstances in which she found herself and her son.

The boy began to cry, and an angel from God appeared on the scene saying, "Arise, lift up the lad and hold him with your hand" (v. 18 NKJV). In modern language, we understand that the word *arise* means "stand up." God certainly knew Hagar had been mistreated, but through the angel, He told her to stand up anyway. When she stood, something amazing happened. She saw a well of water (v. 19). The well had been there all along, but Hagar could not see it until she stood up. Once she saw it, she was able to draw water for her son and herself, and they both survived. God's message to Hagar and Ishmael that day was: "It's not time for you to die. If you'll simply stand up, you can live."

Hagar's story makes an important point: you do not have to be defined by what has happened to you. She looked at her circumstances and she felt powerless; that's why she sat down. You can look at your circumstances and assess them differently. You can view them as catalysts for your next step toward greatness, or you can view them as blockades to the bright future God has for you. God takes us from glory to glory (2 Cor. 3:18 NKJV), from one good thing to another, even though He may lead us through some rough patches as we're headed toward the next stop on our journey. Based on this verse and others like it (Jer. 29:11; Prov. 4:18), I know better things are ahead for you. The question is: Will you allow your hope for the future to define and direct your life, or will you let what has happened in the past paralyze you and cause you to fear moving forward?

Move Forward

I was not born into a happy family. My mother and father divorced when I was only six months old. For many years, the fact that my father was not there for me controlled my life. I became angry, reckless, and destructive. I felt that my father did not love me, and therefore I did not love myself. At one point, I even bought a pair of hazel-colored contacts to try to change my appearance. I could not accept myself, even down to the color of my eyes, because I felt unaccepted by my father. My mother raised my sister and me to know God, and as I grew older, I began to question Him about my circumstances. Over and over, I asked, "Why, God? Why did my father leave me? Why am I having to grow up without a dad?" The more I questioned God, the more clearly I heard one phrase repeating itself in my mind: *Stand up to it.* What that meant to me was I needed to stand strong and move ahead in my life without allowing the frustrations and challenges of my past to hold me back.

Over time, I did learn to stand up to my situation. I acknowledged the pain of my circumstances and I decided not to let myself become so comfortable in those familiar circumstances that I would not try to reach beyond them. I also made an intentional choice to move on with my life, refusing to define myself or let others define me by the deficiency of a father in my life. These things all helped me break free from a victim mentality and ultimately come to know and appreciate my dad. Even more than that, though, had I never stood up to the negativity inside of me, I am sure I would not have been capable of marrying the phenomenal woman who is now my wife and would not enjoy being a father to my two amazing children. My past tried to highjack my future, but once I decided to stand up to it, it lost the battle.

Even if the specific circumstances do not apply, the principles in these stories apply to many situations. Whatever has weighed you down or held you back does not have to hinder you any longer. If you will recognize what needs to change and stand up to it, you'll find yourself on the path to breakthrough and turn around.

Are You Ready for the Chains to Come Off?

Do you remember what happened to Peter after the angel came to his cell, struck him, and told him to get up? The chains fell off Peter's wrists. The angel did not touch them; they miraculously dropped to the ground. The fact the guards were silent implies that they did not even wake up (Acts 12:7).

I believe that's what will happen in your life as you break free from negative mind-sets and limiting thoughts about yourself. If you will ask God for the piercing revelation only He can give, He will be faithful to show you what you need to see about yourself and how your thinking needs to change. If you will learn from the pain you've suffered and allow it to be a catalyst for change instead of a snare that keeps you trapped in your past, you will be equipped for a better future than you've ever imagined. If you will choose to walk boldly into your future with a mind-set that says, "Everything is possible for him who believes" (Mark 9:23), then the chains that have held you back will fall to the floor and you will find yourself free to fulfill your destiny, live your dreams, and experience the greatness for which you were created.

Internal Building Blocks

- The importance of the mind cannot be overestimated. If you'll change your thinking, you'll change your life.
- One of the greatest powers you have is the ability to choose your thoughts and discipline your mind. People with strong I-factors understand and use this power.
- To stand up and break free from mind-sets that may be holding you back in life, acknowledge your situation and its limitations.
- To free yourself from the thought patterns that may be holding you captive, resist the temptation to become comfortable in your confinement.
- To move beyond the mind-sets that have kept you stuck, it's important not to allow your circumstances to paralyze you.
- To break free from the ways of thinking that have trapped you in the past, you must determine that you will move forward—and then get going!

Strengthening Your I-Factor

1. Pinpoint an aspect of your life that needs to change. How can you change your thinking about it?
2. If you are stuck in a cycle of the same type of problem, what can you do to break free?
3. What is in the cockpit of your life right now—your emotions, your physical desires, or your mind? If it's not your mind, how

can you get your emotions or physical desires to take a back seat to your thoughts?

4. You can take four basic steps that will help you stand up and break free from mind-sets that have held you back. How can you apply each of these in your specific situation?

- Acknowledge your situation and its limitations.
- Resist the temptation to become comfortable in confinement.
- Don't allow circumstances to paralyze you.
- Move forward.

The Power of Perspective

*To change ourselves effectively, we first
have to change our perceptions.*
—STEPHEN COVEY

A YOUNG MAN IN ENGLAND WENT TO CATCH A TRAIN ONE morning. Being a little early for the train, he decided to sit down with a cup of coffee and some cookies to work the crossword puzzle in the newspaper. Without a word, a businessman sitting across from him casually leaned across the table, picked up the pack of cookies, opened it, and popped one in his mouth before placing the cookies back on the table.

The young man was appalled and perplexed. He judged the businessman's behavior as odd and rude. Staring at his puzzle for a moment, he thought about how to respond. Finally, he decided to simply reach over and take a cookie for himself, believing that the businessman would realize the cookies belonged to him. But apparently he didn't. A little while later, the businessman ate another cookie. The two men continued alternately eating cookies, without a word, until the pack of eight was empty. When they finished, the businessman nodded at the young man and went to catch his train. Before too long, the young man realized he needed to move toward the platform for his train, so he gathered his belongings—his coffee cup and newspaper. When he picked up his newspaper, there on the table sat his unopened pack of cookies.[1]

The young man thought the businessman was exhibiting bad manners and stealing from him, while in reality he was the one behaving strangely and stealing the businessman's cookies. He made certain assumptions based on what he saw and experienced, but they were wrong. Once he moved his newspaper, he had a whole new perspective on the situation and on the businessman. He did not understand the truth about what was really happening until he saw something he had not seen before—his cookies under the newspaper.

How many times in your life has everything changed because you saw something from a different point of view? If your experience is similar to mine, you have learned over the years that there is no substitute for a proper perspective. Wrong perspectives lead us to wrong conclusions and cause us to make bad decisions; right perspectives help us properly perceive and understand what is happening in our lives, see how we can benefit from it, and use it as a stepping-stone to success.

Proper Perspective Leads to Accurate Understanding

Like the young man who misplaced his cookies, we can also make faulty assessments about circumstances in our lives if we do not look at them with the proper perspective. If we see them from the wrong point of view, we almost always misinterpret them. Having the right perspective on the situations we face is the only way to understand them accurately and handle them well.

Having an accurate perspective is especially vital with regard to the hardships and problems we face in life. It's so important that I think many people owe God an apology. This statement may be shocking to you, but let me explain. I think we owe God an apology because we have misjudged, misunderstood, and jumped to the wrong conclusions about what He has done or allowed to happen in our lives or in the world at large. Many of us have been quick to blame God when we experience circumstances that are hurtful or disappointing. We've had the propensity to get an attitude and hold a grudge against God because of the issues, problems, challenges, and difficulties we have had to face. We've asked, "Where is God in this situation?" when God is exactly where He's always been—on the throne and in loving control of our lives and the world. We have often misread these situations completely. We have not seen them from God's perspective, so we have not understood His intentions in allowing these hardships or disappointing times in our lives.

When we encounter struggles in life, their purpose is not to punish us for being bad or to teach us harsh lessons. The issues and adversities we face are strategically designed to draw out all the good God has put inside of us. They are God's way of mining the gold He has deposited in our lives so it can enrich us and everyone around us.

One of my favorite stories from the business community is about Steve Jobs. There was a time in Apple's history when the company's board of directors fired him. They forced him to leave the company he envisioned, the one he started from nothing and built from the ground up. When Jobs left Apple, he took a few months to find his footing and then got busy building other companies. One of those companies was Pixar, which revolutionized animated films.[2] He did

> When we encounter struggles in life, their purpose is not to punish us for being bad or to teach us harsh lessons. The issues and adversities we face are strategically designed to draw out all the good God has put inside of us.

not rob the world of his genius just because a board was no longer happy with him; he found new and different ways to impact society.

A lot of people would have been angry over being asked to leave their own company, and many would have fallen into deep discouragement or even depression over such a traumatic demotion. Most people would see the firing as a problem—a big problem—but Jobs saw it as an opportunity. He had a different perspective than others would have had, and instead of marking the end of his career, that situation laid a foundation for future success. The wrong perspective could have caused him to slide into obscurity, but the right one catapulted him to new levels of greatness.

Who Me? A King?

Earlier in the book, I wrote about the Old Testament king David but did not share much about his background. There was no royal family in Israel at the time of his birth, so he was not born under the same circumstances as Prince William, the Duke of Cambridge, or his son, Prince George, in line to inherit the throne. No, he was born into a fairly ordinary family with a mom (who is not mentioned in Scripture), a dad named Jesse, and seven brothers. As King Saul's life began to spin out of control, God asked Samuel to anoint a new king—not one to assume rule immediately, but one who would know he was chosen and could prepare himself to ascend at the appropriate time. God did not give Samuel a name or a physical description; He simply sent him to Bethlehem and told him He would show him once he arrived which one of Jesse's sons would be the future king (1 Sam. 16:1–3).

Samuel invited Jesse and his sons to a service where a sacrifice would be offered to the Lord. There, he looked at each young man and knew none was the chosen one. Finally, he asked Jesse, "Are these all the sons you have?" (v. 11). Jesse said no, he had one more son, David, the youngest, who was tending the sheep that day. When Samuel saw David, he knew instantly that he would eventually become king, though David would not take the throne for many years. Once David was anointed, he did not pack his bags and move into the palace; he went back to tending sheep in the hills. He may have thought, *Me? A king? You've got to be kidding!*

This background is important because it gives us insight into how David must have seen himself. He was the youngest of seven brothers and a shepherd boy. His job was a common, dirty, physically demanding task that did not command much respect. No one can know for certain what David thought about himself, but I suspect even after Samuel anointed him, he still saw himself as a shepherd. I believe one reason David was anointed king so many years before the beginning of his rule was that God knew the process of preparing David for leadership would take time. Not only did David have a lot to learn about leading a nation, he also needed to undergo an internal transformation from viewing himself as a simple sheepherder to viewing himself as a capable leader of a strong nation.

Just as David had to work on his understanding of identity and change his self-perception, your perspective on yourself will also change over time as you move toward the greatness God intends for you. You may be thinking, *I could never undergo such a drastic change in the way I see myself.* But you can, and to do it you have access to the very thing that empowered David to change his mind about himself and grow into all he was destined to be—a relationship with God and a proper perspective on the things God allowed to happen in his life.

Inspiration for Modern-Day Giant-Slayers

As much as I've mentioned David in this book, I have not yet gone into detail about what I view as the foundation of his greatness.

After his anointing as king, while he was still tending sheep, his first major accolades and public acclaim came because he killed the fierce Philistine giant, Goliath. But that's not where his greatness began. He killed Goliath because he was not afraid of him when other people were. But that was not the birthplace of his greatness either. The reason he had the courage to fight and slay Goliath was that he understood who he was. He understood his identity, and that understanding of identity came from his relationship with God. That relationship with God enabled him to view life from the proper perspective.

As I have already pointed out, before David became a king or even a king-in-waiting, he was a shepherd boy. Let me say a bit more about that. It was hard, messy, sometimes dangerous work. And it was very lonely. David did not have other young men around to talk to, so he talked to God. We know this because some of what David said to God made its way into the book of Psalms. Many of the psalms we now know by heart, the ones we lean on in times of trouble and the ones we declare in times of victory, started as songs or prayers of David during his days as a shepherd. All we have to do is read some of these psalms to see that David had an intimate and powerful relationship with God. I'm convinced this deeply personal relationship provided David with his strong sense of identity and perspective, and that's why he was able to face Goliath and numerous other enemies victoriously for most of his life. Where other people saw problems, enemies, and obstacles, David only saw opportunities.

When Goliath came against the Israelites, he was a fearsome sight. First Samuel 17:4–7 (NLT) describes his appearance this way:

He was over nine feet tall. He wore a bronze helmet, and his bronze coat of mail weighed 125 pounds. He also wore bronze leg armor, and he carried a bronze javelin on his shoulder. The shaft of his spear was as heavy and thick as a weaver's beam, tipped with an iron spearhead that weighed 15 pounds. His armor bearer walked ahead of him.

As Goliath approached the Israelites that day, he roared at them: "Am I not a Philistine, and are you not the servants of Saul? Choose a man and have him come down to me. If he is able to fight and kill me, we will become your subjects; but if I overcome him and kill him, you will become our subjects and serve us" (vv. 8–9). When Saul and the Israelites heard this, they were "dismayed and terrified" and "they all fled from him in great fear" (vv. 11, 24).

No one stepped up to fight Goliath that day, so he continued issuing the same challenge for forty days. One day, David happened to be walking near the battlefield and heard Goliath's taunts. Unlike his fellow Israelites, David was not afraid. He asked, "Who is this uncircumcised Philistine that he should defy the armies of the living God?" (v. 26). That's the most important question any Israelite could have asked about Goliath. Except for David, it appears no one else even thought about this crucial point.

When David said, "Who is this uncircumcised Philistine?" he was hitting the very heart of an identity and perspective issue— the issue that separated him from Goliath and the one that would bring him victory and deal the giant a deathblow. When Goliath first threatened the Israelites, he started by stating his perspective on the situation: "Am I not a Philistine?" He said this because Philistines were known as mighty, victorious warriors, and by identifying himself with them, he was basically saying in his mind, *And you know the Philistines always win!*

David understood that, but he also understood the deeper perspective issue in play. Yes, Goliath was a Philistine, but he was an *uncircumcised* Philistine. That changed everything, and David knew it. The Philistines were not God's chosen people. For Goliath to be uncircumcised meant he did not have access to God's covenant promises. Goliath had no foundation or identity in God, and God was not on Goliath's side. David was circumcised. He was in covenant with God, and he understood that one of the provisions of the covenant was that God would fight for him.

That's why young David volunteered to take on Goliath when the rest of the Israelites ducked and ran. Saul tried to talk him out of it, perhaps because by that time Saul had forgotten the power of Israel's identity as God's covenant people. He told David, "You are not able to go out against this Philistine and fight him; you are only a young man, and he has been a warrior from his youth" (v. 33). After David stood up to Saul and told him about fighting lions and bears while on shepherd duty, Saul gave in. In fact, Saul put his own armor on David, put his own big bronze helmet on David's head, and gave the young man his sword. That's when David indicated once again his deep understanding of identity.

"I cannot go in these," David said, referring to the king's heavy armor, "because I am not used to them" (v. 39). This shows us how thoroughly David understood who he was. He knew he was a shepherd, not a soldier. Saul's armor was fine for Saul, but David was not impressed with it. It was unwieldy and he was uncomfortable in it. He knew he could not win this contest wearing another man's gear or using another man's weapon. He had to be true to who he was. So he took off the armor, put down the sword, and picked up five smooth stones from a nearby stream (v. 40). Confident that he could kill the giant by shooting the stones from his slingshot, David walked toward Goliath as Goliath mocked him and made fun of his weapon.

David's response to Goliath indicates the strength of his sense of perspective and his confidence in God:

> You come against me with sword and spear and javelin, but I
> come against you in the name of the LORD Almighty, the God of

the armies of Israel, whom you have defied. This day the Lord will deliver you into my hands, and I'll strike you down and cut off your head. This very day I will give the carcasses of the Philistine army to the birds and the wild animals, and the whole world will know that there is a God in Israel. All those gathered here will know that it is not by sword or spear that the Lord saves; for the battle is the Lord's, and he will give all of you into our hands. (1 Sam. 17:45–47)

In other words, "Goliath, you're going *down*. And not only that, but the whole mighty Philistine army is going down with you. God is on my side, and when I finish with this slingshot, you're all history." Quite a bold statement for a boy to make to a giant.

Why was David confident enough to face the armored Goliath, the experienced warrior more than nine feet tall, with only five stones and a slingshot? Because his sense of identity was surging that day, and it formed the basis for his proper perspective on Goliath. First, he knew the power of his covenant with God. Second, he had been shooting slingshots for years. He'd had a lot of time to practice, and that's what he was good at. He refused to compromise his identity. Instead, he had it in perspective and he capitalized on it— even though others thought he was crazy. At the end of the day, the mighty Goliath lay dead, facedown on the ground from a slingshot wound to the forehead.

There are three key lessons all of us can learn from David's willingness to fight Goliath and the fact that he overcame him. His story is a study in how to deal with the giants we face in life. First, we learn that no matter how big the giants in our lives may seem, we can still bring them down. Second, when we find ourselves up against tremendous obstacles, we can choose to see them as opportunities. Third, part of what God is trying to show us through the difficulties we face is that we are good enough to win every challenge we face and to embrace every opportunity He gives us. Let's explore each of these points.

No Giant Is Too Big to Fall

According to *The Guinness Book of World Records*, the tallest person in recorded history was an American male named Robert Wadlow, who stood just over eight feet, eleven inches and died in 1940.[3] But even Wadlow would have seemed small compared to Goliath. When David took on Goliath, he did not simply agree to fight someone considerably bigger than any other man he had ever seen, he agreed to go up against someone truly *enormous*.

There is a direct correlation between our I-factors and the way we deal with our challenges. People with a strong I-factor tackle difficulties head-on, like David, while people with a weak I-factor try to run from their hardships or pass the responsibility for dealing with them to someone else. From time to time, everyone faces much-larger-than-usual problems. They are the Goliaths in our lives—so big we cannot see over them or around them, so daunting we may want to run and hide from them, so formidable we feel defeated before we even try to overcome them. When we see our giants, as huge as they are, as possibilities for greatness instead of as problems, we take the first step toward bringing them down.

Obstacles and Difficulties Are Opportunities That Will Reveal Your Greatness

There was something great in David that no one knew about until he stepped up to fight Goliath. Until that moment, I suspect no one thought much about the young shepherd. But when David said, "Give me a shot at him," the first response from the people around him was negative. No one believed in him. Perhaps there is hidden greatness in you too, greatness that will not be evident to the people around you until you face a challenge that puts a demand on it.

Any time you face a Goliath in your life, the first thing to do is refuse to be intimidated because you understand that it does not exist to defeat you; it exists to showcase the greatness inside of you. Facing giants is part of life and it is part of any significant pursuit you may embark on over the course of your lifetime. If you can understand the purpose of those massive obstacles,

> People with a strong I-factor tackle difficulties head-on, like David, while people with a weak I-factor try to run from their hardships or pass the responsibility for dealing with them to someone else.

you can allow them to do what they are designed to do—reveal to you and to the people around you the strength, the character, the calling, and the destiny that is waiting to come from your life.

In David's life, the Goliath encounter was designed to be a stepping-stone to the throne and a long, victorious reign over a prosperous nation. That makes me wonder, what is your Goliath designed to reveal about you?

You Are Good Enough

A lot of people feel called to do certain things and then get nervous when they have a chance to step into those callings. Similarly, many people find the doors they need to walk through open to them, but when they get those opportunities they long for, they hesitate to embrace them. Too often, the reason people are reluctant is not that they don't think the opportunities are good ones, it's that they don't think they are good enough for the opportunities. Deep inside, they wonder if they are ready for such good things to come their way. Know this: part of the purpose behind your present or future Goliath is to confirm in you that you are good enough.

How to Slay Your Giants

Hardly anyone gets a free pass all the way through life. Almost everyone fights some kind of battle at some point. Some of these battles can be fiery and some can last a long time. Regardless of how intense or frequent your battles are or how long they last, David's story highlights several characteristics of people who know how to be victorious over their enemies.

Sometimes, the biggest giants in our lives are within us. We can manage the outside forces acceptably; our real struggles are things like fear, jealousy, comparison, insecurity, inferiority, excessive anger, bitterness, or hopelessness. These enemies and others like them are invisible, but they rage just as fiercely as conflicts against outside sources. In some ways, they can have a stronger hold on us than external situations can. This is because we can always walk away from battles involving others and get at least a bit of a break, but no one can escape the threats and taunts from the giants in his or her own soul. Whatever your giant is, whether it's internal or external, you can handle it. Here's how.

Don't Undervalue What You Have

When Saul realized that David's only weapon against Goliath was a slingshot, he offered David his royal weapons and his armor. As I mentioned earlier, these were not what David needed. David's expertise was with a slingshot, so a slingshot was his weapon of choice. It didn't seem like much to the people around him, but in his hands and from his perspective, it was lethal. He understood the importance of being himself. He did not try to pretend he was someone else, so he rejected the king's armor and weapon.

Many times when you face an opportunity to grow by embracing a challenge, you may question yourself or feel tempted to stray from your authentic self. You may find yourself thinking, *I'm not sure I'm ready for this. I don't think I have what I need. I may not be good enough for this.* The truth is, when God is leading you, you do have everything you need and you *are* everything you need to be. He makes sure of that. Your job is simply to trust in the person He has created you to be and act from it. Even if people around you try to convince you to use the weapons they prefer or wear the armor that fits them, always stick with who you are and what works for you. The greatest thing you can ever do is mine the gold of your authentic self and be comfortable living from that powerful resource.

Focus on Promises Instead of Problems

Being able to see Goliath from the perspective of God's promises to the Israelites instead of as a problem was the key to David's victory. His knowledge that he was one of God's covenant people, and therefore heir to covenant promises, gave him the confidence to take on Goliath. Everyone else hid because they viewed Goliath as a problem; David stepped up because he remembered and believed God's promises to his nation and God's personal promise to make him king. Clearly, he understood that if a giant is standing in the way of something God has promised you, it's simply something you have to go *through* in order to get what God is bringing you into.

When you find yourself up against a giant in your life, the key to defeating it is not to view it as a problem, but to focus on God's promises. If you will see your obstacles through the lens of His promises instead of viewing them as problems, you will understand that dealing with them is not a trick to keep you from possessing your promise, but a God-given opportunity to get you into it.

Don't Let Your Critics Limit You

I mentioned earlier that Saul tried to talk David out of fighting Goliath because Saul saw Goliath as a problem, while David saw him as an opportunity. But before that happened, David's own brother, Eliab, became furious with David and said, "Why have you come down here? And with whom did you leave those few sheep in the desert? I know how conceited you are and how wicked your heart is; you came down only to watch the battle." To this, David replied, "Now what have I done? . . . Can't I even speak?" (1 Sam. 17:28–29).

The fact that David asked, "Now what have I done?" indicates that perhaps his older brother had a history of talking down to David or at least of not encouraging him. The situation is not uncommon. To apply this incident to your life today, I would say the older brother represents your family members or close friends. Any time you move toward a new level of greatness, someone will speak negatively or attempt to discourage you. Often, that negativity and lack of support start with the people closest to you. Giant-slayers understand that sometimes everyone else is wrong.

What's interesting to me about Eliab's comments to David is that they were dead wrong. His perspective on David was so skewed that he did not recognize David's potential. He should have known David could be deadly with a slingshot, having killed lions and bears, but that was nowhere in his thinking. He simply viewed David as his silly little brother making a fool of himself by saying he could slay Goliath. He specifically said David had a "wicked heart," but God saw David totally differently. Check out what God said about him: "I have found David son of Jesse, a man after my own heart; he will do everything I want him to do" (Acts 13:22).

Whenever you take a step toward destiny, know that you will encounter opposition and that it's likely to come from people you'd least expect. Understand also that their perspectives on you may be terribly flawed, as Eliab's perspective on David was. Don't let anyone try to limit you or convince you that you can't do what you know you can do. Stay true to what you know about yourself, keep the right perspective on your challenges (which is that they are designed to help you reach a new place of greatness), and move forward with strength and courage.

Build on Past Success and Personal Experience

When David volunteered to stand up to Goliath, the Israelites wondered why he thought he could do it. He remembered something they did not. He knew he had faced threats from lions and bears and come out a winner. From David's perspective, perhaps going up against Goliath was not much different than confronting a lion or a bear. After all, lions and bears were frightening—just like Goliath was. And just like Goliath, lions and bears could have killed David as easily as he ultimately killed them. In all these situations, it would seem David was at a disadvantage. Perhaps facing Goliath was the biggest disadvantage, but David may have thought, *I have been outsized before.* I believe, from his perspective, David simply viewed Goliath as the next level of challenge he needed to face and defeat.

This is why dreams and destinies do not manifest overnight. If we were to identify our dreams or understand our destinies and then immediately step into them, we would be completely unprepared to fulfill them properly. Instead of being ready to handle them, we would end up frustrated. But when we walk into these things gradually, learning and growing as we deal with challenges along the way, then we are ready when we finally reach our moment of fulfilled destiny.

While you and I remain unaware at times of God's plans and purposes for us, those plans and purposes are never far from His mind. He begins training and equipping us for them very early in life, guiding us through the years in ways that will prepare us for what He has in store for us later.

David received much of his training for greatness on the backside of the mountains, tending sheep and fighting lions and bears. I believe every time a rock flew out of David's slingshot to slay a lion or a bear with pinpoint accuracy, God not only saw it, but also saw ahead to the day David's deadly zinger would kill Goliath. God didn't train David with giants, though; He trained him with animals.

You may be wondering why you are facing some of the seemingly minor challenges in your life right now. They are your lions and bears. They are the things God is using to prepare you for victory in bigger battles in days to come, battles that may be fierce against enemies that may be huge. You may be going through some tough times right now, but the important point is that you not only *go* through them, you also *grow* through them. They're designed to strengthen and mature you and to plant seeds of greatness that will one day become evident not only to you, but also to everyone else around you.

Proper Perspective Leads to Success

While there are many lessons to be learned from the story of David and Goliath, one principle that stands out is this: our sense of identity determines our perspective. In other words, the way we see ourselves affects how we see other people and the circumstances of our lives. David did not hesitate to take on the seemingly impossible task of fighting Goliath because his strong sense of identity empowered him to see the situation clearly and assess it properly. When everyone around him looked at Goliath and felt terrified, David looked at him and could taste victory.

David saw the truth about Goliath—that he was not in covenant with God—when no one else even thought to consider that important fact. Joshua and Caleb saw the truth about the promised land—that God had promised it to the Israelites—when everyone else felt intimidated by the people already living there. In both stories, these men knew their God and knew their relationship to Him. That relationship gave them confidence and strong identities, strong enough to tackle daunting situations without fear. Their identities were partially based on the same truths you and I have access to today, truths about who God is. When we understand and believe that, in addition to believing what God's Word says about who we are, we have a winning combination—all the time.

Let me share with you some realities about God, because the way you see Him affects the way you see yourself. If you see Him accurately, that perspective will cause you to also see yourself properly—and that will take you to a whole new level of strength, courage, and confidence to fulfill your destiny.

- God is not like human beings who sometimes fail you. He tells the truth, and you can count on Him (Num. 23:19).
- God has good plans for you, plans to bless you and lead you into a great future (Jer. 29:11).
- God makes you strong and leads you in the right way (2 Sam. 22:33–37).
- God is always ready to help you, protect you, and deliver you in times of trouble (Ps. 18:2–3).
- God gives you the grace you need in every situation, every time you need it (2 Cor. 9:8).
- God is the greatest, most powerful force in the universe. Nothing can stand against Him (1 Chron. 29:11).
- God fights your battles and gives you victory (2 Chron. 20:15; 1 Cor. 15:57).
- God is able to do even more for you than you could ever imagine (Eph. 3:20).
- God gives you unconditional, never-ending love and faithfulness (Ps. 86:15; Lam. 3:21–23).

I hope, starting right now, that these words are beginning to transform the way you see God and the way you see yourself. Your perspective on yourself, your potential, and the obstacles you face can determine whether you succeed in life or not. In David's life, his path to greatness followed a pattern. First, he was anointed, and the knowledge that he was chosen sparked a transformation in the way he saw himself. Then he was prepared for his future responsibilities. This preparation included a conflict with Goliath that not only solidified David's trust in God, it also taught him the importance of fighting battles God's way. Ultimately, David became Israel's greatest king.

As you look toward your future, remember how powerful perspective is. Wrong ways of seeing yourself, your life, and your God can derail you completely, but proper perspectives can propel you to heights of the destiny and greatness you were made for.

——————— Internal Building Blocks ———————

- The right perspective on the situations we face empowers us to understand and process those situations accurately, while the wrong perspective leads us to incorrect conclusions, which lead to wrong actions.
- David's successful slaying of Goliath teaches us at least three important lessons: first, no giant in your life is too big to come down; second, obstacles and difficulties will reveal your greatness; and third, when opportunities for greatness present themselves to you, it's vital that you believe you are good enough to embrace them.
- No one goes through life without facing difficulty. Some of those difficulties are gigantic, seemingly as impossible to overcome as Goliath himself.

- How to slay the giants in your life: don't undervalue what you have, focus on God's promises instead of your problems, don't let your critics limit you, and build on past success and personal experience.
- Proper perspectives are critical to success in every area of your life.

Strengthening Your I-Factor

1. Why is a right perspective on the situations you face in life so important?
2. Is there a Goliath in your life right now? If so, what is it? In what ways does dealing with this giant give you and the people around you a chance to see the greatness in you?
3. This chapter mentions the importance of not undervaluing what you have, just as David did not undervalue his simple slingshot and smooth stones. What do you have that may be more powerful than you think?
4. Do you have any critics who are trying to limit you? How has this chapter taught you to deal with them more effectively?
5. What past successes and personal experiences have you had that can help you deal with giants you face today or in the future?
6. How do you see yourself? In what ways do you feel your perspective is accurate? In what ways does it need to change?

13

Seven Steps to Greatness, Part 1

Greatness and goodness are not means, but ends.
—Samuel Taylor Coleridge

SOMETHING ABOUT THE WORD *GREATNESS* STIRS OUR souls and inspires us. At times, it feels out of reach, and yet there's something inside of us that wants to go for it. Even if we cannot define *greatness* in a succinct, dictionary-type way, we know intuitively what it is. It's both an aspiration and an invitation, something we hope and want to work for and something that calls out to us, "Come and get me!" Deep down, people who have a healthy I-factor and those working toward one regularly think about greatness, dream about greatness, and want to ultimately achieve whatever greatness means to them.

As I was writing this chapter, I began to wonder what various people have said about greatness through the years. I found some interesting quotations from a variety of people whose names might never appear together under any other circumstances except that they had something valuable to say about greatness. Each one gives us a different and important perspective on what greatness is.

- Musician Bob Marley put it simply, "The greatness of a man is not in how much wealth he acquires, but in his integrity and his ability to affect those around him positively."[1]

- English playwright George Bernard Shaw said, "Just do what must be done. This may not be happiness, but it is greatness."[2]
- Russian novelist Leo Tolstoy said, "There is no greatness where there is no simplicity, goodness, and truth."[3]
- Former British Prime Minister Winston Churchill noted rightly, "The price of greatness is responsibility."[4]
- The Olympic great Wilma Rudolph said, "Never underestimate the power of dreams and the influence of the human spirit. . . . The potential for greatness lives within each one of us."[5]
- Indian leader Mahatma Gandhi observed, "As human beings our greatness lies not so much in being able to re-make the world . . . as in being able to remake ourselves."[6]

My personal definition of *greatness* is simpler and less eloquent than some others, but it encapsulates what I have come to believe greatness is. In my view, to achieve greatness is to become and accomplish everything God has purposed for you to be and do. For some people, that may include accolades, applause, and life in the spotlight. For others, it may take place behind the scenes, away from cameras, by living faithfully and lovingly every day. Greatness is not the same as fame. We could just as easily say a missionary whose name we do not know, but who cares for the sick and feeds the hungry in a place we never heard of, has reached greatness as we could say Billy Graham has attained it.

Whatever greatness means to you (and if you aren't sure yet, I'm going to help you figure it out), I hope this book has increased your hunger for it and elevated your belief that you can achieve it.

I have a feeling you are reading this book not just to gain information, but also for the sake of transformation. I believe you want your life to change and you've realized that the best changes always begin on the inside. You can change your hairstyle, your fashion, your car, your address, your name, or your career, but those adjustments are only skin deep. Sooner or later, unless the right adjustments take place within you, the external changes won't matter.

Throughout this book, I have offered insights into the importance of having a healthy I-factor, meaning an accurate assessment of your identity, a proper understanding of your significance, and a good relationship with yourself. I've also tried to provide some helpful advice about strengthening areas of your I-factor that might be weaker than others. But I don't think you've read the book simply to increase your knowledge about the I-factor or even to find out how to make your I-factor healthier. I think you've read it because there is a dream, a passion, and a deep longing for greatness inside of you, and you realize that your I-factor will be a major determinant in whether you get to fulfill your dreams, live your passion, or experience your greatness.

While I don't know the specifics of your life, I do believe you are a person of destiny and you were born for greatness. You are not on earth at random; you're alive today for a reason. You're not the result of biology; you were lovingly crafted and uniquely designed by a Creator whose good plans are unfolding for you day after day.

I've written many times in this book about the greatness I believe you're destined for, and in this chapter I'd like to offer several specific steps that will help you achieve it. Before I share the steps,

> Your I-factor will be a major determinant in whether you get to fulfill your dreams, live your passion, or experience your greatness.

though, it's important to do something else first. You need to know where you're going. I call it "defining your greatness."

Define Your Greatness

Most people hunger for something greater than they're currently experiencing. In the faith community, where I spend a lot of my time, I sense that hunger everywhere I go. It's a combination of people's deep yearning to be more, do more, and experience more, and God is always in the business of doing greater things. When we walk with Him, we constantly live within earshot of His beckoning us to new levels and next steps. It's a divine call to step up and experience something different and better than we have ever known.

Paul said this about God: "He creates each of us by Christ Jesus to join him in the work he does, the good work he has gotten ready for us to do, work we had better be doing" (Eph. 2:10 MSG). Notice there is good work God already has prepared for us to do. We aren't waiting for Him to come up with something great; He's waiting for us to discover it and commit to it.

Only you can define the greatness you were made for. Whether you feel destined to come up with a cure for cancer, to walk on another planet, to be an executive of integrity in an industry known for corruption, or to be the best second-grade teacher who ever lived, your greatness is a personal matter. Although it will most likely involve what you do in this world, it will not be rooted in your doings; it will be rooted in your being.

No one can tell you what your greatness is; you have to dig deep inside yourself and mine it like gold. I can, however, offer you a list of a dozen questions that will help you on this great adventure of discovery. I don't expect you to answer them before you read the rest of this chapter because answering them well will require some time and energy, and perhaps some reflection and prayer. I simply want to leave them with you at this point. Allow them to hover over your thought process as you keep reading, but also realize you will want to go back to them later.

- What do you really like to do? What brings you the most fulfillment in life?
- What do you do well?
- What are your natural gifts and talents?
- What is your best skill set? What kinds of training have you received?
- What qualities do you admire in other people? What accomplishments have you seen other people achieve that make you think, *I'd like to do something like that*?
- Which character traits are strongest for you?
- If you could speak to a large group of people for fifteen minutes with your only assignment being "Inspire them," what would you say?
- If you did not need a job in order to make money to live, how would you spend your time each day?
- What lessons have you learned from the challenges you've faced, and how could those lessons help other people?
- What do you enjoy so much that you totally lose track of time when you are engrossed in it?
- Under what circumstances do you feel you are your best self?
- When you reach the end of your life and look back, what would you most regret not doing?

The more clearly you can define your greatness, the better you can take specific steps to help yourself get there. In the next two chapters, I'd like to share the seven steps to greatness that I'm confident will take you from the person you are right now to the person you long to be.

Step 1: Make Quality Decisions

Perhaps you remember a game I remember from childhood days on the playground. When we chose teams for games like dodgeball or basketball, we often pointed our little fingers at people saying, "Eenie, meenie, miney, mo . . ." Whoever the finger landed on was the person who joined our team. Children still play that game, especially when they struggle to make a decision, such as whether to wear pink socks or purple socks with a new dress or whether to play with toy construction trucks or with plastic farm animals. When choosing teams, clothes, or playthings, eenie, meenie, miney, mo is harmless. It helps children make decisions and go on about their days.

But to adults, random decisions can be devastating. A mature individual cannot say to a potential spouse, "Hold this spoon in one hand and put both hands behind your back. If I choose the one that has the spoon, I'll marry you. If I choose the one that's empty, you'll need to find someone else." Nor can we approach a job interview with a coin toss, thinking, *Heads, I'll take the job if they offer it; tails, I won't.* No, the more we grow, the more important our decisions become. That's why the first step to greatness is to make quality decisions.

You face all kinds of decisions every day, and one of the most important understandings you will ever reach is that life itself is a series of choices and the sum of the decisions you make. The late preacher and ministry leader Myles Munroe said, "Our life is the sum total of all the decisions we make every day, and those decisions are determined by our priorities."[7] Some choices seem relatively insignificant while others seem enormous, but the truth is that *every decision matters.* Decisions cause you to take certain actions, which lead to certain habits, which shape your character and impact your future. If you want to know what your life is going to look like at the end of this year or five or ten years from now, you can get a preview by looking at the decisions you are making right now. Nothing will position you for your destiny in the future as effectively as making quality decisions today. If you can manage your decisions well, you can chart the course of your life.

Let me offer some brief suggestions to consider each time you face a decision. First, take all the time you need. One of the biggest reasons people make bad decisions is that they rush into them. In some cases, you may need to move quickly, but you can almost always take a night to sleep on a decision. In other matters, you may have weeks or months to think about what to do. Sometimes, you know in your heart what you need to do and you can act swiftly, but when that is not the case, I encourage you not to allow yourself to be rushed or pushed into a decision that does not feel 100 percent right to you.

> Nothing will position you for your destiny in the future as effectively as making quality decisions today.

Second, as you're trying to decide what to do in certain situations, it's worth taking time to get all the information you can on all the options you have. Whether you read books about your choices, wisely and strategically look up things on the Internet, or take advantage of a chance for hands-on practice or observation, be ravenous for information. The more you know about a potential course of action, the better you can decide whether to take it or not.

Third, get all the wise counsel and input you can get. One of the great blessings of life is that until we are very old, we can almost always find someone older, wiser, and more experienced than we are. This is true in most career fields, and it's certainly true in life in general. Chances are, someone somewhere has faced a decision similar to yours and would probably be able to provide you with helpful insights about the decision-making process. They may also be able to explain unanticipated consequences—positive or negative—you would not think of on your own. Whenever you want to make a quality decision, it's smart to listen to the people who have gone before you.

Fourth, look at your situation from as many perspectives as possible. For example, you may have to decide whether to take a promotion at work or not. From the perspective of your career, it seems like a no-brainer. It would put you exactly where you want to be. But if you're married and have a family, it's important to consider the opportunity from a family perspective. If the job would take you away from home for several days each week, your spouse would have to pick up the slack and find ways to compensate for your absence. If your children are at a point in life where you really want to be available to support and influence them, then being gone several days a week would not help you fulfill that desire.

Anytime you have a decision to make, think about it from every angle because while one decision would be good from one perspective, it might not be good from other points of view. Once you've explored the various angles, you can choose which ones to prioritize and you'll know what to do.

Step 2: Make God's Word
Your Manual for Life

Because each decision you make has an impact on your health, happiness, overall well-being, and destiny, it's important to make every one according to the Word of God. That's the second step to greatness: make God's Word your manual for life. You can't make wise decisions based on emotions or information you gather from the world around you. The only way to make wise decisions, decisions that can withstand changing circumstances and fickle feelings, is to base them on the time-tested, never-failing Word of God.

The Bible does so much more than help you make decisions. It can be your manual—your guidebook—for life. "Every part of Scripture is God-breathed and useful one way or another—showing us truth, exposing our rebellion, correcting our mistakes, training us to live God's way. Through the Word we are put together and shaped up for the tasks God has for us" (2 Tim. 3:16–17 MSG). What is the task God has for you? It's to move into the greatness He's purposed for your life.

The great writer Charles Dickens said this about the New Testament: "The New Testament is the very best book that ever was or ever will be known in the world."[8] Given Dickens's expertise as an author and that some people think *he* wrote the best books in the world, his comment is amazing. It's also true. As a pastor, I spend much of my life studying and teaching God's Word, and I have seen firsthand how powerful it is in people's lives when they live by what it says. The impact this Word has on people's lives is completely transformative. I have seen depressed people become filled with hope; sick people healed; addicted people break free; and confused, frustrated people finally find their way—all because they committed to know and live by God's Word. It's life, it's truth, and it works.

If you're serious about living in the greatness for which you were created, you won't find a plan for it in *People* magazine, or *Essence*, or the *Wall Street Journal*. You'll find it in God's Word. The pages of Scripture are full of inspiration, encouragement, wisdom, and stories that are highly relatable to the circumstances you may find yourself in today, even though they took place centuries ago. From Genesis to Revelation, you'll discover a proven path to greatness as you read about many ordinary people who went from obscurity to tremendous significance. The way to greatness is there; you simply have to choose to follow it. By following, you're taking ownership of your destiny, realizing you have a part to play in it. I am convinced the best way to greatness is through God's life-changing Word.

Step 3: Change Your Thinking to Change Your Life

Our thoughts are powerful, and over the years, all kinds of research have shown how much we can influence our lives by the way we think. Our words and actions are rooted in our mind-sets. Everything about the way we live starts with a thought. A well-known quote attributed to everyone from Lao Tzu to the father of Margaret Thatcher to a man named Frank Outlaw who founded Bi-Lo Supermarkets says this: "Watch your thoughts, for they become words. Watch your words, for they become actions. Watch your actions, for they become habits. Watch your habits, for they become character. Watch your character, for it becomes your destiny." Regardless of its origin, these words are full of truth. Our thoughts form the foundation of everything else that happens in our lives.

The way you are living today is directly related to the way you are thinking right now or to the way you have thought in the past. For example, if you are living at a high level of health and fitness, the reason is you *think* physical well-being is important; you eat right, exercise, and avoid things that are bad for your body. The same is true financially. The way you *think* about money, savings, and debt directly impacts your financial habits. The same principles apply to every aspect of your life: how you think determines what you do, and what you do determines how you live.

If you want to change your life and experience the greatness that awaits you, you start by changing your thinking, which almost always means making it more positive. People who think positively tend to enjoy their lives more, have better relationships, and experience greater success than those who think negatively. If we want to change our lives for the better, we must change our thoughts for the better, replacing negative mind-sets with positive thinking.

One reason learning to think more positively is an important step to greatness is that negative thinking can hold you back from the things you want to do in life, jeopardize your potential success, or even keep you from fulfilling your destiny. One way to change negative thinking is to look for the positive instead of the negative in every situation. Everything you encounter has a bright side somewhere. It may be hard to see at first, but if you look for it, you will find it. If you'll discipline your mind to recognize the good things instead of the bad things in the circumstances you face, you'll take a giant step toward breaking free from negative thinking. Retraining your brain in this way may take some time and practice, but the benefits of a more optimistic outlook will be worth the effort.

Another way to change negative thinking to positive thinking is to learn to view every problem as a possibility. Sometimes when we face a problem, we see nothing but an obstacle standing in our way. But if we will learn to see our problems as stepping-stones instead of stumbling blocks, we will soon find ourselves using them to help us instead of allowing them to hinder us.

I want to mention that the power of thoughts cannot be underestimated where the I-factor is concerned. The way you think about yourself is foundational to your I-factor because it determines how you relate to yourself and how you present yourself to others. If you would like to strengthen your I-factor, start paying attention to the negative thoughts you have about yourself, then replace them with more positive ones. So much good will happen if you replace your negative thinking. If you'll make a commitment to think good thoughts about yourself instead of negative ones, your enjoyment of life will improve and your potential for success will increase.

You really do have the power to change your life for the better. You can make it so much better than it is by changing the way you think. Replacing negative thoughts with positive ones will make all the difference.

Step 4: Utilize the Power of Words

When you start to think in fresh, new ways, one of the first differences you will notice is you will also speak differently. Your words will be more positive, more hopeful, and more confident. You may remember the old saying, "Sticks and stones may break my bones, but words will never hurt me." It was popular; children said it all the time, but it was wrong! The truth about words is in Proverbs 18:21: "The tongue has the power of life and death, and those who love it will eat its fruit." The point of this verse is that your *words have power*; they are not neutral. They exert profound influence in your life and in the lives of others.

American novelist Nathaniel Hawthorne said, "Words, so innocent and powerless . . . when standing in a dictionary, how potent for good or evil they become in the hands of one who knows how to combine them."[9] The words you speak can make a situation better or worse. They can hurt someone or heal someone. What you say to someone can drive a relationship apart or bring it back together. Words can give people exactly the encouragement they need to get through a tough situation, or they can make them want to give up. The right words can calm down an angry person, while the wrong ones can inflame him. They can completely change the atmosphere around you from negative to positive. Yes, indeed, words are powerful, and because you have so many words at your disposal, you are powerful too.

Think about it: How many times in your life has someone said something that changed the way you felt about yourself, the way you viewed a situation, or a course of action you planned to take? How many times has someone's comment either lifted you out of a hopeless place or made you feel like a million bucks? If you're anything like I am, you've had numerous experiences with the power of other people's words, both positive and negative. Your words are just as powerful as anyone else's. In your own life when you talk to yourself, as most of us do, usually in the form of our thoughts, no one's words carry more weight or make more difference than yours.

As you move toward greater and greater things, let me encourage you to make your words work for you, not against you. Avoid negative, discouraging, critical words or complaints, and instead use words that are hopeful, happy, faith-filled, honest, wise, and encouraging. Speak these types of words to yourself, because positive self-talk is effective in strengthening your I-factor. What you speak to yourself about yourself will eventually manifest in your life. Also, speak positive, supportive, uplifting words to others. When you are the one with good things to say instead of bad things, people are drawn to you. They tend to view optimistic people as leaders and as good colleagues and friends. Every time you speak positively, you create an opportunity for something good to happen. Why? Because words have power.

Hopefully, these first four steps toward greatness have given you a lot to think about and plan for as you continue your journey to the greatness only you can define and only you can achieve. In the next chapter, I'll explain and encourage you in the next steps, which I believe will get you all the way to the greatness you envision for yourself if you will practice them.

Internal Building Blocks

- To me, achieving greatness means becoming and accomplishing everything God has purposed for you to be and do. You must decide what greatness means to you.
- You face all kinds of decisions every day, and it is important you understand that life itself is a series of choices and the sum of the decisions you make.
- The first step to greatness is to make quality decisions, choices that will move you toward greatness, not away from it.
- The second step to greatness is to make God's Word, the Bible, your manual for life. Seek wisdom and instruction in its timeless truth and allow it to guide you in every situation.
- The third step to greatness is to change your thinking to change your life. Your thoughts are powerful. If you want to live differently, start by thinking differently.
- The fourth step to greatness is to utilize the power of words. Words can be a negative force or a positive force. Use them for good!

Strengthening Your I-Factor

1. People define greatness in all kinds of ways. What does greatness mean to you?
2. Think about a couple of situations in which you need to make decisions right now. How can you make the best quality decisions under these circumstances?
3. What would you tell a person struggling with the idea that God's Word is the only trustworthy manual for life? What specific step

can you take to challenge yourself to read, study, know, believe, and obey God's Word as the best way for your life?

4. What areas in your life do you need to change? How can you change your thinking in order to bring about the changes needed to move you toward greatness?

5. Have you ever thought about how powerful your words are, or is this a new concept to you? Are you intentional with your words or have you been using them carelessly? How can you begin to use the power of words more effectively?

Seven Steps to Greatness, Part 2

You must remain focused on
your journey to greatness.
—LES BROWN

GOD DID NOT CREATE YOU FOR INSIGNIFICANCE; HE CRE-
ated you to fulfill an awesome destiny and to achieve the greatness
for which you were born. But greatness does not happen overnight.
It's not something you can order at the drive-through of life and get
in a matter of minutes. It's the result of a process that takes time,
energy, and commitment—a process that sometimes unfolds with
one step forward and two steps backward.

Hardly anyone takes the journey to greatness without some
missteps and stumbles, but part of what makes the journey so rich
and rewarding is that people who have greatness inside of them
pick themselves up after a fall and keep going. I want to encourage
you, if you find certain steps more difficult than others, or if you
think you've got one nailed and then find out you don't, do not let
yourself become discouraged. Just keep moving forward. That's the
way to reach your goal.

In chapter 13, I wrote about the first four steps to greatness, and
now I want to write about the last three. I'll address the necessity

of managing your emotions instead of allowing them to manage you, the importance of putting the past behind you, and the need to embrace changes that produce growth in your life.

Step 5: Take Charge of Your Emotions

I'd like you to think for a moment about fire in someone's home. When you envision it, what do you see? Do you see a cozy hearth with flames flickering to warm the room while a family sits comfortably around the room, reading books and drinking hot chocolate? Or do you see a fire started by a child experimenting with matches, a fire that quickly devours everything around it and almost destroys the house? My point in asking these questions is to show that fire in a house can be good or bad; it can bring comfort and warmth, or it can wreak destruction. This proves that fire itself is not necessarily good or bad; it can go either way.

The same principle that applies to fire is true for human emotions. When I say we must take charge of our emotions, I'm not implying that emotions are intrinsically bad. Certainly, problems can arise when a person's life is based entirely on his or her feelings and when decisions are based on emotion alone. But emotions are God-given. They help us feel alive, give us sympathy for people who are hurting, help us grieve when we suffer losses, allow us to rejoice when great things happen, and cause us to feel outrage over injustice. God created us with the capacity to experience emotion, and He can use our feelings for our good when we manage them according to His Word. Our emotions were never intended to govern us; we are supposed to manage them and use them for our good.

Emotions, positive or negative, can be intense. They can result in destructive rage or unspeakable joy. We can have all kinds of emotions over the course of one day, or even in one hour. They are also fickle and they can change like the wind, which makes them unpredictable at times and almost always undependable. Emotions can be the fuel that propels us toward our destiny or the fuel that causes us to run a long way off course before we get there—if we get there. That's why it's a good idea not to let them in the driver's seat of our lives. No matter how strong our emotions are or how often they fluctuate, the best way to handle them is not to grit our teeth and try to keep from expressing them, but to learn to deal with them in healthy ways and submit them to the Word and will of God.

If you have ever let your feelings take the lead in your life and suffered the consequences, you understand why taking charge of your emotions is a step to greatness. For example, I believe one reason the divorce rate in the United States is so high is that people marry based on emotion. Of course, good feelings are important when it comes to committing the rest of your life to someone, but they need to be in their proper place.

> Emotions can be the fuel that propels us toward our destiny or the fuel that causes us to run a long way off course before we get there—if we get there.

To illustrate my point about submitting our emotions to God's Word, think about a sweet young Christian woman who falls in love with a handsome young man who does not follow God and is known for being unfaithful to the women he is in relationships with. But, this man says and does all the right things and makes her feel more special than anyone ever has. When he asks her to marry him, she is so deeply in love with him and with the idea of being married that she says yes. Ten years later, he's not as handsome as he was at the altar, her attempts to convert him have failed, he mistreats her, he mishandles their finances, and she is pretty sure he is involved with another woman.

She finally awakens to the fact that she made a bad emotional decision when she married him. Had she submitted her emotions to common sense alone, she would have known that a man who cheats on a series of women is likely to cheat on the next one. Had she submitted her emotions to the wisdom of God's Word, she would have known not to yoke herself with an unbeliever (2 Cor. 6:14). Paying attention to that one scripture could have saved her years of suffering.

The same principle applies when people make emotional purchases. Whether it's a new designer suit, a stylish pair of shoes, a shiny new sports car, or a boat, emotions can easily get involved. We feel we deserve something or we think we will feel better about ourselves if we have it. Those feelings are emotions. God's Word cautions us time and time again not to spend more than we have and to use our resources wisely. Simply submitting emotions to God's Word could save us month after month after month of payments and interest.

I can't think of anyone who has ever achieved any measure of greatness while being led by emotions. Along your journey to destiny, you will no doubt have strong feelings about certain things. The feelings are fine, as long as you make them subordinate to God's Word and handle them in healthy ways. As long as your emotions don't control you, but you control them by letting God lead them, they will help you instead of hinder you.

The people at greatest risk for allowing their emotions to rule their lives are those who are not emotionally healthy. Those who do have a healthy grasp on their feelings are much more likely to keep those feelings in proper perspective. Before I close this section, I want to mention six habits of emotionally healthy people, which are based on biblical principles.

1. Emotionally Healthy People Do Not Give In to Fear

Of all the emotions people can have, perhaps fear causes more trouble for more people than anything else. Fear—along with its offspring: dread, worry, and intimidation—holds more people back from going after their greatness than anything else I know. If we're going to be emotionally healthy, we have to let biblical truth be our standard, and God's Word says over and over again, "Do not fear." Fear is a negative emotion, one that threatens us in many ways under lots of different circumstances. In various situations, we will feel fear; it's a fact of life. Trying not to be afraid is fruitless, but learning how to handle our fears will help us for the rest of our lives. As we stand up to fear and refuse to succumb to it, we become healthier emotionally.

2. Emotionally Healthy People Maintain a Positive Outlook on Life

I have already written in this book about being positive, so I won't elaborate on it here except to say that genuine positivity is an indicator of emotional health. It's not the only indicator, because we have all known people who come across as extremely friendly and positive, only to find out later that it's all a charade and they use their outgoing personalities to mask emotional deficiencies. But generally speaking, people who are emotionally healthy are optimistic and upbeat, choosing to look on the bright side of things instead of focusing on the negative. They go through life expecting good things, not bad things, to come their way.

3. Emotionally Healthy People Deal with Minor Issues Before They Become Major Issues

People who are emotionally healthy choose to deal with little things before they become big things. Most of us know that problems in business, in relationships, and in life in general start small; they don't start big. They only get big because someone doesn't stop them before they begin to grow. Even if they don't like conflict, emotionally healthy people handle small problems before they become serious problems. Addressing potentially bad situations before they get out of hand is not always easy, but it's important to do so. I hope you'll develop the skills to recognize when something is heading in the wrong direction and have the courage to stop it before it becomes truly detrimental.

4. Emotionally Healthy People Know What to Accept and What to Try to Change

People who are healthy in their emotions change what they can change and accept what they cannot do anything about. It's important to know the difference. If you're trying to change something you really can't change, you'll end up frustrated and angry. And if you refuse to change something you can change, you may end up disappointed and full of regret. So let me encourage you to take stock of the situations in your life. Determine which ones you can do something about and which ones are beyond your control. Change what you can, and accept the rest.

5. Emotionally Healthy People Look Toward the Future, Not the Past

I'll write more about this later in this chapter, but for now I'll say that I've noticed one common denominator among emotionally healthy people is an ability to leave the past behind and look forward to the future. They know you can't move ahead in life if the burdens of the past are weighing you down. The only way to make progress toward the bright future before you is to learn the lessons of previous mistakes and let the rest of it go.

6. Emotionally Healthy People Forgive

I devoted an entire chapter of this book to the importance and the process of forgiveness, but I would be remiss to write about habits of emotionally healthy people without mentioning that, without a doubt, one of the best things they do is to forgive. Because they know anger, bitterness, and unforgiveness act like poison to their souls, they don't let that happen. They also realize that choosing to forgive someone is not the same as forgetting about an offense, and it doesn't mean trusting an offender again or restoring a relationship. It means making a healthy choice to release anger and a desire for revenge—and moving on in peace.

As you keep working toward new levels of greatness in your life and new levels of strength in your I-factor, emotional health is crucial. At times, people need professional help or therapy to guide them successfully through the most difficult seasons of life. I hope you have come to understand in this chapter how important it is to keep your emotions under control and that if you ever need a helping hand under emotionally intense circumstances, you will seek it. I encourage you to be willing to do whatever it takes to remain emotionally healthy and in charge of your feelings.

Step 6: Put the Past Behind You

Have you ever thought about how powerful your past can be? It's not something you're currently experiencing; it's something you have already experienced—yet sometimes it seems to come alive in your thoughts in such a way that it sabotages your present and hijacks your future. I've said many times, "If the past is your focus, the past will be your destination." It's true. Living in the past and thinking about it too much will keep you stuck in the past; there is no way to reach the heights of greatness you are destined for without putting your past behind you once and for all.

I understand this can be difficult, especially when the past has been deeply painful or life altering. That's one reason I have placed it close to the end of the steps to greatness. Each previous step helps and supports you as you deal with your past. For example, no one can make quality decisions about the future while tied to the past. Being able to change your thinking about the past will definitely change your life, and being able to manage your feelings and emotions about past relationships or past experiences will also help you break the grip the past may have on you. In addition, making God's Word your guide for finally dealing with the past is tremendously helpful. It's the best way I know to put your past in its proper perspective, break the hold it has on your present, and set you free to embrace the future.

I'd like to mention a couple of points I believe will empower you to deal with the past. First, in Christ, the past is insignificant. Second, whatever your story is, even if your past is a chronicle of mistakes, failures, bad decisions, shame, guilt, or filth, God wants to rewrite your story starting today.

In Christ, the Past Is Insignificant

I believe one of the most desperate needs among people is to gain a clear understanding of how God sees us. It will revolutionize the way we see ourselves and the way we view others. All believers accept Jesus' death on the cross as an intellectual reality, but some fail to grasp in their hearts how dramatically His sacrifice impacts our everyday lives.

The crucifixion means that every sin in our past has been washed away, every wound has been healed, and every bondage has been broken. The tide of blood that flowed from Calvary has carried away everything that would make us feel guilty, ashamed, bitter, and regretful, and has made possible a life of total freedom, healing, wholeness, and redemption. It gives us a fresh start every single day.

I like to say that because of the cross, our pasts no longer belong to us. "All things are yours, whether Paul or Apollos or Cephas or the world or life or death or *the present or the future*—all are yours, and you are of Christ, and Christ is of God" (1 Cor. 3:21–23, emphasis added). Notice the dimensions of time mentioned in this verse: the present and the future. All things are yours, including the present and the future, but not the past. That's why it's not on this list!

Many times, people allow the past to define the present and the future. I have seen this happen time and time again. I have known women who felt guilty about wanting to have children and thought they did not deserve the joy of motherhood because they had abortions in their pasts. I know divorced people who are afraid to fall in love again because the pain of broken marriage still haunts them. I know businesspeople who will not even try to fulfill their potential because someone stole from them or cheated them out of what they had worked for years ago. I know people who cannot even see their good qualities because they grew up being told they were stupid, worthless, irresponsible, or ugly. Perhaps you also know people who have suffered these same situations or something similar. Maybe I've even described you.

> Now is the time—I mean right now, this minute—to make up your mind that your past no longer matters.

Now is the time—I mean right now, this minute—to make up your mind that your past no longer matters. When it doesn't matter, it can't influence you. Until the past is rendered impotent in your mind, it will affect the way you see yourself, the way you view others, and the way you think about your future, whether you realize it or not. It's time for that to stop. Jesus said,

"You will know the truth, and *the truth will set you free*" (John 8:32, emphasis added).

Here's the truth: Your past does not belong to you. It does not have to haunt you or hover over your mind anymore. It belongs to God and that's why He can rewrite it as He chooses.

God Wants to Rewrite Your Story

In Genesis 18:9–15, something unbelievable happened. At least it's unbelievable to the lady at the center of the story, the one destined to receive it. An angel sent from God visited a man named Abraham. He was one hundred years old and his wife, Sarah, was ninety, way past their reproductive years. God's message to Abraham that day was this, "I will surely return to you about this time next year, and Sarah your wife will have a son" (Gen. 18:10).

Though the angel was speaking to Abraham outside near the tent where he and Sarah lived, she was standing at the door listening. When she heard the angel's announcement, "Sarah laughed to herself as she thought, 'After I am worn out and my lord is old, will I now have this pleasure?'" (v. 12). This was her way of saying, "Not a chance! Abraham and I are as old as the hills!"

God heard Sarah's thoughts and asked Abraham, "Why did Sarah laugh and say, 'Will I really have a child, now that I am old?' Is anything too hard for the LORD?" (vv. 13–14). Then He declared, "I will return to you at the appointed time next year, and Sarah will have a son" (v. 14).

Sarah denied laughing because she was afraid. Then God spoke to her saying, "Yes, you did laugh!" (v. 15). In the original language of the Old Testament, the word for *laugh* indicates that Sarah was not saying, "Oh, God, you are so funny! The thought of having a child at my age must be a joke!" No, the word indicates that she was frustrated and angry with God.[1] Nothing about her response indicated that she believed Him. Instead, she got an attitude toward Him.

But look at how the writer of the book of Hebrews remembered Sarah's story, generations after it happened:

> By faith Sarah herself also received strength to conceive seed, and she bore a child when she was past the age, because she judged Him faithful who had promised. Therefore from one man, and him as good as dead, were born as many as the stars of the sky in multitude—innumerable as the sand which is by the seashore. (Heb. 11:11–12 NKJV)

Clearly, the Hebrews account of Sarah's response to God differs greatly from the Genesis account. While I can't prove it from a scholarly perspective, I believe God rewrote Sarah's story when He inspired the writer of Hebrews. The doubt, anger, and frustration of her past were wiped away, and this once-skeptical, scoffing woman is listed in Scripture as a great person of faith.

The reason I am so confident God rewrites stories is that I know what the Bible says about sin. When a person has a painful past, sin is almost always involved on some level. Either the person has been sinned against—as in the case of rape, abuse, or other forms of violence—or the person has done something sinful, as in hurting someone else or making decisions contrary to God's Word. But the Bible says that as soon as we confess our sins, God is faithful to forgive them and cleanse us from our unrighteousness—not a little bit, but completely (1 John 1:9). It says, "As far as the east is from the west, so far has He removed our transgressions from us" (Ps. 103:12 NKJV) and that He will "forgive their wickedness and will remember their sins no more" (Heb. 8:12). Furthermore, Scripture declares, "There is now no condemnation for those who are in Christ Jesus" (Rom. 8:1).

The moment we repent, God changes our history and sets us back on the path of our destiny. The moment we ask Him to heal the wounds others have inflicted on us, healing begins to flow. The moment we ask Him to set us free and make us whole and strong, He goes to work. Every day is a new day with God. Whether the problems in our pasts occurred many years ago or as recently as this morning, they're all subject to the same supernatural erasing. That doesn't mean we may not have to deal with consequences.

We often find ourselves wrestling with the after-effects of our own sins and with the impact of the ways people have sinned against us. For example, people who turn their backs on God's Word and engage in sex before marriage may end up with the stress and financial strain of having a child before they're ready. People who damage their own bodies through drug or alcohol abuse may have to handle the physical or mental problems that result from substance abuse. But consequences do not have to be painful reminders of the past. They must be dealt with in the present, and by God's grace, their potential to sting and be burdensome can be removed. They can even become blessings in the future.

If you have a story you are not proud of or one that causes you great pain, I hope you are encouraged that you can turn the page. God wants to remove the weight of your past from you, setting you free to live in the present and look forward to the future. He is eager to rewrite your story, and I believe it will be better than anything you've ever dreamed.

Discipline Your Mind to Live in the Present and Look Toward the Future

It's important to learn the lessons your past experiences can teach you, but once you've learned them, discipline your mind to move on. That way, you can enjoy what's happening now and look forward to what is to come.

Recognize When the Past Is Influencing Your Decisions, and Stop It

Even though the past is over and done with, we sometimes have trouble *really* putting it behind us because we think about it too much. When that happens, our present decisions can be influenced by our past mistakes. We make certain choices in order to avoid repeating things we did wrong months or years ago. Let me encourage you to be mindful of the way you think when you make decisions. Learn from the good lessons of the past, but don't let the past influence you to choose anything less than what you know to be the best for you in your current situation.

Focus on Today

Some people have painful pasts, while others are blessed to have pleasant memories of days gone by. Some vilify the past, while others glorify it. People with hurtful pasts are at risk of dwelling on their pain to the point of never getting healed, while people with happy pasts are at risk for missing the present and the future because they want to recreate the past. If that's you, I want to encourage you today to be glad for your good memories, but don't try to relive them. Today is full of its own goodness, so let the past rest and embrace the great things available to you right now.

Be Open to New Things

If you will make a deliberate effort to be open to new things—new people, new skills or hobbies, new social or career opportunities, and other new things—those new experiences will crowd out your memories of the past. You'll be so busy filling your current life with good things that you'll have less desire to focus on the past. I encourage you to be intentionally open to new things and to enjoy the present.

Step 7: Embrace Change
That Produces Growth

The way we handle change can determine whether or not we reach our destiny, and the last step to greatness is to embrace growth that produces change. Growth and change are two different dynamics. A change does not necessarily lead to growth, but growth always involves change.

Think about it: you can decide to take a different route to work one morning. That's definitely a change, but it doesn't produce growth. It just gets you to the same place you go every day. Or, you can decide to reduce the amount of sugar and carbohydrates in your diet, replacing them with vegetables, fruits, whole grains, and lean protein. That type of change will result in growth—growth in physical health and well-being. On your journey to greatness, it's important to embrace the type of change that leads to lasting, sustainable growth. You want growth that catapults you into your destiny, not change for the sake of simply mixing things up and doing them differently.

Change can cause our lives to shrink or to expand. Let's say a woman who loves knitting decides that she needs to make some changes in the way she manages her time. If she chooses to withdraw from others and spend more time at home knitting, she will likely minimize her opportunities for growth. But if she decides to spend a couple of hours a week teaching knitting to local senior citizens, the change will produce growth as she listens to their stories and benefits from their wisdom. Either way, she is involved in knitting. One scenario helps her grow and makes her world bigger; the other makes it smaller.

Every change you make has the potential to bring new experiences, new challenges, and new relationships into your life—and each of these new things brings unique benefits and opportunities.

Each one gives you a chance to learn more, do more, and become more than you have ever been before. The question is: Will you embrace the growth these changes offer?

Let me share a few characteristics of change that produces growth.

Changes That Produce Growth Challenge Your Current Level of Determination and Persistence

One way change gives us a chance to grow is that it breeds determination and perseverance. Many times, changes worth making take time, and sometimes they present us with obstacles. If we believe these changes are for our good, we will develop determination and perseverance in new ways. These fresh levels of determination and perseverance will serve us well not only through current changes, but in the future as we grow, develop, and go after our destiny.

Changes That Produce Growth Require You to Find New Levels of Strength

The types of changes that help you grow are the ones that present you with a chance to dig deep into yourself and draw out strength and courage you may not have needed before. In order to maximize the changes life sends your way, you have to be willing to face uncertainty and be courageous enough to move forward without always knowing exactly how things will turn out. When you do, you may likely find you are stronger than you thought, and that will give you greater courage to accept the next challenge you face.

Changes That Produce Growth Offer Experience, Wisdom, and a Fresh Perspective

Each change you encounter can offer you an opportunity to gain experience, wisdom, and perspective you might never gain without it. Think about it: Can you remember a time or situation of great change in your life that gave you a whole new insight or perspective? Maybe you once saw things a certain way, but after going through some kind of change, you saw them differently. Or perhaps, the experience of going through that change gave you important wisdom and insight needed to help someone dealing with a similar situation. That would have been a growth-producing change.

Sometimes, change comes to our lives on its own as a result of circumstances such as graduating and needing to get a job, a work promotion requiring a geographical move, retirement, aging, illness, or any number of other situations. When those changes come, we have no choice about them and we simply must deal with them. At other times, though, we can choose change. We may decide the time is right to leave an old job and start a new business, to marry or start a family, or to take off on a new adventure. People who are serious about going after greatness are not afraid to initiate changes that will produce the growth they want and need. For those changes to be most beneficial, they need to happen at the right time. So how do you know when the time is right to make a change? You know it's time for a change when

- things that were once fun become dull or boring.
- you no longer feel challenged or invigorated.
- things that have always come easily begin to seem like a chore, as though the grace to do them has lifted.
- you find yourself daydreaming continually about what you'd *like* to do instead of focusing on what you *have* to do.
- you develop a sustained interest in something new. This is not a burst of enthusiasm that will fade, but a long-term, genuine interest that causes you to think

more about the new thing than what you're currently involved in.

- you find yourself wondering about changes you could make and entertaining new possibilities. You start asking yourself, *What if I did this?* or *What if I did that?*
- you feel a sense of confidence and courage when you think about the change you want to make.
- you believe the downsides of doing nothing are worse than the potential risks of making a change.

If now is the time for you to make a change that produces growth in your life, I encourage you to go for it with all your might. It may be the one adjustment that changes everything for you.

Change, Growth, and Greatness

A healthy I-factor depends on many components I have written about in this book. Although I mentioned the ability to manage change last, it's no less important than anything else. Many of the topics I have addressed, such as understanding your identity, dealing with fear and developing courage, and following your dreams help prepare you to handle change well. These things were designed to help you understand yourself better, relate to yourself more effectively, and empower you to live at your full potential.

I trust that growth-producing change has taken place within you as you have read this book. For those changes, I am thankful. But I know that in order to become all you were created to be and to achieve all you were designed to do, growth and change will continue to unfold for as long as you live. The goal of a strong I-factor is for you to be your best self and live your best life, and I've tried to equip you to do that. I wish you well on your journey to greatness!

────────────── Internal Building Blocks ──────────────

- Greatness is the result of a process that takes time, energy, and commitment—a process that sometimes unfolds with one step forward and two steps backward.
- The fifth step to greatness is to take charge of your emotions. You need to lead your emotions instead of letting them lead you.
- Emotionally healthy people do not give in to fear. They also maintain a positive outlook on life, deal with minor issues before they become major issues, know what to accept and what to change, look toward the future instead of the past, and forgive.
- The sixth step to greatness is to put the past behind you. The past is insignificant when you are in Christ. God wants to rewrite your story.
- You can put the past behind you by disciplining your mind to live in the present and look to the future, realizing when the past is influencing your decisions and stopping it, focusing on today, and being open to new things.
- The seventh step to greatness is to embrace change that produces growth. Changes that produce growth challenge your current level of determination and persistence; require you to find new levels of strength; and offer experience, wisdom, and a fresh perspective.
- You will continue to grow and change for as long as you live. Let the growth and changes always move you to new levels of greatness.

────────────── Strengthening Your I-Factor ──────────────

1. Based on the qualities of emotionally healthy people, how would you rate your emotional health? In what specific ways do you need to become more healthy emotionally?

2. Have you successfully put the past behind you or does it still have a hold on you? What specific circumstances or events are most difficult for you to break free from, and how can you begin to break their grip on you?

3. What specific changes can you initiate in your life right now that will produce growth?

4. How can you continue to strengthen and develop your I-factor so that it supports you on your lifelong journey of increasing greatness?

5. Do you believe God wants to rewrite your story? Are you willing to surrender your life to Him and let Him do it?

A Final Word

I WROTE *THE I-FACTOR* TO HELP PEOPLE DEVELOP BETTER relationships with themselves and to strengthen themselves internally. Therefore, the book has called you and challenged you to focus on yourself. That's a good and healthy thing to do for certain periods of time, seasons of life when you need to grow and change. But an entire lifetime of self-focus is a recipe for misery. If we never look beyond ourselves, so much good would fail to be done in the world. So much kindness, encouragement, and support would be missing from the lives of those who need it. While building a strong I-factor is vital to your personal greatness, that greatness should never stop with you. It's meant to be shared.

The first great task in life is to find yourself; the second is to lose yourself. You find yourself in various ways, one of which is to develop a healthy I-factor. You lose yourself when you use the growth and greatness you have experienced to benefit others. Finding yourself allows you to achieve a measure of success. Losing yourself enables you to experience an unprecedented measure of joy, fulfillment, and reward.

I've concluded that most people are driven by one of three internal desires: survival, success, or significance. Some are happy simply to stay alive and make it through each day. Some want to reach a certain level of success. And some not only want to survive and succeed, they want to take the next step and become significant. True significance only happens when we impact other people in positive ways. Success is all about you; significance is all about others.

I believe God wants everyone to have a strong I-factor—to be confident in who He has created us to be and at ease with who we are, to be emotionally and spiritually healthy, and to be able to deal with our challenges effectively as we pursue our personal greatness. But I don't think He wants us to stop there. He wants us to be intentional about getting beyond ourselves and putting others first. After all, that's how He made a difference in the world. He gave us the original model of giving when He sent and sacrificed His Son for our salvation. "For God so loved the world that he gave his one and only Son, that whoever believes in him shall not perish but have eternal life" (John 3:16).

God asks us to do the same. "We know what real love is because Jesus gave up his life for us. So we also ought to give up our lives for our brothers and sisters" (1 John 3:16 NLT).

I'd like to close this book with a story and a poem I hope will inspire you to make a difference in the world around you, based on your strong and growing I-factor. Around 1980, vandals approached a statue of Jesus at Christ the King Catholic Church in San Diego, California, and broke off the hands. The church's powerful and creative response was not to restore Christ's hands to the statue, but to leave the statue broken and install a plaque at its base. The plaque reads: "I have no hands but yours." This is a reference to an ancient poem by St. Teresa of Avila, who lived from 1515–1582.[1]

> *Christ now has no body on earth but yours;*
> *no hands but yours; no feet but yours.*
> *Yours are the eyes through which the compassion*
>   *of Christ must look out on the world.*
> *Yours are the feet with which He is to go about doing good.*
> *Yours are the hands with which He is to bless His people.*[2]

Acknowledgments

BETH CLARK: THANK YOU FOR YOUR FRIENDSHIP, WISDOM, and expertise.

Mel Berger and Margret King: Thank you for fighting for me.

Brian Hampton: Thank you for believing in me.

Webster Younce, Janene MacIvor, and the Thomas Nelson editorial and production teams: Thank you for your heart for this project! You are a breath of fresh air!

Jeff James, Aryn VanDyke, and the Thomas Nelson Marketing and Sales Departments: Thank you for all of your creativity and efforts in promoting *The I-Factor.*

To all my family and friends who offered prayer, support, and encouragement for this project: I *remain* grateful!

Notes

Introduction

1. Van Moody, *The People Factor* (Nashville: Thomas Nelson, 2014), xiv.

Chapter 1: More Than Meets the Eye

1. *Titanic*, directed by James Cameron (Hollywood: Paramount Pictures, 1997), DVD.
2. "American Originals," *National Archives and Record Administration*, updated April 15, 1998, http://www.archives.gov/exhibits/american _originals/titanic.html.
3. "History: Titanic," BBC, accessed February 15, 2016, http://www.bbc.co.uk /history/titanic.
4. "Interesting Facts," *TheTitanicStory.com*, 2000, http://www.titanicstory .com/interest.htm.
5. Ibid.
6. Brian Stelter, "Brian Williams: My 'Ego' Caused Me to Make Things Up," CNN Money, June 19, 2015, http://money.cnn.com/2015/06/19/media/brian -williams-nbc-speaks-on-today-show/.
7. Jack Shafer, "Why Did Brian Williams Lie?" *Politico*, February 5, 2015, http://www.politico.com/magazine/story/2015/02/brian-williams-lie -114950.
8. Stelter, "Brian Williams."
9. Warren Patrick Baker and Spiros Zodhiates, eds. *The Complete Word Study Dictionary Old Testament* (Chattanooga: AMG International, 2003), 140.
10. Annotation on 1 Samuel 2:12. *The NIV Study Bible* (Grand Rapids: The Zondervan Corporation, 1985).
11. Pamela L. McQuade with Paul Kent, *The Dictionary of Bible Names* (Uhrichsville, OH: Barbour Publishing, 2009), 302, 157.
12. Baker and Zodhiates, *The Complete Word Study Dictionary*, 43, 493.

13. *Merriam-Webster*, s.v. "glory," accessed February 16, 2016, http://www
.merriam-webster.com/dictionary/glory.

Chapter 2: It's Time to Peel the Onion

1. Joyce Meyer "Learning to Like Yourself", http://www.joycemeyer.org
/articles/ea.aspx?article=learning_to_like_yourself
2. "George Washington Carver," National Peanut Board, January 29, 2016,
http://nationalpeanutboard.org/peanut-info/george-washington-carver.
3. Ibid.
4. Ibid.

Chapter 3: The Best-Kept Secret of Sustained Success

1. Gene Edwards, *The Tale of Three Kings* (Wheaton, IL: Tyndale House
Publishers, 1980, 1992) pp. 37–39.
2. Nelson Mandela, as quoted in Maureen Biwi, *Nelson Mandela's Quotes and
Tributes* (Swindon, UK: AA Global Sourcing Ltd., 2013), 24.
3. Charles Spurgeon, as quoted in Roy B. Zuck, *The Speaker's Quote Book*
(Grand Rapids: Kregel Publications, 2009), 268.
4. Jim Bakker, *I Was Wrong* (Nashville: Thomas Nelson, 1996).

Chapter 4: Your True Self Is Your Best Self

1. Socrates, as quoted in "The Death of Socrates," PBS, accessed February 16,
2016, http://www.pbs.org/empires/thegreeks/characters/socrates_p12.html.

Chapter 5: Proof of Identity

1. Geoff Mulvihill, "Bernard Pagano, 81, Priest Cleared of Armed Robberies,"
The Boston Globe, August 8, 2006, http://www.archive.boston.com/news
/globe/obituaries/articles/2006/08/08/bernard_pagano_81_priest_cleared
_of_armed_robberies/.
2. Robin Warder, "10 Weird and Tragic Cases of Mistaken Identity," *Listverse*
(blog), May 26, 2014, http://listverse.com/2014/05/26/10-weird-and-tragic
-cases-of-mistaken-identity/.

Chapter 6: The Journey to Significance

1. Gen 29:32, *NIV Thinline Bible* (Grand Rapids: Zondervan Publishing
House, 2005).
2. Ibid., annotation on Gen. 29:33.
3. Ibid., annotation on Gen. 29:34.

4. *Dictionary.com Unabridged*, s.v. "Leah," Random House, Inc., accessed February 17, 2016, http://dictionary.reference.com/browse/leah.

5. *Strong's Concordance*, s.v. "repent," *Bible Hub*, accessed February 17, 2016, http://biblehub.com/greek/3340.htm.

6. Erma Bombeck as quoted in John C. Maxwell, *Success: One Day at a Time* (Nashville: Thomas Nelson, 2014), 113.

7. *Strong's Exhaustive Concordance*, s.v. "yadah," *Bible Hub*, accessed February 17, 2016, http://biblehub.com/hebrew/3034.htm.

Chapter 7: A Training Ground for Greatness

1. Walt Disney Biography http://www.biographyonline.net/artists/walt -disney.html.

2. Renee Jacques, "16 Wildly Successful People Who Overcame Huge Obstacles to Get There," *Huffington Post*, updated February 13, 2014, http://www.huffingtonpost.com/2013/09/25/successful-people-obstacles _n_3964459.html.

3. Ibid.

4. "Marie Curie Biography," *Biography.com*, A&E Television Networks, accessed February 17, 2016, http://www.biography.com/people/marie-curie -9263538#early-life.

5. Jacques, "16 Wildly Successful People."

6. "10 Famous People Who Overcame Their Disabilities," *Smashing Tops* (blog), September 9, 2011, http://smashingtops.com/people/10-famous -people-who-overcame-their-disabilities/.

7. Maya Angelou as quoted in Ann Kannings, *Maya Angelou: Her Words* (Raleigh: Lulu Press, Inc., 2014).

8. "Maya Angelou Biography," *Biography.com*, A&E Television Networks, accessed February 17, 2016, http://www.biography.com/people/maya -angelou-9185388#early-years.

9. Annotation on Psalm 84:5, *NIV Study Bible* (Grand Rapids: The Zondervan Corporation, 1985).

10. "Nelson Mandela Biography," *Biography.com*, A&E Television Networks, accessed February 17, 2016, http://www.biography.com/people/nelson -mandela-9397017#early-life.

11. Ibid.

12. Ibid.

13. Ibid.

14. Ibid.
15. Ibid.
16. "Nelson Mandela—Biographical," *Nobelprize.org*, accessed February 18, 2016, http://www.nobelprize.org/nobel_prizes/peace/laureates/1993/mandela-bio.html.

Chapter 8: The Biggest Favor You Can Do Yourself

1. Al and Lisa Robertson, *A New Season* (Nashville: Howard Books, 2015). 153–159; 165–172; 179–188, 193–201, 213–215.
2. T.D. Jakes. *Let It Go* (New York: Atria Books, 2012), 33.
3. Pamela Rose Williams, "Bible Verses About Forgiveness: 20 Encouraging Scripture Quotes," *What Christians Want to Know* (blog), accessed February 18, 2016, http://www.whatchristianswanttoknow.com/bible-verses-about-forgiveness-20-encouraging-scripture-quotes/.
4. Annotation on Matthew 17:22, *NIV Study Bible* (Grand Rapids: The Zondervan Corporation, 1985).

Chapter 9: Success Is an Inside Job

1. *Merriam-Webster*, s.v. "courage," accessed February 18, 2016, http://www.merriam-webster.com/dictionary/courage.
2. *Merriam-Webster*, 1913 ed., s.v. "courage," accessed February 18, 2016, http://www.webster-dictionary.org/definition/courage.
3. "Steve Jobs' 2005 Stanford Commencement Address: 'Your Time is Limited, So Don't Waste It Living Someone Else's Life,'" *Huffington Post*, December 5, 2011, http://www.huffingtonpost.com/2011/10/05/steve-jobs-stanford-commencement-address_n_997301.html.
4. *The Pursuit of Happyness*, directed by Gabriele Muccino (Culver City, CA: Columbia Pictures, 2006).

Chapter 10: Don't Stop Now

1. Spiros Zodhiates, ed., *The Complete Word Study Dictionary New Testament* (Chattanooga: AMG Publishers, 1992), 333.
2. Warren Wiersbe, *The Bible Exposition Commentary New Testament, Vol. 1. Matthew-Galatians* (Wheaton, IL: Victor Books, 1996), 304.
3. "Abraham Lincoln Biography," *Biography.com*, A&E Television Networks, accessed February 18, 2016, http://www.biography.com/people/abraham-lincoln-9382540#childhood.
4. Ibid.

5. "President Abraham Lincoln Timeline," *Apples 4 the Teacher*, accessed February 18, 2016, http://www.apples4theteacher.com/holidays/presidents -day/abraham-lincoln/timeline.html.

6. "Tad Lincoln," *Lincoln Bicentennial 1809–2009*, Library of Congress, accessed February 18, 2016, http://abrahamlincoln200.org/lincolns-life /lincolns-family/tad-lincoln/default.aspx.

7. "Emancipation Proclamation," January 1, 1863, http://www .emancipationproclamation.org/.

8 Gregory Y. Titelman, *Random House Dictionary of Popular Proverbs and Sayings* (New York: Random House, 1996), 154.

Chapter 11: Head First

1. "Profiles in Greatness: Rowland H. Macy" http://www.success.com/article /profiles-in-greatness-rowland-h-macy.

2. "Macy's: A History," Macy's Inc., accessed February 18, 2016, https://www .macysinc.com/press-room/macysinc-history/macys-a-history/default.aspx.

3. Ibid.

4. Ibid.

Chapter 12: The Power of Perspective

1. Lauren Bringle, "A Funny Story About Perspective," *In Search of the Great Perhaps* (blog), July 20, 2013, https://searchfortheperhaps.wordpress.com /2013/07/20/a-funny-story-about-perspective.

2. Joel Siegel, "When Steve Jobs Got Fired by Apple," ABC News, October 6, 2011, http://abcnews.go.com/Technology/steve-jobs-fire-company/story ?id=14683754.

3. http://www.guinnessworldrecords.com/world-records/tallest-man-ever.

Chapter 13: Seven Steps to Greatness, Part 1

1. Bob Marley as quoted in "Causes and Charities," *BobMarley.com*, accessed February 18, 2016, http://www.bobmarley.com/charity/.

2. George Bernard Shaw as quoted in Joseph Demakis, *The Ultimate Book of Quotations* (Raleigh: Lulu Press, Inc.), 172.

3. Leo Tolstoy, *War and Peace*, Richard Pevear and Larissa Volokhonsky, trans. (New York: Vintage Books, 2007), 1071.

4. Winston Churchill, "The Price of Greatness Is Responsibility" (speech, Harvard University, Cambridge, Massachusetts, 1943).

5. Wilma Rudolph as quoted in Corinne J. Naden and Rose Blue, *Wilma Rudolph* (Chicago: Raintree, 2004), 7.
6. Mahatma Ghandi as quoted in Samiksha Jain, "10 Mahatma Ghandi Quotes to Inspire Young Entrepreneurs," *Entrepreneur.com*, September 30, 2015, http://www.entrepreneur.com/article/251235.
7. Myles Munroe as quoted in "Myles Munroe: Uncover Your Potential," *700 Club*, CBN, accessed February 18, 2016, http://www1.cbn.com/700club /myles-munroe-uncover-your-potential.
8. Charles Dickens as quoted in William Joseph Federer, *America's God and Country: Encyclopedia of Quotations* (St. Louis: Amerisearch, 2000), 207.
9. Nathaniel Hawthorne as quoted in "Quotes of Famous and Wise People on the Power of Words," *Power of Words*, accessed February 18, 2016, http:// www.prdaily.com/Main/Articles/12_inspiring_quotes_about_words_and _writing_9620.aspx.

Chapter 14: Seven Steps to Greatness, Part 2

1. Warren Patrick Baker and Spiros Zodhiates, eds., *The Complete Word Study Dictionary Old Testament* (Chattanooga: AMG Pulishers, 2003), 946.

A Final Word

1. Robert Prater, "Christ Has No Hands Here but Yours," *Words of the Preacher* (blog), May 13, 2010, http://preacherprater.blogspot.com/2010/05 /christ-has-no-hands-here-but-yours.html.
2. "Prayer of Saint Teresa of Avila (1515–1582)," *CatholiCity.com*, accessed February 18, 2016, http://www.catholicity.com/prayer/prayer-of-saint -teresa-of-avila.html.